BUYING A HOME IN FLORIDA

by

David Hampshire

First published 1996

Survival Books
25 Kenilworth Road
Fleet
Hampshire GU13 9AX
United Kingdom
tel/fax 01252-815995

British Library Cataloguing in Publication Data
A CIP record for this book is available from the British Library
ISBN 0 9519804 6 7

Printed and bound in Great Britain by The Bath Press, Lower Bristol Road, Bath
BA2 3BL

ACKNOWLEDGEMENTS

My sincere thanks to all those who contributed to the successful publication of this book, in particular the many people who provided information and took the time and trouble to read and comment on the many draft versions. I would especially like to thank Sarah Sherman, Debbie Bartlett, Kevin Logan, Tom Cowell (Florida Dream), Mark Prescott, Peter Stanhope (Florida Brits Club), Keith Harpham (Florida Homes and Travel), Marjann Shawler, Christopher (Kip) Palmer, Veronica Orchard, Julia & Michael Thorpe, Philip & Jane Read, Ron & Pat Scarborough, Adèle Kelham and Erik Gottschalk for their help and everyone else who contributed in any way whom I have omitted to mention. Also a special thank you to Jim Watson (tel. UK 01788-813609) for the superb illustrations, cartoons and cover.

By the same author:

Buying a Home Abroad
Buying a Home in France
Buying a Home in Spain
Living and Working in America
Living and Working in Britain
Living and Working in France
Living and Working in Spain
Living and Working in Switzerland

What Readers and Reviewers Have Said About Survival Books

When you buy a model plane for your child, a video recorder, or some new computer gizmo, you get with it a leaflet or booklet pleading 'Read Me First', or bearing large friendly letters or bold type saying 'IMPORTANT - follow the instructions carefully'. This book should be similarly supplied to all those entering France with anything more durable than a 5-day return ticket. — It is worth reading even if you are just visiting briefly, or if you have lived here for years and feel totally knowledgeable and secure. But if you need to find out how France works then it is indispensable. Native French people probably have a less thorough understanding of how their country functions. — Where it is most essential, the book is most up to the minute.

Living France

We would like to congratulate you on this work: it is really super! We hand it out to our expatriates and they read it with great interest and pleasure.

ICI (Switzerland) AG

Rarely has a 'survival guide' contained such useful advice — This book dispels doubts for first-time travellers, yet is also useful for seasoned globetrotters — In a word, if you're planning to move to the US or go there for a long-term stay, then buy this book both for general reading and as a ready-reference.

American Citizens Abroad

It's everything you always wanted to ask but didn't for fear of the contemptuous put down — The best English-language guide — Its pages are stuffed with practical information on everyday subjects and are designed to compliment the traditional guidebook.

Swiss News

A complete revelation to me — I found it both enlightening and interesting, not to mention amusing.

Carole Clark

Let's say it at once. David Hampshire's *Living and Working in France* is the best handbook ever produced for visitors and foreign residents in this country; indeed, my discussion with locals showed that it has much to teach even those born and bred in *l'Hexagone*. — It is Hampshire's meticulous detail which lifts his work way beyond the range of other books with similar titles. Often you think of a supplementary question and search for the answer in vain. With Hampshire this is rarely the case. — He writes with great clarity (and gives French equivalents of all key terms), a touch of humor and a ready eye for the odd (and often illuminating) fact. — This book is absolutely indispensable.

The Riviera Reporter

The ultimate reference book — Every conceivable subject imaginable is exhaustively explained in simple terms — An excellent introduction to fully enjoy all that this fine country has to offer and save time and money in the process.

American Club of Zurich

What Readers and Reviewers Have Said About Survival Books

What a great work, wealth of useful information, well-balanced wording and accuracy in details. My compliments!

Thomas Müller

This handbook has all the practical information one needs to set up home in the UK — The sheer volume of information is almost daunting — Highly recommended for anyone moving to the UK.

American Citizens Abroad

A very good book which has answered so many questions and even some I hadn't thought of — I would certainly recommend it.

Brian Fairman

A mine of information — I might have avoided some embarrassments and frights if I had read it prior to my first Swiss encounters — Deserves an honoured place on any newcomer's bookshelf.

English Teachers Association, Switzerland

Covers just about all the things you want to know on the subject — In answer to the desert island question about *the one* how-to book on France, this book would be it — Almost 500 pages of solid accurate reading — This book is about enjoyment as much as survival.

The Recorder

It's so funny — I love it and definitely need a copy of my own — Thanks very much for having written such a humourous and helpful book.

Heidi Guiliani

A must for all foreigners coming to Switzerland.

Antoinette O'Donoghue

A comprehensive guide to all things French, written in a highly readable and amusing style, for anyone planning to live, work or retire in France.

The Times

A concise, thorough account of the DO's and DON'Ts for a foreigner in Switzerland — Crammed with useful information and lightened with humourous quips which make the facts more readable.

American Citizens Abroad

Covers every conceivable question that might be asked concerning everyday life — I know of no other book that could take the place of this one.

France in Print

Hats off to Living and Working in Switzerland!

Ronnie Almeida

CONTENTS

1. WHY FLORIDA ?   15

DO YOU NEED A PERMIT OR VISA ?   17
RETIREMENT   20
WORKING   21
SELF-EMPLOYMENT   22
KEEPING IN TOUCH   25
GETTING THERE   30
GETTING AROUND   31
DRIVING IN FLORIDA   33

2. FURTHER CONSIDERATIONS   45

CLIMATE   46
GEOGRAPHY   48
REGIONS   49
HEALTH   52
INSURANCE   53
SHOPPING   65
PETS   70
TELEVISION & RADIO   72
CRIME   75
LEGAL SYSTEM   78
EDUCATION   80
LEISURE & SPORTS   81

3. FINANCE   87

US CURRENCY   88
IMPORTING & EXPORTING MONEY   89
CREDIT RATING   91
BANKING   92
MORTGAGES   97
INCOME TAX   104
PROPERTY TAXES   113
CAPITAL GAINS TAX   115
ESTATE & GIFT TAX   117
SALES TAX   117
WILLS   119

COST OF LIVING   120

4. FINDING YOUR DREAM HOME   123

AVOIDING PROBLEMS   124
CHOOSING THE LOCATION   125
RENTING   130
FLORIDA HOMES   132
COST   134
FEES   137
NEW HOMES   138
RESALE HOMES   142
COMMUNITY PROPERTIES   144
MOBILE HOMES   148
TIMESHARE & PART-OWNERSHIP SCHEMES   149
REAL ESTATE AGENTS & BROKERS   151
HOME INSPECTIONS & SURVEYS   154
GARAGES & PARKING   155
CONVEYANCING   156
PURCHASE CONTRACTS   157
CLOSING   164
REMODELING   165
MOVING HOUSE   167
MOVING IN   168
HOME SECURITY   168
UTILITIES   170
HEATING & AIR-CONDITIONING   174
GARBAGE COLLECTION & DISPOSAL   175
RENTAL INCOME   176
SELLING A HOME   182

5. ARRIVAL & SETTLING IN   187

ARRIVAL/DEPARTURE RECORD   188
IMMIGRATION   189
CUSTOMS   191
REGISTRATION   192
FINDING HELP   193
CHECKLISTS   194

APPENDICES 199

APPENDIX A: USEFUL ADDRESSES   200
APPENDIX B: FURTHER READING   203
APPENDIX C: WEIGHTS & MEASURES   205
APPENDIX D: MAP OF FLORIDA   210
APPENDIX E: GLOSSARY   212
APPENDIX F: SERVICE DIRECTORY   217

ORDER FORM 220

INDEX 221

IMPORTANT NOTE

Readers should note that the laws and regulations for buying property in Florida aren't the same as in other countries and are even different in certain aspects to those in other US states. They are also liable to change periodically. **I can't recommend too strongly that you always check with an official and reliable source (not always the same) and take expert legal advice before paying any money or signing any legal documents. Don't, however, believe everything you're told or read, even, dare I say it, herein!**

To help you obtain further information and verify data with official sources, useful addresses and references to other sources of information have been included in all chapters and in appendices A and B. Important points have been emphasized throughout the book **in bold print**, some of which it would be expensive and foolish to disregard. **Ignore them at your peril or cost.** Unless specifically stated, the reference to any company, organization, product or publication in this book *doesn't* constitute an endorsement or recommendation. Any reference to any place or person (living or dead) is purely coincidental.

AUTHOR'S NOTES

- **All prices quoted in this book should be taken as estimates only,** although they were mostly correct when going to print.

- His/he/him/man/men, etc. also mean her/she/her/woman/women, etc. (no offence ladies). This is done simply to make life easier for both the reader and, in particular, the author, and **isn't** intended to be sexist.

- To help you familiarize yourself with the American language, the spelling and terminology used in this book is mostly American English and not British English.

- Warnings and important points are shown in **bold** type.

- For those unfamiliar with the metric system of weights and measures, conversion tables are included in **Appendix C**.

- A map of Florida showing the regions and counties is included in **Appendix D**.

- A list of property, mortgage and other terms used in this book is included in a **Glossary** in **Appendix E**.

- A **Service Directory** containing the names, addresses, telephone and fax numbers of companies and organizations doing business in the countries featured in this book is contained in **Appendix F**.

If you have any suggestions or comments about anything contained in this book, particularly concerning changes or information you would like to see in the next edition, we would like to hear from you. If your suggestions are used in the next edition, you will receive a *free* copy.

INTRODUCTION

If you're planning to buy a home in Florida or even just thinking about it — this is THE BOOK for you! Whether you want a villa, townhouse or apartment, a holiday or permanent home, this book will help make your dreams come true. The purpose of *Buying a Home in Florida* is to provide you with the information necessary to help you choose the most favorable location and the most appropriate home **to satisfy your individual requirements.** Most important of all it will help you avoid the pitfalls and risks associated with buying a home in Florida, which for most people will be one of the largest financial transactions they will undertake during their lifetimes.

You may already own a home in your home country, however, buying a home in Florida (or in any foreign country) is a different matter altogether. One of the most common mistakes people make when buying a home in Florida is to assume that the laws and purchase procedures are the same as in their home country. **This is certainly not true!** The system of buying property varies considerably from country to country and in the US it even varies from state to state. Buying property in Florida is generally very safe, particularly when compared with certain other countries. However, if you don't follow the rules provided for your protection, a purchase can result in serious financial losses as many people have discovered to their cost.

Before buying a home in Florida you need to ask yourself *exactly* why you want to buy a home there? Is your primary concern a good long term investment or do you wish to work or retire there? Where and what can you afford to buy? Do you plan to rent your home to offset the running costs? What about property, capital gains and inheritance taxes? *Buying a Home in Florida* will help you answer these and many other questions. It won't, however, tell you where to live and what to buy, or whether having made your decision you will be happy — that part is up to you!

For many people, buying a home in Florida has previously been a case of pot luck. However, with a copy of *Buying a Home in Florida* you'll have a wealth of priceless information at your fingertips. Information derived from a variety of sources, both official and unofficial, not least the hard won personal experiences of the author, his friends, colleagues and acquaintances. This book doesn't, however, contain all the answers (most of us don't even know the right questions to ask). What it *will* do is reduce the risk of making an expensive mistake that you will bitterly regret later and help you make informed decisions and calculated judgments, instead of costly mistakes and uneducated guesses (forewarned is forearmed). **Most importantly of all, it will help you save money and will repay your investment many times over.**

The worldwide recession in the early 1990s caused an upheaval in world property markets, during which many 'gilt-edged' property investments went to the wall. However, property remains one of the best long term investments and it's certainly one of the most pleasurable. Buying a home in Florida is a wonderful way to make new friends, broaden your horizons and revitalize your life — and it provides a welcome bolthole to recuperate from the stresses and strains of modern life. I trust this book will help you avoid the pitfalls and smooth your way to many happy years in your new home in Florida, secure in the knowledge that you have made the right decision.

Good Luck!

David Hampshire
May 1996

1.

WHY FLORIDA?

Florida is the third most populous state in the US (with around 14m inhabitants) and receives around 250,000 new residents every year plus over 40m visitors. However, contrary to popular belief it isn't primarily populated by aging retirees (it's often derided as 'the land of the newly wed and the nearly dead') and has one of the youngest resident populations of any US state (the average age is around 36). Despite the state's huge growth in the last few decades, Florida remains one of the least understood parts of the US, with a character, history and variety of landscape unrivalled by virtually any other region. As a location for a holiday or retirement home, Florida has few rivals and in addition to its outstanding property values it offers a superb climate and an incomparable choice of affordable leisure and sports pursuits.

There are many excellent reasons for buying a home in Florida, but it's important not to be under any illusions regarding what you can expect from a home there. The first question you need to ask yourself is *exactly* why do you want to buy a home in Florida? For example, are you seeking a holiday or a retirement home? Do you plan to rent it to offset some of the mortgage and running costs? How important is the rental income? Are you primarily looking for a sound investment or do you plan to work or start a business there? Often buyers have a variety of reasons for buying a home in Florida, for example many people buy a holiday home with a view to living there during the North American or European winter when they retire (North American retirees who winter in Florida are known as 'snowbirds'). If this is the case, there are more factors to take into account than if you're 'simply' buying a holiday home which you will occupy for a few weeks a year only (when it's probably wiser not to buy at all). If on the other hand you plan to work or start a business in Florida, you will be faced with a whole set of different criteria.

Can you really afford to buy a home in Florida? What of the future? Is your income secure and protected against inflation and currency fluctuations? In the 1980s, many people purchased holiday homes in Florida by taking out second mortgages on their family homes and stretching their financial resources to the limits. Not surprisingly, when the recession struck in the early 1990s many of them lost their Florida homes when they were unable to keep up the mortgage payments. Buying a home abroad can be an excellent long term investment, although in recent years many people have had their fingers burnt in the volatile property market in many countries. Fortunately the Florida property market is one of the most stable in the world and property values there weren't affected by the recession nearly as much as those in most other popular holiday-home destinations (and most other US states).

In Florida, property values increase at an average of around 5 per cent a year or in line with inflation, although in some fashionable resorts and communities prices rise faster than average, which is generally reflected in much higher purchase prices. There's generally a stable property market in Florida, which acts as a discouragement to speculators wishing to make a quick profit, particularly when you consider that capital gains tax can wipe out much of the profit made on the sale of a home (particularly a second home). **You shouldn't expect to make a quick profit when buying property in Florida, but should look upon it as an investment in your family's and friends' future happiness, rather than merely in financial terms.**

There are both advantages and disadvantages to buying a home in Florida, although for most people the benefits far outweigh the drawbacks. Among the many advantages of buying a home in Florida are guaranteed year-round sunshine (nowhere in Europe compares); excellent value for money; quality and spaciousness of homes; stable property market; safe purchase procedure (providing you aren't reckless); integrity of licensed real estate brokers; English-speaking; low cost and high standard of living;

relatively low taxes (for residents); inexpensive flights; good rental possibilities (in most areas); excellent local services; and a vast range of affordable leisure (including the largest concentration of theme parks in the world) and sports activities on your doorstep.

There are of course a number of drawbacks, not least the restrictions regarding the amount of time non-residents can spend there (a maximum of six months a year); the difficulty in retiring to Florida; the high crime rate in some areas; the high humidity and threat of hurricanes in summer (although overplayed); overcrowding in popular tourist areas (particularly in winter when the snowbirds arrive)); overdevelopment in many areas; high traffic congestion, particularly in urban areas; relatively high running costs of a home (compared with some other countries); the expense of getting to and from Florida (if you own a holiday home there); and the high cost of health and homeowner's insurance.

Unless you know exactly what you're looking for and where, it's advisable to rent a property for a period until you're more familiar with an area. As when making all major financial decisions, it's never advisable to be in too much of a hurry. Many people make expensive (even catastrophic) errors when buying homes in Florida, usually because they do insufficient research and are in too much of a hurry, often setting themselves ridiculous deadlines (such as buying a home during a long weekend break or a week's holiday). Not surprisingly, most people wouldn't dream of acting so rashly when buying a property in their home country! It isn't uncommon for buyers to regret their decision after some time and wish they had bought a different type of property in a different region (or even in a different country).

Before deciding to buy a home in Florida it's advisable to do extensive research and read a number of books especially written for those planning to live or work there (like this one and *Living and Working in America*, also written by your author). It also helps to study specialist property magazines such as *International Property Magazine* and *World of Property* (see **Appendix A** for a list), and to visit overseas property exhibitions such as those organized by Overseas Property Match and Homebuyer Events Ltd. in Britain. **Bear in mind that the cost of investing in a few books or magazines (and other research) is tiny compared with the expense of making a big mistake!**

This chapter provides information about permits and visas, retirement, working, buying a business, communications (e.g. telephones), getting to Florida and getting around, particularly regarding driving in Florida.

DO YOU NEED A PERMIT OR VISA ?

Before making any plans to buy a home in Florida, you must ensure that you will be permitted to use the property when you wish and for whatever purpose you have in mind, and whether you will need a visa. While foreigners are freely permitted to buy property in the US, most aren't permitted to remain longer than three months a year without an appropriate residence permit (a so-called 'green card') or visa. If there's a possibility that you or a family member may wish to work or live permanently in Florida, you should enquire whether it will be possible before making any plans to buy a home there. **Permit infringements are taken seriously by the American authorities and there are penalties for breaches of regulations, including fines and even deportation for flagrant abuses!**

With the exception of certain visitors (see **Visa Waivers** on page 19) all non-resident foreigners wishing to enter the US require a visa. The US issues a bewildering range of visas, which are broadly divided into immigrant (permanent resident) and non-immigrant (temporary resident) visas. An immigrant visa gives a person the right to live and work in the US (and change jobs freely) on a permanent basis and qualify for US citizenship after five years' residence. A non-immigrant visa allows someone to enter and remain in the US on a temporary basis, e.g. from six months to five years, and in certain cases to accept employment. Work permits aren't issued as the appropriate visa serves the same purpose.

American immigration and naturalization laws are enforced by the Immigration and Naturalization Service (INS) of the United States Department of Justice, who are responsible for the processing of foreigners entering the US and those seeking permanent residence. The INS maintains four regional service centers and over 60 local offices throughout America, and also has representatives in most American embassies and consulates. Entry into the country is strictly controlled and anyone who doesn't comply with visa requirements can be fined, jailed or deported. The US attempts to restrict entry of undesirables and misfits (of which it evidently has more than its fair share already) and anyone who's a threat to the health, welfare, and security of America.

Only holders of visas permitting employment may work in the US and holders of other categories of visas may not accept employment. Your passport must usually be valid for a minimum of six months after the termination of your planned stay in Florida and if it's close to its expiry date it's better to renew it before traveling to the US.

Note that immigration is a complex subject and that the information contained in this chapter is intended as a general guide only. You shouldn't base any decisions or actions on the information contained in this or any other book without confirming it with an American Embassy or Consulate. There are many books detailing how to obtain a visa to live or work in the US, a number of which are listed in **Appendix B.**

Visitors

Anyone wishing to visit Florida for a holiday or on business who doesn't qualify for a visa-free trip (see **Visa Waivers** on page 19) or who wishes to remain longer than 90 days and less than 180 days (six months), must apply for a category B visa. Visitors' visas aren't required by Canadian citizens and most foreign residents of Canada (landed immigrants) who wish to enter the US as visitors, or by Mexican nationals with a US border crossing card. Visitors' visas are the most commonly issued visas and are valid for visits of up to six months a year for business or pleasure. B-1 visas are granted to business persons and B-2 visas to tourists, although combined B1/B2 visas are also available.

Both B-1 and B-2 visas may be valid for a single entry only or for 10 years, when they allow multiple entries. Note that since January 1st 1995 indefinite visas have been replaced by a 10-year visa and indefinite visas issued more than 10 years before the date of travel (perhaps contained in an old passport) are no longer valid. Whether you receive a single or a 10-year visa is decided by the issuing embassy or consulate. A 10-year visa allows the holder to enter and leave the US as often as he wishes during its validity period. However, B visas are always valid for a maximum stay of six months at any one time or a total of six months in a calendar year (the actual period is decided by an immigration officer), although extensions may be granted. Factors which affect the time limit of a B visa include the expiration date of the visa, the date stamped on your I-94 card (see page 188), the number of entries made, the expiration date of your passport, and your history of travel to the US.

B visas *don't* give visitors the right to work (termed 'productive labor') in the US, even if payment is made outside the country. This doesn't, however, apply to business conducted as a visiting businessman, e.g. as a representative of an overseas company, when no payment is received from an American source. The holder of a B-1 visa may consult with business associates, lawyers or accountants, take part in business or professional conventions, and negotiate contracts and look for investment opportunities. A category B-1 visitor must have a permanent overseas residence and must remain on the payroll of an overseas company.

In addition to completing form OF-156 (see page 188), supporting documentation may be required in the form of an invitation from the person whom you will be visiting or staying with in America, if applicable. For a B-1 visa, you may require a letter from your employer verifying your continued employment, the reason for your trip, and your itinerary in America. You may be required to 'submit evidence substantiating the purpose of your trip and your intention to depart from the US after a temporary visit.' Examples of the evidence required are given on form OF-156. In the case of pleasure trips, this includes documents outlining your plans in the US and stating the reasons why you would return abroad after a short stay such as family ties, employment (a self-employed person may require a letter from his accountant or solicitor stating that he's known to them and how long he's been in business), home ownership or similar binding obligations in your home country. **The issue of a B-2 visa allowing a stay of six months is usually straightforward for a retiree owning a home in Florida, but should never be regarded as a formality (owners are sometimes required to attend an embassy interview before being granted a visa).**

Applications for B visas can usually be made in person and be issued the same day, although some embassies (e.g. London) insist that applications are made by mail, except for bona fide emergency travel. You can usually leave your application and documents at an embassy (a 'drop-box' is provided) and collect your visa the next day or have it mailed to you. If time doesn't allow an application by mail, you can apply through a travel agent or visa courier service, who can usually obtain visas within a few working days. If you apply for a visitor's visa by mail, you should allow up to four weeks for processing (it varies depending on the time of year). Note that if you make an application for a visitor's visa in a country other than your home country or country of residence (called an 'out-of-district' application), your application will be subject to increased scrutiny as it may be suspected that you're 'shopping around' for an easier port of entry.

Note that a B visa *doesn't* automatically allow you to remain in the US for six months at a time. However, it's possible to extend a B visa for a maximum of six months, when the application must be accompanied by a letter from your employer (if applicable) explaining why you need an extension. There's no entitlement to an appeal if the extension isn't granted. Technically you can leave the US after six months, return the following day and stay for a further six months, although this is illegal. A condition of the B visa is that you intend to leave the US at a specific time in the future *and not to remain indefinitely.* **You must also maintain a permanent home abroad.** Although many people use a B visa to remain in the US for a year or two, most eventually get caught and are refused admission.

Visa Waivers

Nationals of certain countries can visit the US under a temporary Visa Waiver Pilot Program (VWPP), including the citizens of Andorra, Austria, Belgium, Brunei,

Denmark, Finland, France, Germany, Iceland, Ireland, Italy, Japan, Liechtenstein, Luxembourg, Monaco, the Netherlands, New Zealand, Norway, San Marino, Spain, Sweden, Switzerland and the United Kingdom. If you're a citizen of one of these countries, you don't require a visa to visit America, providing:

- you have a valid passport issued by a participating country and are a citizen of that country (not just a resident);
- your trip is for pleasure or business;
- your stay is for a maximum of 90 days;
- you have a return or onward non-transferable ticket for a destination outside North America, issued by a participating carrier (i.e. most major airlines) and non-refundable except in the country where issued or your home country. If you enter the US by land from Canada or Mexico, the return ticket requirement isn't applicable.
- you have proof of financial solvency;
- there are no reasons or 'grounds of exclusion' why you shouldn't be admitted to America.

A *Nonimmigrant Visa Waiver Arrival/Departure Form* (form I-94W) must be completed and is available from participating carriers (airlines and shipping companies), travel agents, US tourist offices, American embassies and consulates, and land-border posts (Canada and Mexico). Note that if you enter the US under the visa waiver pilot program, you can't obtain an extension beyond three months and you waive your rights to a hearing of exclusion or deportation, except for asylum.

RETIREMENT

It's impossible for foreigners without a permanent residence permit to retire in Florida or elsewhere in the US. In order to live permanently in Florida you require an immigrant (permanent resident) visa, which is difficult to obtain. Proof of owning a home or self-sufficiency (unless you're *very* rich and famous) isn't a qualification for long term residence. Therefore if you don't qualify to live in the US by birthright or relationship, it may be impossible to obtain a residence permit. There are, however, a number of ways to obtain a residence permit, but it's necessary to obtain expert legal advice from an immigration lawyer (see **Appendix F**).

Some people who are interested in living permanently or 'retiring' to Florida purchase a small business (see **Self-Employment** on page 22), which providing you have a partner or manager may necessitate little actual involvement in the day-to-day operation of the business. Anyone with a B visa can spend up to six months a year in Florida and many retirees from North America and northern Europe do so each year, usually during the northern hemisphere's coldest months, i.e. October to March.

WORKING

If there's a possibility that you or any family members may wish to work in Florida, you must ensure that it will be possible before buying a home. If you don't qualify to live and work in the US by birthright or family relationship, obtaining a work permit may be difficult or impossible. Apart from buying a business in Florida (see **Self-Employment** below), one of the easiest methods of working in the US is through an L-1 Intracompany Transfer visa. With an L-1 visa a foreigner owning or employed by a business abroad can form a branch, subsidiary, affiliate or joint venture partner of the same company in Florida, and have himself transferred there to work for the American company. It's essential to engage an immigration lawyer when applying for an L-1 visa.

Investors who create employment for at least 10 full-time American workers (not family members) by investing capital in a new commercial enterprise in the US are granted an immigrant (permanent resident) visa. The minimum amount of capital required is usually $1m, although it depends on the unemployment rate in the proposed area. It may vary from $500,000 in a rural area with high unemployment to $3m in an urban area with low unemployment.

Immigration Lawyers: It isn't always essential to employ an immigration lawyer when applying for a visa to work in the US, but it's usually advisable. Many visa applications are rejected because the paperwork is incorrect, e.g. the wrong information has been provided; a form hasn't been completed correctly; the wrong visa application has been made; or the incorrect approach has been made to the Immigration and Naturalization Service (INS). The correct method depends on each individual case and the procedure can be complicated (INS rules and regulations also change frequently). Before hiring a lawyer you should ensure that you know exactly how much you must pay and precisely what you will receive for your money. There are US visa consultants in many countries (see **Appendix F**), many of whom advertise in the local press, e.g. those publications listed in **Appendix A**.

Information: The US Department of Labor, Bureau of Labor Statistics, publishes an abundance of information about employment trends and job prospects in the US including the *Occupational Outlook Handbook, Job Outlook in Brief, Tomorrow's Jobs: Overview, The Job Outlook for College Graduates to the Year 2000* and *Matching Yourself With the World of Work*, all of which are available from the Superintendent of Documents, US Government Printing Office, Washington, DC 20402 (tel. 202/783-3238). State and local job market and career information is available from state employment security agencies and State Occupational Information Coordinating Committees (SOICCs). There are a number of books written for those planning to work in the US including *Living and Working in America* (written by your author and published by Survival Books), *Finding a Job in the USA* (Island Publishing) and *How to Get a Job in America* by Roger Jones (How To Books).

Anyone interested in working in Florida should note that the economy is largely based on tourism, which for most employees means low wages. A high percentage of the workforce is employed in hotels, restaurants, department stores and small shops, all businesses which usually pay relatively low salaries or the minimum wage. Even skilled workers are paid significantly less in Florida, where hourly rates are much lower than those paid in northern US states and northern Europe. You can get an idea of local wage rates for various occupations from local Chambers of Commerce or the Florida Department of Labor and Employment Security.

SELF-EMPLOYMENT

One of the most common ways for foreigners to live permanently in Florida is to buy or start a business, which entitles citizens of many countries to obtain a Treaty Investor Visa (see page 24) valid for up to five years. The US welcomes small businessmen (i.e. those employing less than 100 people) who represent around 97 per cent of all Florida businesses. However, before investing in a business in Florida it's essential to obtain expert professional and legal advice. An application for a visa should be made by an experienced immigration lawyer or a business broker, as well prepared applications are usually processed quickly and successfully. Visas can be approved and issued in as little as two weeks if the paperwork is in order, although you should allow one to two months.

The purchase of a business *must* always be conditional on obtaining visas, licenses, permits, loans or any other necessary funding, and anything else that's vital to the successful operation of a business. You aren't required to make an investment before making an application for an E-2 visa, but the necessary funds must be available. This allows you to make an offer to purchase a business which is conditional upon you being granted an E-2 visa. Note that if you require financing, it must meet with the rules and is usually limited to a maximum of 25 per cent of the value of a business costing around $100,000. While it's easier to buy an existing business (which gives you an immediate cash flow) than start a new one, you must thoroughly investigate the financial status, turnover and value of a business (*always* obtain an independent valuation). It's important to engage an accountant and lawyer at the earliest opportunity.

Licensed Business Brokers: Many people use the services of a licensed business broker when buying a business in Florida, a number of whom advertise in the publications listed in **Appendix A**. **It's important to confirm that a broker is licensed and not to take his word for it (don't believe a piece of paper, but check with the authorities)!** It's advisable to use a buyer's broker who represents only you (the buyer) and not the seller, thus eliminating potential conflicts of interest. It's important to note that most real estate brokers offer businesses for sale through a multiple listing service (see page 153) and therefore primarily represent the seller and not the buyer. A business buyer's broker will not only find you a suitable business in a particular area, but will negotiate the price on your behalf and may arrange for an E-2 visa. Business brokers have a huge number and range of businesses for sale including everything from a sandwich bar to a restaurant, a laundromat to a motel, plus a variety of franchise operations.

Don't pay a broker's fees in advance and deal only with a company that operates on a success basis, where payment isn't due until a business is purchased and the visa approved. Compare brokers' commissions, which usually vary depending on the price of the business. Note that it isn't normal practice in Florida for a seller to divulge details of his accounts (turnover, profit, etc.) until a prospective buyer has entered into a preliminary or main contract to purchase the business and a good faith deposit has been placed in an escrow account. You should also engage a lawyer who's acting solely for you and not for any other parties involved in a transaction (and who isn't receiving commissions from anyone involved). **Take care as there are crooks around who prey on greenhorn foreigners!**

Choosing a Business: The key to buying or operating a successful business in Florida is research, research and more research. Bear in mind that choosing the location for a business is even more important than the location for a home. Always thoroughly investigate an existing or proposed business (including the location, catchment area, competition and history) before investing a dime. Check the trading and profit accounts and confirm them with the local tax office (they may be false!) by checking sales tax returns for the last two or three years. It's also advisable to have a certified public accountant (CPA) do an independent audit as some businesses use dual accounting. Some sellers deliberately try to sell an ailing business to an inexperienced and unsuspecting foreigner. A professional crook may offer owner financing knowing that you will be unable to maintain the payments and that they will be able to foreclose later and regain control of the business for nothing. Always check how long a business has been on the market. If it's longer than six months it may be that it's overpriced and isn't a good investment.

Generally speaking it isn't advisable to run a business in a field in which you have no experience, although obviously this isn't always practical (and some businesses require little specialist education, knowledge or training). When experience or training is necessary, it's often wise to work for someone else in the same line of business to gain experience, rather than jump in at the deep end. Note that assistance, including hands-on help, from the seller could be made part of a purchase contract. **As any expert will tell you, the US isn't a country for amateur entrepreneurs, particularly amateurs who don't do their homework and are unfamiliar with Americans and the American way of doing business.**

Note that certain businesses, e.g. a hair and beauty salon, must be licensed, which require an owner to go back to school and pass exams in Florida. It may, however, be possible to operate a business under the existing owner's license until you have your own, in which case there should be a clause in the contract. Note, however, that it's a federal offense to operate without a license, e.g. you need a license to sell cigarettes, alcohol, gasoline, food and provide accommodations. It's common practice (and invaluable) for the previous owner to stay on for a period (e.g. 30 days) after a sale to show the new owner the ropes. If applicable and you can afford it, it will also pay you to hire any existing staff. It isn't necessary to employ US nationals if a business will initially support the buyers only, although it's a big plus point with the authorities when applying for a visa. Employees can be full-time, part-time or contract staff. A number of free commercial real estate/business guides are published in Florida including the monthly *Harmon Commercial Real Estate* (tel. 1-900-773-7356 for a copy).

Local Information: There are many local, state and federal government agencies and departments providing information and advice about starting and running a business. The best places to start are local Chambers of Commerce, which are a mine of information about every aspect of business and relocation to a particular town or area (many produce relocation and business information packages). The Florida Department of Commerce, Division of Economic Development (tel. 1-800-342-0771 or 904/488-9357) also publishes a wealth of information including a useful free Florida *Business & Newcomers* guide. *Florida Trend* business magazine is essential reading for business people and it also publishes a *Newcomer's Guide to Florida Business*.

The US Small Business Administration (SBA) has offices in most counties (many located in Chambers of Commerce) and provides a wide variety of free business counseling concerning finance, accounting, record keeping, business start-up and management, taxes, marketing, sales promotion, advertising, retailing, manufacturing, and sales and service businesses. The SBA has two offices in Florida, one serving southern Florida (1320 South Dixie Highway, Suite 301, Coral Gables, FL 33146, tel. 305/536-5521) and the other northern Florida (7825 Baymeadow Way, Suite 100-B, Jacksonville, FL 32256-7504, tel. 904/443-1900). The Small Business Development Center has programs for budding entrepreneurs at most state universities and community colleges in Florida. If you're thinking of starting a business or becoming self-employed you may also find it beneficial to join the National Association of Self-Employed (NASE), PO Box 612067, DFW Airport, TX 75261-2067 (tel. 1-800-232-NASE). NASE publish a wealth of information for small businesses (including the *Small Business Resource Guide*) and can save you considerable time, trouble and *money* through a multitude of services and discounts.

General Information: Most international firms of accountants have offices throughout the US and in many other countries and are an invaluable source of information (in English and other languages) on subjects such as forming a company, company law, taxation and social security. Many publish free booklets concerning doing business in the US including *Doing Business in the United States* (Ernst & Young and Price Waterhouse) and the *AT&T Business Guide to the USA* (available from American Chambers of Commerce).

Wealth Warning: Whatever people may tell you, working for yourself isn't easy and it requires a lot of hard work (self-employed people generally work much longer hours than employees); a sizeable investment and sufficient operating funds (most businesses fail due to a lack of capital); good organization (e.g. bookkeeping and planning); excellent customer relations (in the US the customer is always right, even when he's wrong!); and a measure of luck (although generally the harder you work, the more 'luck' you will have). Don't be seduced by the apparent laid-back way of life in Florida — if you want to be a success in business you can't play at it. Bear in mind that almost two out of three new American businesses fail within three to five years and that the self-employed must provide their own health and pension plans, and don't qualify for unemployment insurance and workers' compensation.

Treaty Investor Visas

One of the main attractions of buying or starting a business in the US is that it provides one of the easiest and quickest ways to obtain a non-immigrant visa, namely an E-2 Treaty Investors Visa. E-2 visas are available only to citizens of countries with which the US has a trade investment treaty including Albania, Argentina, Australia, Austria, Bangladesh, Belgium, Bosnia, Bulgaria, Cameroon, Canada, Colombia, Congo, Costa Rica, Croatia, Czech Republic, Ecuador, Egypt, Ethiopia, Finland, France, Germany, Grenada, Honduras, Iran, Ireland, Italy, Japan, Kazakhstan, Korea (South), Kyrgyzstan, Latvia, Liberia, Luxembourg, Macedonia, Mexico, Moldova, Mongolia, Morocco, Netherlands, Norway, Oman, Pakistan, Panama, Paraguay, Philippines, Poland, Romania, Russia, Senegal, Slovakia, Slovenia, Spain, Sri Lanka, Suriname, Sweden, Switzerland, Taiwan, Thailand, Togo, Tunisia, Turkey, Uzbekistan, the United Kingdom and Zaire.

At least 50 per cent of the owners of a treaty business must be citizens of a single investor country. An E-2 visa holder must be a principal owner who controls at least 50 per cent of the company or a key employee (with the same nationality as the principal owner) who's a manager, executive or a person with specialized knowledge essential to the business. E-2 visas are issued subject to certain requirements, but there's no restriction on the number issued each year. It isn't always necessary to use an immigration lawyer to make an E-2 visa application, although it's usually advisable. Always obtain a quotation in writing and shop around a number of immigration lawyers (check their credentials and references), as fees can run into thousands of dollars depending on the amount of work involved. **Note that the purchase of a business should always be contingent on obtaining an E-2 visa.**

An E-2 visa is granted to the principal owner or a key employee of a company that has invested a 'substantial amount of money' in a business enterprise in America. The minimum investment figure isn't fixed (although some people will tell you otherwise), but the investment must be 'substantial' and mustn't be 'marginal', i.e. it mustn't usually provide a living solely for the investor and his family. **The investment necessary depends on the kind of business and while most investments are over $100,000, E-2 visas may be approved for as little as $50,000.** Note, however, that for an investment under $500,000, asset-backed financing is usually limited to 25 per cent of a business' value. When establishing a new business, you must invest a sum which would normally be considered necessary to start the particular type of business envisaged and you must have reasonable cash reserves to cover emergencies. You must also allow around 20 per cent of the purchase price for working capital. Sellers are often prepared to offer owner financing, whereby they finance a percentage of a sale themselves.

Note that due to the relatively high sum required to buy or start a business in Florida, many people initially rent rather than buy a home there. A business can be jointly owned with a spouse or partner, who can be an American citizen. Although an investor must be actively involved in the enterprise and serve in directing and managing the investment, it's possible with an active partner or manager to be almost a 'sleeping partner' in a business (although you keep this from the authorities). The investment must be in an active business or an ongoing commercial operation, for example a service industry or manufacturing. It must additionally create jobs for American workers, either immediately or in the near future, although there's no set minimum number. The enterprise therefore can't be just for the sole purpose of providing a living for the investor and his family. It's generally easier to obtain an E-2 visa for an existing rather than a new business.

E-2 visas are initially granted for a period of up to five years and can be extended for up to five years at a time. **Note, however, that an E-2 visa is valid only so long as a business continues to be viably operated.** The spouse and children under 21 of an E-2 visa holder are included in the visa, but may not work in America. Children can attend college or university in the US until the age of 21, when they must qualify for a visa in their own right. No educational standards, job offer or experience are required for an E-2 visa, which permits multiple entries and a potentially indefinite stay in the US.

KEEPING IN TOUCH

Like the rest of the US, Florida enjoys a high standard of communications services such as telephone (including mobile phones), fax, mail and courier services.

Telephone: The American telephone system is the most modern and cheapest in the world and you can get a telephone installed within a few days in most areas. Call charges levied by American telephone companies are much lower than in most other countries, particularly if you take full advantage of off-peak periods and toll-free numbers. Florida's 9m telephones are run by around 13 companies, although the market is dominated by Southern Bell with some 60 per cent, followed by GTE Florida with around 20 per cent and United Telephone with about 15 per cent. Telephone companies charge a connection fee (e.g. $55) and a deposit (e.g. $100) for new customers. In addition to fixed-line telephones, there's also an extensive cellular, mobile (wireless) phone network in the US covering the whole of Florida (shop around as there are numerous deals and discounts). **Emergency numbers are listed at the front of most telephone directories (the general emergency number in the US is 911).**

Public telephones or payphones are plentiful in cities and towns (where they are usually located on street corners), airports, rail and bus stations; hotel and office building lobbies; bars and restaurants (many provide cordless telephones); libraries and other public buildings; stores, department stores and drug stores; laundromats; shopping malls; gas stations; and at rest stops on major highways. The minimum cost for local calls is 25¢ for the first three minutes and 10¢ for each additional minute.

Installation: Homes in the US (both new and old) are invariably wired for telephone services, although no telephone is installed. Many American homes have telephone points in almost every room, although you should check the number and type of telephone points in advance (there are usually only two in standard new homes). If you need additional wiring or points you can have it done by your telephone company, a contractor or you can do it yourself. When you aren't doing the installation yourself, obtain quotations from a number of companies. You aren't required to rent (lease) or purchase a telephone from your local telephone company and can buy one from any retailer (costing from around $10).

Using the Telephone: Using a telephone in the US is much the same as in any other country, with the exception of a few American idiosyncracies. Telephone numbers consist of a three-digit area code (123), a three-digit exchange code (456) and a four-digit subscriber number (7890), written variously as (123) 456-7890 (standard), 123-456-7890 or 123/456-7890. An area code may cover a suburb in a large city (212 is Manhattan, New York), a Metropolitan area (213 is Greater Los Angeles) or an entire state (207 is Maine). There are seven area codes in Florida, three of which (352, 941 and 954) were introduced in the last few years. Florida codes are 305 (covering Miami, the Florida Keys and the southern part of the southeast coast); 352 (14 central and northern counties, nine of which also use another code); 407 (Orlando and its surrounds and the central area of the east coast); 813 (central west coast including Tampa and St. Petersburg); 904 (northern Florida); 941 (13 counties in southwest Florida ranging from Polk County to Collier and Monroe counties); and 954 (Broward County). If you're making a call to a number within your local calling or service area, you dial the seven-digit telephone number only (exchange + subscriber). When making a call to another area code, you dial 1 + the area code + the seven-digit telephone number. Local calling and service areas are shown in telephone directories.

Calls outside your local calling or service area are termed 'toll calls' and are handled by a long distance telephone company. In America, states or regions are served by local telephone companies, such as Southern Bell in Florida. For long distance, e.g. interstate and international calls, there are completely independent long distance telephone companies such as AT&T, MCI and Sprint. AT&T are the leading long distance telephone company with over 60 per cent share of the US market, followed by MCI (around 20 per cent) and Sprint (10 per cent). Rates for domestic long distance and international calls vary depending on the telephone company, and one company may be cheaper for long distance calls, but more expensive for international calls. AT&T,

MCI and Sprint compete vigorously for customers and offer special deals to new customers.

Most areas are served by a number of long distance companies, although some have one only. You must designate (or pre-subscribe) a primary long distance company when you apply to be connected and all calls made by dialing 1 (or 0) plus an area code are then routed through that company. If you wish to place a call via an alternate long distance company, you must make arrangements with that company. Some areas have an Easy Access System, where each long distance company has its own code, which is dialed before dialing 1 + area code + telephone number.

Toll-Free Numbers: Toll-free numbers are indicated by an 800 code and are provided by businesses, organizations and government agencies in America. When calling a business such as an airline or car rental company, always use their toll-free number, which can be obtained from the national toll-free directory assistance number (1-800-555-1212). Note, however, that most toll-free numbers are for interstate callers only and must be prefixed with a '1' (a local number is usually provided for in-state callers). Don't confuse toll-free 800 numbers with 700 or 900 information or entertainment numbers, which are expensive.

Extra Services: All telephone companies provide a range of extra services, usually called custom calling or optional services, most of which require a touch-tone telephone which provides faster dialing plus access to a range of computerized services. These include call waiting, call diversion, repeat call, priority call and call return. Person-to-person, collect and other 'special' calls can be made via the operator.

Costs: Florida telephone companies offer a variety of 'monthly calling plans' or measured services to residential customers. Plans are based on direct-dial calls made to exchanges within the area covered by your local telephone company and rates vary depending on the area, the number of free calls permitted and the cost of calls. Your local telephone company will help you decide the best service for your requirements and budget. The lowest monthly fee is usually around $15. It's cheaper to make long distance and international calls after 5pm and before 8am on weekdays, and at weekends.

Part-Time Residents: If you're away from your Florida home for from two to nine months a year, your telephone company may offer a 'seasonal service' whereby they will disconnect your telephone while you're away and charge a reduced fee. This is advisable for owners who will be renting their home and don't want visitors to use the telephone. You can also reroute all your calls to a local number while you're away (e.g. a friend or a management company) and simply disconnect the telephone, although the socket will remain active. Owners who are renting their home can install a special telephone allowing visitors to make free local and 800 calls, but requiring long distance and international calls to be charged to a credit card.

Billing: Telephone bills in the US are sent out monthly. Both local and long distance calls are usually itemized with the date, time, place, area and number called, rate, duration and cost. Bills are sent by your local telephone company and include charges from long distance call companies, although there's no connection between them. If you're planning to buy a holiday home in Florida from which you will be absent for long periods, you should pay your telephone bill (and all other regular bills) by direct drafting (direct debit) from a local bank account. If you fail to pay a bill on time your service could be cut and it can take weeks to have it reconnected.

International Calls: To make an international call, you dial the international access code (011), the country code (e.g. 44 for Britain), the area code *without* the first zero, and finally the subscriber's number. For example, to call the number 123-4567 in central London, England (area code 0171) you would dial 011-44-171-123-4567. The reason you don't get the operator after dialing the first 0 of 011, is that there's an automatic delay after you dial 0, during which time you can dial additional numbers. When making a person-to-person, collect call (not accepted by all countries), calling card or billing to a third number international call, you need to dial 01 instead of 011, followed by the country code, city code and number. The operator will come on the line and ask for details, such as the name of the person you're calling or your calling card number. If you can't dial an international number directly, you must dial 00 and make the call via the international operator, when the cost will be the same as dialing yourself.

American long distance telephone companies (e.g. AT&T, MCI and Sprint) compete vigorously for overseas customers and all offer US citizens and residents calling (credit) cards, and calling cards which allow foreign customers to bill their international calls to a credit card. The benefits of international calling cards are that they are fee-free; calls can be made to and from most countries; calls can usually be made from any telephone, including hotel telephones; calls are made via an English-speaking operator in the US (foreign-language operators are also available) and, **most important of all, calls are charged at American rates (based on the cost between the US and the country you're calling from and to) and are usually much cheaper than calls made via local (foreign) telephone companies.**

You should be aware that telephone calling card fraud is a huge and growing international problem. If someone gets hold of your card and code numbers they can make calls at your expense (in the US crooks train zoom cameras on public telephones to watch people entering their code numbers). Don't let anyone overhear your code number, which in the US must be said out loud rather than dialed.

Internet 'Telephone' Services: The success of the Internet is built on the ability to gather information from computers around the world by connecting to a nearby service for the cost of a local telephone call. If you have correspondents or friends who are connected to the Internet, you can make international 'calls' for the price of a local telephone call to your Internet provider, which may even be free. Once on the Internet there are no other charges, no matter how much distance is covered or time is spent on-line. Internet users in the US can buy software from companies such as Vodaltec and Quarterdeck (costing around $50) that effectively turns their personal computer into a voice-based telephone (both parties must have compatible computer software). You also need a sound card, speakers, a microphone and a modem, and access to a local Internet provider (costing around $20 a month). While the quality of communication isn't as good as using a telephone (it's similar to using a CB radio) and you need to arrange call times in advance, making international 'calls' costs virtually nothing.

Fax: In addition to being home to the world's most prolific telephone users, the US also has the largest number of fax (facsimile) machines in the world. Faxes can be sent from a payphone-type machine and credit card operated machines (e.g. provided by the Pay Fax Company) which are provided in public places such as airports, railroad stations, photocopy centers and even book shops. There are public telex and fax bureaux in most cities (see **Business Services** below), and most hotels provide telex and fax services for non-residents (e.g. fax machines in lobbies) and in-room fax for guests in some hotels. You can also obtain a fax pager which allows you to call and obtain information about your fax messages, e.g. the SkyTel Skyfax service uses a standard SkyTel pager to notify travelers of an incoming fax. The pager display tells you the name of the sender and his telephone number and you can have the fax sent to a laptop computer or a nearby fax machine.

Mail Services: Although the United States Postal Service (USPS) isn't the most efficient in the world, it's certainly not the worst and is supplemented by many excellent domestic and international courier companies. The delivery standards for first-class mail are next day delivery in the same metro area, two-day delivery within 600 miles and three-day delivery over 600 miles. Airmail from Florida to Europe takes around a week. Post office business hours in the US are usually from 9am to 5pm, Monday to Friday, and some offices are open on Saturdays, e.g. from 8am to noon. Main post offices in major towns don't close at lunchtimes. Some main post offices are open 24-hours Monday to Saturday for important services and have a self-service section for weighing packages and buying stamps. In rural areas and small towns, post offices usually have restricted and varied business hours.

Domestic mail in the US can be sent by first, second, third or fourth class (who said the US had no class system!). First class mail is generally used to send letters and written and sealed matter; second class is for newspapers, magazines and other periodicals with second-class mailing privileges (however, it can't be used by the general public); third class is for circulars, books, catalogs, printed matter, merchandise, seeds, cuttings, bulbs, roots, scions and plants; and fourth class mail is for merchandise, books, printed matter, and all other items that don't come under first, second or third-class.

Domestic letters weighing up to one ounce cost 32¢, airmail international letters 60¢ up to half an ounce and $1 up to one ounce, and postcards 20¢ within the US and 50¢ international airmail. Aerogrammes (pre-paid airmail letters) cost 50¢ to all countries and are available from post offices and stationery stores. **Note that a surcharge is usually levied when stamps are bought anywhere other than at a post office.** It's important to use the zip (post) code when mailing items to US addresses (without which mail may take longer to be delivered or be lost entirely) and to put your address on the back of the envelope. When sending a parcel abroad you need to complete a customs declaration form. Note that there are strict rules regarding the packaging of items sent by mail and it's advisable to use the special packaging available from post offices (or use a courier company).

Telegrams: Telegrams (or cables) can't be sent from post offices in the US and are handled by Western Union or American Telegram, both of whom have offices in most towns (to wire someone means to send them a cable). You can send telegrams by telephone and charge them to your telephone bill or a major credit card. For information or to send a telegram telephone 1-800-325-6000 for Western Union and 1-800-343-7363 for American Telegram. Both companies accept telegrams, mailgrams, cablegrams or radiograms from a home or business number. Local companies, listed under 'Telegraph Service' in the Yellow Pages, also provide a national and worldwide service.

Courier Services: The post office operates a domestic guaranteed overnight express mail service, as do private companies such as DHL, Emery Worldwide, Federal Express and UPS (who also provide express international parcel services). Companies guarantee next day delivery for domestic express items mailed before a certain time of day and offer a money-back guarantee if the stated delivery time isn't met. Pick-up (collection) services are provided by both the post office and private companies.

Business Services: Except for the delivery of letters, most mail services are also provided by private postal, business and communications service companies such as Mr. Mailbox and Mail Boxes Etc. (the 'post office alternative'), who have offices throughout Florida. Their services include a mailbox service, mail-hold, mail forwarding, call-in service and 24-hour access, stamps, envelopes, postcards, packing supplies, air shipping/receiving, postal metering, American Express money orders, Western Union money transfers, telegrams, mailgrams, cablegrams, computer letters, voicemail, E-mail, Internet services, fax (Minute Mail), telex, copy service, telephone message service, and various other business services.

GETTING THERE

Although it isn't so important if you're planning to live permanently in Florida and stay put, one of the major considerations when buying a holiday home is the cost of air transportation from your home country to Florida. How long will it take to get to your home in Florida, taking into consideration journeys to and from airports? How frequent are flights at the time(s) of year when you plan to travel? Are direct flights available? What is the cost of flights from your home country to the region in Florida where you're planning to buy a home? If a long journey is involved, e.g. from Europe or further afield, you should bear in mind that it takes many people a day or two to recover from jet-lag after a long flight. It's also possible to travel to Florida by train from Los Angeles and New York and Greyhound buses operate numerous routes from other US states to all major towns in Florida.

Florida has seven international airports (in order of passenger numbers): Miami, Orlando (the second largest in the US), Tampa, Fort Lauderdale/Hollywood, Palm Beach, Jacksonville and Sanford Orlando (a new airport serving the Orlando region). There are scheduled flights to Miami from most major countries and also to other major international airports such as Orlando and Tampa (although less frequently). However, only a few airlines fly non-stop from Europe to Florida, with the majority having one-stop links. There are also frequent charter flights to Miami, Orlando and Tampa from Britain and some other European countries. Connections from other US airports to Florida are plentiful and every major US airline and many minor airlines fly to Florida from other US states. Air Canada and the major US airlines such as American Airlines and Delta fly non-stop from Toronto and Vancouver to Miami and either Orlando or Tampa. Miami is designated a gateway airport and acts as a hub for American carriers and regional/commuter airlines, operating services to scores of smaller airports. Note, however, that there can be long immigration queues at Miami, which is the second busiest gateway to the US and the main hub between North and South America and the Caribbean. Arrivals are often subject to delays lasting up to two hours as stringent checks are made for drug traffickers and smugglers.

International air fares to and from the US are among the lowest in the world and have been slashed even further in recent years. When traveling to Florida from Europe it's usually cheaper to travel from a major city such as London, where a wide choice of low-cost fares are available. For example, from London's Gatwick and Heathrow airports there are scheduled flights to Miami by American Airlines, British Airways, Continental (via Newark), Delta, Northwest (via Boston), United, USAir (via Charlotte) and Virgin Airlines. Economy returns from Britain cost from around $300 return in low season and $700 in high season. Full list price flights on scheduled airlines cost from around $1,500 for an economy return to over $6,000 first class. Always shop around for the lowest fares available and book early for public and school holiday periods. British and other European travelers should compare the fares listed in newspapers such as the *Sunday Times*, *Observer* and the *European*, and London's *Time Out* entertainment magazine.

Note that the high season for flights from Europe to Florida is June to August (and a week either side of Christmas), which is the low season in central and southern Florida.

However, although you will pay more for your flight at this time of year, the cost of accommodations and other essentials should be cheaper. The low season for flights to central and southern Florida from Europe is November to March. Northern Florida has the same high and low seasons as Europe. Discounts are available from low-cost flight agents ('bucket shops' and 'consolidators') and can save you $150 to $300 on regular fares and agents and travel agents also offer frequent special offers. Package deals including flight and accommodations are plentiful in most European countries and they usually work out cheaper than do-it-yourself holidays, although accommodations are usually in the upper bracket and expensive. However, some budget travel agents offer hostel accommodations. Fly-drive deals are also common, although you should check extra costs which can add $100 to $200 a week to the 'cost' of a 'free' car rental (see **Car Rental** on page 40). Bear in mind that if you need to take a flight to Florida at short notice it can be prohibitively expensive as you may be unable to get an inexpensive charter or APEX flight. If you own a holiday home in Florida, it's possible to insure against emergency travel in some countries.

Always allow plenty of time to get to and from airports in Florida, particularly when traveling during peak hours when traffic congestion can be horrendous.

GETTING AROUND

Travel in Florida is rarely difficult or particularly time-consuming if you have your own car and avoid rush hours and bottlenecks. Using public transport is a different matter altogether and anything but a short journey requires careful planning. With the notable exception of air travel and rush-hour urban rail and bus services in a few areas, public transport in Florida is generally slow and infrequent (or non-existent). Cities and large towns have bus links and some have an intermittent train service, but many rural and coastal areas are inaccessible without your own transport (in some areas you may be able to make use of Florida's numerous waterways). If you don't drive or aren't planning to own a car in Florida, you will usually need to buy a home in a city or large town where there's adequate public transport. Due to the total dominance of the automobile over public transport, it's almost mandatory to own or rent a car in the US.

Almost everything in the US is designed with the motorist in mind, particularly shopping malls, and there's a surfeit of drive-in services including banks, movies, fast food joints, espresso bars, grocery stores, religious services, clinics and even marriages. Note that if you don't have a car you will need to carry all your shopping home or have it delivered. Having your own transport allows you a much wider choice of where you can buy a home in Florida as you will be able to live virtually anywhere. Many people with holiday homes in Florida rent or buy a car. Renting a car in Florida is relatively inexpensive and is the best option if you're planning to spend only a few weeks or months a year there. However, if you plan to spend the winter there, then it's advisable to buy a car, which is inexpensive compared with most other countries.

Note that buying a car in the US and shipping it abroad can result in huge savings, even after paying import duty and taxes in your home country. There are many shipping companies regularly shipping cars from the US to Europe and further afield. One such company is Wilhelmsen Lines (tel. 1-800-342-2721), who ship from Mobile, Alabama (just to the west of Pensacola in northern Florida) and from Savannah, Georgia to British and other European ports.

Bus: Buses are the cheapest way to get around in Florida, where Greyhound long distance buses link all major cities and many smaller towns. However, in rural and isolated areas bus services are rare and there may be one bus a day only, if any.

Greyhound services between the main cities operate 24-hours a day, stopping only for meal breaks and to change drivers. Note that Greyhound, the state's only commercial bus company, no longer publishes a timetable, which makes planning a journey requiring a few changes somewhat difficult. When planning a long journey, obtain the latest schedule from your local bus terminal, otherwise you could find yourself stranded in the back of beyond. There are also local buses in cities and large towns and much of the southeast coast is also covered. Although cheap, local buses are slow and a relatively short trip (e.g. from West Palm Beach to Miami) can take all day.

Train: Amtrak, the US national rail service, operates a limited service in Florida with around two trains a day on most routes. Amtrak services mainly consist of inter-state trains, e.g. the Silver Meteor and Silver Star, which run from Miami to New York (once a day) and the Sunset Limited from Miami to Los Angeles (three a week). A car train runs daily from Lorton, Virginia (near Washington DC) to Sanford, around 30 miles north of Disney World. Amtrak stations in Florida include Chipley, Crestview, Dade City, Deerfield Beach, DeLand, Delray Beach, Fort Lauderdale, Hollywood, Jacksonville, Kissimmee, Lake City, Lakeland, Marianna, Ocala, Okeechobee, Orlando, Pensacola, Miami, Palatka, Sanford, Sebring, Tallahassee, Tampa, West Palm Beach, Waldo (Gainsville), Wildwood, Winter Haven and Winter Park.

Amtrak provide Thruway buses, which can be used only by rail passengers, to link train services and service areas where there's no rail service (e.g. Clearwater and St. Petersburg). Between Miami and West Palm Beach there's an elevated Tri-Rail system, which has 12 stops and costs $2.50 one way. However, most services run during rush hours only, which means that you must travel during the early morning or evening. There are urban Metrorail and MetroMover rail transport systems in Miami, and Jacksonville has a downtown people-mover system. Florida is planning a high-speed rail service (using French TGV trains) between the state's major growth areas of Miami, Orlando and Tampa, the first stage (Orlando to Tampa) of which is scheduled for completion by around 2004 (but don't hold your breath).

Air: If you live near an airport, traveling within Florida by air is a viable alternative to driving or using other public transport. Cut-rate fares are regularly advertised in local newspapers and off-peak fares aren't much more expensive than taking a bus or train and are much faster. Florida has over 130 public airports (including international, regional and municipal) and numerous private airports, together handling around 40m passengers a year. Florida's major airports include Miami, Orlando, Tampa, Fort

Lauderdale/Hollywood, Palm Beach, Southwest Florida regional (Fort Myers), Jacksonville, Sarasota/Bradenton, Daytona Beach, Pensacola, Tallahassee, Melbourne (Cape Kennedy), Gainsville and Key West.

By Road: Florida's road system has been fighting a losing battle against the soaring number of cars for decades and road building and improvements have completely failed to keep pace with the state's population explosion in the last few decades. Although there's now increased funding for roads, Florida's overcrowded highways are likely to be around for many years (possibly decades). If at all possible, it's advisable to avoid rush hours like the plague. They vary depending on the area and are usually between 7 and 9.30am, and 4 to 6.30pm. Florida is infamous for its traffic jams, particularly on coastal highways such as the I-75 and I-95 and US highways 1, 19 and 41. The worst areas are around Miami, Fort Lauderdale, West Palm Beach, St. Petersburg, Clearwater, Tampa and Orlando.

It can be difficult to find a parking space at peak times in shopping malls and towns in urban areas, and gridlock (jams) is common in major metropolitan areas, particularly during peak holiday periods. Because of the traffic congestion many people consider any journey over a few miles to be a major outing, which is why there are shopping centers and restaurants every few blocks in most towns.

DRIVING IN FLORIDA

Like motorists in all countries, Americans have their own idiosyncracies and customs, many of which are peculiar to a particular region, state or city. Wherever you drive in America, the traffic density and different road rules (or lack of) can be intimidating. In American cities, one of the main causes of accidents is drivers 'running' (driving through) red stop lights. However, Americans generally have a reputation as good and careful drivers and most take their driving seriously. Drivers tend to be relaxed, courteous and considerate and, unlike many Europeans, are usually happy to give way to a driver waiting to enter the traffic flow or change lanes. As in most countries, drivers are usually more polite and respectful of pedestrians in small towns than in major cities. In country or wilderness areas, you should keep an eye open for alligators, deer and other wildlife which may stray into your path.

The standard of Florida roads varies enormously from eight-lane freeways in urban areas, to gravel or dirt tracks in remote rural areas. Generally American roads have fewer road markings (e.g. studs or 'cat's eyes') than European roads. Streets in most cities are laid out in a grid pattern (hence 'gridlock' meaning a traffic jam), with all roads running north-south or east-west. In the downtown areas of main cities every alternate street is usually a one-way street. Streets are usually marked as north, south, east or west of a dividing line and each corner is designated a block number indicating whether it's N/S/E/W of the dividing line. It's usually important to know whether you want uptown or downtown when asking for directions. Direction signs are often sparse (particularly on freeways), inconsistent and poorly placed. They are usually unlit at night in urban areas and hence difficult to read. In many suburbs, counties may be posted but not major towns. **If you get lost and end up in a 'rundown' area, don't stop a stranger to ask the way, but find a policeman or police station or at the very least a brightly lit gas station or other establishment.**

A combination of straight wide roads, big comfortable cars, low maximum speeds (although federal speed limits have been abolished), and vigilant police, tend to result in a relaxed and civilized driving style. The extra comforts provided as standard in many American cars, such as automatic transmission, power steering and brakes, and air-conditioning, also help make driving more relaxing. That's not to say that there aren't crazy, incompetent and aggressive drivers in Florida, rather that they are very much in the minority. Fortunately you will meet few of the crazies portrayed on TV and in American movies. Wherever you drive, it's considered bad taste to annoy other drivers, e.g. by making rude signs or gestures, and can be dangerous (some people carry guns in their cars!).

One of the most surprising differences between motoring in the US and in other western countries is that on most roads with more than one lane, it's legal to pass (overtake) on the inside, i.e. on the right. Most foreigners find this strange at first and it can be particularly unsettling when you're being passed by giant trucks on both sides. Always take particular care when changing lanes as it's the cause of most freeway accidents. It's advisable to look over your shoulder before changing lanes, as wing mirrors (particularly on monster American cars) usually have a blind spot as big as a house. Although freeways usually have a through (slow) and a passing (fast) lane, because of the passing either side rule, many motorists stick to one lane. It's legal to stay in the outside lane and be passed on the inside, partly because some freeway exits are from the outside rather than the inside lane.

Officially it's illegal to overtake on an inside lane, i.e. to deliberately move to an inside lane to overtake a slower vehicle and then return to the outside line. Passing, however, is legal, i.e. when you're already in an inside lane in which traffic is moving faster or you have a clear road. Needless to say, there's a thin dividing line between 'passing' and 'overtaking' and inside lane overtaking is common. Note, however, that lane hopping can earn you a ticket (in dollars or to the next life). Although illegal, many Americans swap lanes continuously and dodge in and out of cars without signalling (Americans rarely signal when changing lanes on freeways). Slow-moving traffic is supposed to remain in the right-most lane on a freeway or multi-lane road. Take care when passing American trucks as they are often very large and long and can create considerable side winds.

There are a number of toll roads in Florida including the 345-mile Florida Turnpike, also known as the Sunshine State Parkway, which runs from the I-75 south of Wildwood near Ocala in central Florida south to Miami and Homestead. Tolls range from 25¢ to around $15 for cars, depending on the length of your journey. You're advised to use toll roads whenever possible as they are generally less busy than non-toll roads. There are also a number of toll bridges (cars from 50¢ to around $3) and car ferries in Florida.

Like motorists in many other countries, American drivers often drive too close to the vehicle in front of them (called 'tailgating'), particularly on freeways, and have no idea of safe stopping distances. This is particularly true of truck drivers, who often try to intimidate you into driving faster or moving over by driving a few feet from your fender (trucks aren't allowed in the outside lane of freeways with three or more lanes). After passing manoeuvres, driving too close to the vehicle in front is the biggest cause of accidents in the US. As a safety precaution, always try to leave a large gap between your car and the vehicle in front. This isn't just to allow yourself more time to stop should the vehicles in front decide to get together, but also to give a tailgater more time to stop. **The closer the vehicle is behind you, the further you should be from the vehicle in front.**

Many Americans, particularly Floridians, are fair-weather drivers and are totally lost in heavy rain (or any weather other than bright sunlight), when they're likely to slow to walking pace and are a hazard to other motorists. Despite their idiosyncrasies, most American drivers are above average and more polite than drivers in many other countries, although road manners have deteriorated in recent years, particularly in urban areas. Wherever you drive in the US, it pays to drive defensively and always expect the unexpected from other drivers. However, providing you avoid rush hours, you will probably find driving in the US less stressful than in many countries. If you come from a country where traffic drives on the left, take it easy at first and bear in mind that there are other motorists out there just as confused as you are. The best news regarding driving in Florida is that gas costs only around $1.30 a gallon.

Drivers' Licenses

A valid driver's license is required to drive or hire a car in Florida and most foreigners can drive in the US for up to one year with a foreign driver's license. However, if your foreign license doesn't contain a photograph or is written in a language other than English, it's advisable (but not mandatory) to obtain an International Driver's Permit (IDP). Always carry your foreign license as well as the IDP. If you don't have an IDP it may be necessary to obtain a certified English translation of your foreign driver's license, usually obtainable from your country's embassy in the US. Check whether your license is legal in the US with a motoring organization or US consulate in your home country. You must always carry your driver's license when driving in the US, where a driver's license is the most common form of identification (in some states you can have your car impounded if you're stopped by the police and don't have your license).

Anyone resident in Florida must obtain a Florida driver's license within 30 days of establishing residence (or obtain a new license within 10 days of changing their address or name). If you plan to buy and register a car in Florida, you will also need a Florida driver's license. This particularly applies to homeowners spending up to six months a year in Florida, when buying a car is much cheaper than renting. There are two kinds of license issued in Florida. A full license, valid in all US states and issued only to US citizens and resident aliens (all foreigners are referred to as 'aliens' by the US authorities), and a Florida only license, which is issued to non-residents and resident aliens wishing to retain their foreign license. Note, however, that US immigration officials are often suspicious of non-residents with a Florida or other US driving license and may suspect you of planning to remain or work illegally in the US (however, if you're retired and spending the winter in Florida, this is a valid reason for needing a Florida license).

To obtain a Florida driver's license it's necessary for foreigners to take written and practical driving tests, plus an eyesight test. There are in fact two written tests (driving law and road signs) each comprising 20 multi-choice questions (of which you must get 15 correct on each paper), which are followed by the eyesight test. Before taking the written tests, which can be taken at any driver's license office without an appointment, you should study the Florida Driver's Handbook (available free from driver's license offices or the Department of Highway Safety and Motor Vehicles, 2900 Apalachee Pkwy., Room B-443, Tallahassee, FL 32399-0500, tel. 904/922-9000). To take the test you need two forms of identification (ID) such as your passport and foreign driver's license, plus proof of insurance for the car you're currently driving, e.g. the rental agreement, and proof of your address in Florida. If you fail the written tests you can retake them until you pass. After passing the written and eyesight tests you must take a short practical driving test, which is a cakewalk by European standards (it's easier to get a driver's license than a fishing license in Florida!). After you have passed the driving test your photograph is taken, you sign the application form, pay the fee of $20 and are issued with your license on the spot, which is valid for six years.

ID Cards: Driver's license offices also issue photo ID cards for a few dollars which can be used to prove your identity and home address in Florida. This is necessary when paying by check and an ID card also allows you to claim resident discounts at many Florida attractions. You require a passport-size photograph, your passport and proof of your Florida address, e.g. a utility or tax bill or a social security card (although you may get away without this). **Note that ID may be damanded for any number of things from buying a beer (if you look under age) or a lottery ticket to obtaining a fishing license!**

Car Insurance

When driving in Florida (or anywhere in the US), it's important to ensure that you have adequate insurance cover, including passenger cover if applicable. Buying car insurance is more complicated in the US than in most other countries and it may include liability insurance; personal injury protection (PIP) or no-fault insurance; uninsured and under-insured motorists insurance; collision and comprehensive cover (see also **Car Rental** below). It's also advisable to have breakdown insurance which is available from automobile clubs such as the Automobile Association of America (AAA), which also provides a wide range of other services to members.

Liability Insurance: Includes *bodily injury* liability, i.e. injuries you cause to someone else as a motorist, and *property damage* liability, which is damage caused to someone else's property, including other vehicles. In Florida (and most US states), third-party liability motor insurance is compulsory, although unlike most other western countries, bodily injury and property damage in the US *doesn't* include unlimited liability. Most states (including Florida) have 'financial responsibility' laws setting minimum levels for third party claims. These may be as low as $10,000 in respect of personal injury or the death of an individual and $5,000 in respect of property. Minimum financial responsibility limits for Florida are as follows:

- bodily injury liability (BIL) to one person is $10,000;
- bodily injury liability to two or more persons is $20,000;
- and property damage liability (PDL) is $10,000.

The above amounts are usually expressed as three figures, e.g. $10,000/20,000/10,000, although some insurance companies express liability limits as a single figure. The limits are the maximum an insurance company will pay out no matter how many people are involved in an accident or how much property damage is caused. The maximum third-party cover for any one accident is $300,000 or $100,000 per person for personal injury and $25,000 for vehicles or other property. The single figure limit is the best system, as it provides more flexibility in resolving claims against you (and is a lot simpler to understand!). **Note, however, that the minimum liability amounts are derisory and it's imperative to take out additional insurance, e.g. $1m at least.**

No-Fault Law: Florida has a *no-fault* insurance law, which means that if you're involved in an accident, you have minimum cover of $10,000 for both Personal Injury Protection (PIP) and Property Damage Liability (PDL) from your own insurance company, rather than go to court and prove that the other party was at fault. Anyone who owns or has registered a vehicle that has been in Florida for at least 90 days during the past year is required to purchase a no-fault policy in Florida. It's impossible to buy a tag (registration number plate) or register a car in Florida without a no-fault policy issued in Florida. No-fault insurance is compulsory and covers only bodily injury and not vehicle damage. Those insured under PIP insurance receive prompt payment from their own insurance company, but their right to sue for general damages is usually restricted. Note that PIP cover may duplicate other insurance cover provided by health or disability insurance policies. PIP insurance provides benefits for medical and hospital costs (the level depends on your policy), plus lost wages or income continuation (e.g. $2,000 per month or 75 per cent of actual loss), replacement/essential services (e.g. $25 per day), survivors' loss/death benefit (e.g. $10,000) and funeral expenses (e.g. $5,000). Lost wages and replacement services are payable up to a maximum amount for maximum periods, e.g. one to three years.

Insurance premiums are high in the US, particularly for males under 25 and those who live in inner cities, where driving conditions are more hazardous and where car theft is endemic. Premiums are generally lower for women, who have fewer accidents than men. Note that it's often inexpensive for a family to insure two or more cars, when the second and subsequent cars may cost only a few hundred dollars extra a year. Always shop around a number of insurance companies, as rates for the same person for the same cover can vary by from 100 to 400 per cent from different insurance companies. The largest American auto insurers include State Farm, Allstate, Farmers and Nationwide.

Part-time Residents: It's possible to leave a car at your home in Florida and insure it only for the legal minimum and theft when you're absent. However, you need to shop around, as few insurance companies or brokers offer this option. The savings aren't significant, e.g. around $200 on a annual policy costing $1,000 to $1,500 for a six-month absence, but are better than nothing. Shop around for the best deal as some US insurers don't recognize foreign no-claims' records. Retirees should contact the American Association of Retired Persons (AARP), 601 E. Street, NW, Washington, DC 20049 (tel. 202/434-2277), who provide inexpensive auto insurance for members. You may also be able to obtain inexpensive insurance through a professional, business or social organization. The insurance ID card must be kept in the vehicle at all times.

Car Crime

Car theft is rampant in Florida, where a car is stolen every five minutes and thefts of the contents or accessories from motor vehicles are numbered in tens of thousands. If you drive anything other than a worthless wreck you should have theft insurance that includes your car stereo and personal belongings (although this may be prohibitively expensive). If you drive a new or valuable car it's wise to have it fitted with an alarm, an engine immobilizer (the best system) or other anti-theft device, and also use a visible deterrent such as a steering or gear change lock. It's particularly important to protect your car if you own a model that's desirable to professional car thieves, e.g. most new sports and executive models, which are often stolen by crooks to order. If you have a garage, always park your car there overnight.

Radios, cassette and CD players attract thieves like bees to a honey pot in cities and coastal resorts. If you buy an expensive stereo system, always get one with a removable unit or with a removable control panel that you can pop into a bag or pocket. Never forget to remove it (and your mobile telephone), even when parking for a few minutes. A removable unit should be locked in your trunk (boot) or preferably taken with you. Often drivers put a sign in their car windows proclaiming 'No Radio' (or 'No Valuables', 'Trunk is Empty' and 'Doors Open'), to deter thieves from breaking in to steal them.

When leaving your car unattended, store any valuables (including clothes) in the trunk. This shouldn't be done immediately after parking your car in some areas, where it isn't wise to be seen putting things in the trunk. Note, however, that trunks aren't safe unless fitted with a protective steel plate or you have a steel safe installed *inside* your trunk. It's never advisable to leave your original car papers in your car, which may help a thief dispose of it. When parking overnight or when it's dark, it's advisable to park in a secure overnight car park or garage, or at least in a well-lit area. If possible avoid parking in long term parking lots as they are favorite hunting grounds for car thieves. Note that it takes thieves less than 10 minutes to strip most cars clean.

If your car is stolen or anything is stolen from it, report it to the police in the precinct where it was stolen (but don't expect them to find it). You can report it by telephone, but will have to go to the station to complete a report. Report a theft to your insurance company as soon as possible. See also **Crime** on page 75.

General Road Rules

Compared with many other countries, the US has a high accident rate, with some 40,000 motor-vehicle related deaths a year and over 3m injuries, including around 2,500 deaths and almost 200,000 injuries in Florida. The following tips will (hopefully) help you avoid adding to the accident statistics:

• If you come from a country where traffic drives on the left-hand side of the road, e.g. Britain, take extra care until you're accustomed to driving on the right. Be particularly alert when leaving lay-bys, T-junctions, one-way streets and service stations, as it's easy to lapse into driving on the left. It's helpful to display a 'think right!' notice on a car's dashboard as a constant reminder.

• Federal recommended maximum speed limits have been abolished and states are now free to set their own speed limits. Note, however, that Florida has retained the old limits of 55 mph (89 kph) on freeways, referred to as the 'double nickel', and 65 mph (105 kph) on rural interstate highways. Speeds on urban roads vary from 15 mph (e.g school zones) to 40 mph, as posted. Always check local speed limits and look out for local speed restrictions. The use of radar detectors is permitted in Florida. Some towns are 'traffic traps' where the local police hand out tickets like confetti.

• You must use low beams (dipped or dimmed headlights) between sunset and sunrise (usually half an hour after sunset and half an hour before sunrise) and it's prohibited to drive on parking lights. Low beams must also generally be used when visibility is reduced to less than 500 or 1,000ft. Many people drive with low beams on during the daytime in Florida, where heat haze often makes unlit cars difficult to see.

• The sequence of American stop (traffic) lights is usually red, green, yellow and back to red, although some are simply red-green-red. Yellow means stop at the stop line; you may proceed only if the yellow light appears after you have crossed the stop line or when stopping might cause an accident. A green filter light may be shown in addition to the full lamp signal, which indicates you may drive in the direction shown by the arrow, irrespective of other lights. Stop lights are frequently set on the far side of an intersection, sometimes making it difficult to judge where to stop, and are also strung across the road rather than located on posts by the roadside. A 'Delayed Green' sign at some stop lights indicates that the green light opposite will change first, usually to allow motorists to make a turn across your lane. In some suburban areas there are flashing red lights to indicate a stop light ahead. Running (driving through) red lights is a major cause of accidents in America.

Stop lights in cities are usually set for traffic traveling at a certain speed, e.g. 25 mph. These may vary depending on the area, traffic density and the time of day. If you maintain the set speed, you will be able to 'make' (go through) most lights when they are green. At night or in the early hours of the morning, some intersections and crossroads have flashing stop lights. A flashing red light indicates 'STOP' (as at a four-way stop) and a flashing yellow light means 'YIELD', i.e. you can proceed without stopping if it's safe to do so.

- One of the most surprising (although logical) rules in the US is that you may make a right turn at a red stop light, unless otherwise posted. **You must, however, treat a red light as a stop sign and stop before making a right turn.** You must also give way to pedestrians crossing at the lights. Busy intersections often have signs indicating that turning at a red light isn't allowed (e.g. 'NO TURN ON RED') or is allowed at certain times only. If you're stopped in the right-hand lane and the motorist behind you is honking his horn, it probably means you can turn right (so don't get into the right-hand lane unless you wish to turn right).

- You're likely to see some unusual signs in Florida such as 'GATOR XING NEXT 1/2 Mi', which translates into 'alligators crossing the road during the next half a mile', so take care.

- Children getting on or off school (or church) buses, usually painted 'school bus' yellow, have priority over all traffic. All motorists *must* usually stop not less than 20 or 25 feet behind a school bus that's loading or unloading, indicated by flashing (usually red) lights or 'stop arms'. Vehicles must stop even when a school bus has halted on the opposite side of the road (children may run across the road). However, vehicles traveling in the opposite direction on a divided highway (dual carriageway) aren't required to stop. Motorists must remain stopped until the bus resumes movement or the driver signals motorists to proceed. School buses are equipped with flashing yellow lights to warn motorists that a bus is about to stop, followed by flashing red lights when it actually stops. **NEVER PASS A SCHOOL BUS WITH FLASHING RED LIGHTS!** Take care when approaching a stopped school bus without flashing lights as they could have failed. The law regarding school buses is taken very seriously and motorists convicted of passing a stopped school bus may be subject to a fine of up to $1,000, possible imprisonment or community service, and five penalty points on their driving record. School zones and crossings are indicated by a sign showing children on a yellow background in the shape of an arrow facing upwards.

- Seat belts must be worn by all car drivers and front-seat passengers in Florida. Children aged three years and younger must be secured in a federally-approved, child-restraint seat (minimum $150 fine for non-compliance) and children aged five or younger must wear a seat belt in any seat. There's a fine of $27 for not wearing a seat belt and drivers are also responsible for ensuring that passengers in the front seat aged 15 or under wear seat belts. Note that the failure to wear a seat belt may reduce the amount of damages awarded by a court in the event of an accident. In many American cars, shoulder seat belts operate automatically when you close the door (although you must fasten the lap belt yourself).

- Drunken driving is a serious problem in the US, where excessive alcohol is estimated to be a factor in over 50 per cent of all traffic fatalities. Driving under the influence (DUI) is defined as a 0.08 per cent blood-alcohol concentration. Random breath (or sobriety) tests are permitted in Florida, which consist of reciting the alphabet or counting numbers, standing on one foot for a designated period, walking in a straight line, or touching the tip of your nose with an index finger with your eyes closed.

Florida imposes mandatory tests for drivers suspected of 'drunken driving' comprising either a breath, blood, urine or saliva alcohol test (or a test for narcotics). If you have a choice, experts suggest that you request a urine test. A refusal to take a test usually results in your driver's license being automatically suspended or revoked, e.g. for six months or one year. In Florida you're no longer considered fit to drive when your breath contains 35 micrograms of alcohol per 100ml or your blood contains 80mg or 100mg of alcohol per 100ml (or 107mg/100ml of urine). You're considered to be driving while intoxicated (DWI) or driving under the influence (DUI) when your blood-alcohol content (BAC) level is 0.08 per cent. You're entitled to take two chemical tests, which must measure within a certain percentage of each other.

- On-the-spot fines aren't imposed for traffic offenses in Florida. Convictions for many motoring offenses result in license penalty points being imposed (for holders of Florida licenses). Fines can also be exacted for all offenses, although the maximum fine is rarely imposed. Serious offenses such as dangerous or drunken driving involving injury or death to others may result in a mandatory prison sentence. Traffic fines can usually be paid by mail and many communities have a local office (e.g. Violations Bureau) where parking and other fines can be paid.

- Be careful where you park, particularly in cities where you can be clamped or towed away in a flash. *Never* park within ten feet of a fire hydrant; across entrances; at bus stops or taxi ranks; and in front of fire and ambulance stations and schools (which may be indicated by red curbstones). Always read all parking signs carefully and look for curb markings (ask someone if you aren't sure whether parking is permitted).

- The Florida Department of Highway Safety and Motor Vehicles publishes a free *Florida Driver's Handbook* available from local driver's license offices. The American Automobile Association (1000 AAA Drive, Orlando, FL 32746-5063, tel. 407-444-7000) publishes a *Digest of Motor Laws* containing state traffic regulations including motor vehicle registration, taxes, driver's license, traffic rules, towing and trailer information, motorcycle and moped rules, and other information. It's available from any AAA office and is free to AAA members. The AAA Traffic Safety Department also publishes a wide range of brochures, leaflets and maps to help you improve your driving and increase safety. The Florida Department of Transportation publishes a free 'Official Transportation Map' of Florida.

Car Rental

Car rental (or auto rental) is common in America, where public transport is generally poor. Airlines, charter companies, car rental companies and tour operators all offer fly/drive packages (which often include accommodations). It's often advisable to reserve a car in advance, particularly during holiday periods when rental cars are in high demand. Many fly-drive holiday packages (particularly when booked in Europe) include a 'free' rental car. **Note, however, that 'free' rental cars aren't free at all (there's no such thing as a free anything in the States!) and when all the extras (insurance, taxes, etc.) have been added it's often cheaper to rent a car independently, either in advance (see the telephone numbers below) or on arrival. Incredible but true!** You usually need to pay all state taxes and extra insurances (see below) and if you want to leave a car in a location other than where you collected it there's usually a drop-off charge.

A list of the biggest national car rental companies is shown below with their toll-free telephone numbers, many of which have offices in all major cities (e.g. open from 8am to 10pm) and international airports in Florida. Of the major companies, Budget, Alamo and Dollar are generally the cheapest, although all companies offer special deals, e.g. corporate rates, 24-hour rates, weekend and weekly rates, off-peak periods, holidays, extended period low rates on certain categories of cars, and bonus coupons for airline tickets. It's advisable to phone around and haggle over prices, which can vary considerably between companies. Note that rental car drivers have been targeted by muggers in Florida in recent years, although after a spate of attacks rental cars are now indistinguishable from private vehicles (previously they had plates with a 'Y' or 'Z' prefix or 'LEASE', which should be refused). There should also be no stickers on a vehicle indicating that it's a rental car.

There are also cheaper rental companies in all major cities, ranging from companies with a few run-down heaps to medium-sized, state-wide agencies. Some nationwide chains (e.g. Renta-a-Heap, Rent-a-Junk, Rent-a-Wreck and Ugly Duckling) also rent older cars, usually three to five years old. Although cars are well worn, they are usually mechanically sound and rental rates are around half those of new models (although you should beware of high mileage charges and other hidden costs). However, you should steer clear of cowboy rental companies offering 'rental cars from hell', which are unroadworthy and could put your life at risk. Wherever you rent a car, if you suspect that it has a problem you should return it immediately and insist on a replacement.

Note that when renting a car it's imperative to ensure you have sufficient liability insurance (see page 63). Most car rental companies limit liability insurance to the state minimum ($20,000), although some increase it, e.g. to $100,000, which is still far too little ($1m is more realistic). Note that personal liability on travel insurance policies *doesn't* extend to motoring. Check the cost of out-of-state insurance, personal accident insurance (PAI), collision (or loss) damage waiver (CDW/LDW), supplementary liability or extended protection insurance (SL/EPI), and personal effects protection (PEP). Insurance is usually included in the basic cost, although it may be restricted to in-state only and there may be a high surcharge for interstate travel.

If you have American personal auto insurance it may cover you when driving a rental car, although you must usually carry collision insurance on your own policy or your insurer won't cover damage to a rental car if you decline CDW. If you pay for a rental car with a credit card (e.g. American Express or a Mastercard/Visa card), your card company may provide CDW coverage, but check the extent of cover provided as most will pay the deductible only after your insurance company pays on a claim (and CDW may be limited to a maximum rental period of 30 days). In some states (not Florida) CDW has been banned in favor of a mandatory deductible (e.g. $100 or $200) when a rental car is damaged. Paying CDW of around $15 a day should be avoided if at all possible, as it's a rip-off (at $15 a day, it works out at an annual rate of $5,475!). If you decline CDW you will be responsible for all damage to a car (however caused) and will need to pay a large security deposit with a credit card or travelers' checks. Supplementary liability or extended protection insurance (SL/EPI) is also highly recommended (around $10 to $12 per day for cover of $1m), as this will protect you against third-party liability if you're involved in an accident (see above). Note that the cost of CDW and SL/EPI alone can add over $25 a day to the cost of car rental (or a 'free' rental).

Rental cars are graded into classes according to body size, not engine capacity, e.g. economy or sub-compact (the smallest), compact, mid-size or intermediate, and standard or full size. Groups are usually identified by a letter, e.g. A through H. Many companies also rent coupes; station wagons (estates); premium and luxury models; convertibles (or roadsters) and sports cars; four-wheel drive 'off-road' vehicles; and mini-vans. Almost all rental cars have automatic transmission, radios and air conditioning. Many larger models have power steering, cruise control and other 'luxury' features. Vans and pick-ups are available from major rental companies by the hour, half-day or day, or from smaller local companies (usually cheaper). You can also rent a recreational vehicle (RV), motor home, trailer (caravan), or a mini-bus, from a number of companies (prices vary with the season).

Florida is (with California) one of the cheapest states in which to rent a car. An economy car (e.g. Dodge Colt or GM Geo) costs from around $25-30 per day and a compact (e.g. Chevrolet Cavalier or Plymouth Neon) around $35 per day, both with unlimited mileage. With limited mileage, rates may be around $10 per day cheaper plus 25¢ per mile above around 100 free miles per day (most rental cars average around 90 miles a day). Standard or full-size models cost upwards of $40 per day with unlimited mileage. Note, however, that weekly rates are much cheaper than daily rates and the standard budget rate in Florida is around $99 a week for the cheapest economy car. Sales tax at 6 to 7 per cent must be added to the rental fee plus a Florida environmental tax of $2.05 a day, CDW/LDW and other extras, even when a rental car is provided 'free', e.g. as part of a fly-drive deal. You may also be hit with incidental charges such as an airport user access fee (around $3 per day) and a handling fee (around $3 per day). Other charges may include a child car seat (around $3 a day and mandatory for under 4s in Florida) and a surcharge for an additional driver ($5 a day or more). Note that extras such as insurance, taxes and surcharges can easily double the basic daily rental.

Both limited and unlimited mileage rental rates are lower for periods of one week or more. Generally the longer the rental period, the cheaper the daily rate. When comparing rates, always check any minimum periods as some companies' lowest rates are for a minimum period of three days. Many factors affect the rate, including the day of the week and the season. Generally rates vary depending on the size of the town and the popularity of the local tourist attractions. The smaller the town and the more popular the local attractions, the higher the rates.

Many rental companies insist on payment with a major credit card and won't accept cash. This is so that they can trace you if you steal or damage the car and also because they can deduct extra charges from credit cards without obtaining prior approval. The estimated cost of the rental will be deducted or 'blocked off' your card's credit limit as soon as you drive off, so make sure this doesn't leave you short of credit during your trip. When paying by credit card, check that you aren't charged for unauthorized extras or for something that you've already paid for, such as gas.

You must usually be aged at least 21 to rent a car and must have held a license for a minimum of one year. A few companies will rent to 18-year-olds in most cities, although many have a minimum age requirement of 25. However, most rental companies levy a 'young driver' surcharge of from $15 to $20 per day on all drivers under 25, although women under 25 may be charged a lower premium than men as they are less accident prone. If you have a foreign driver's license without a photograph, e.g. a British license, you may be asked to show your passport. It's also advisable to have an International Driver's Permit (IDP), which must be used in conjunction with your foreign license (it won't be accepted on its own). All drivers planning to drive a rental vehicle must provide these documents (there's also a surcharge of $5 to $10 per day for extra drivers). Listed below are the toll-free telephone numbers of the major car rental companies in the US:

Company	Phone No.
Alamo	1-800-327-9633
American International	1-800-527-0202
Avis	1-800-722-1333
Budget	1-800-527-0700
Dollar	1-800-421-6868
Hertz	1-800-654-3131
National	1-800-227-7368
Rent-a-Wreck	1-800-535-1391
Snappy	1-800-669-4800
Thrifty	1-800-367-2277
USA Rent-A-Car System	1-800-872-2277
Value	1-800-468-2583

2.

FURTHER CONSIDERATIONS

T his chapter contains important considerations for most people planning to buy a home in Florida, particularly those planning to live there permanently or semi-permanently, although some topics apply only to those planning to live there permanently. It contains information about the climate, geography, regions, health, insurance, shopping, pets, TV and radio, crime, legal system, education, and leisure and sports activities.

CLIMATE

The major attraction of Florida is its excellent climate (with the possible exception of the hot and humid summer season) and the enviable outdoor lifestyle it affords. Central and southern Florida have long been a refuge from the bitter north American winters, when thousands of retired Canadians and Americans from northern states (known locally as 'snowbirds') and an increasing number of northern Europeans spend the winter there. The southern region experiences mild winters, with warm temperatures and low humidity, although in northern Florida it's much cooler (it has even been known to snow in the Panhandle, although it's rare). Consequently Florida has different tourist seasons for its northern and southern halves, although in summer the north is almost as hot and humid as the south.

The temperature change from north to south is gradual, although anyone after warm winter days shouldn't consider buying a home further north than say Crystal River on the Gulf coast and Daytona Beach on the Atlantic coast. Florida has two main climatic zones, subtropical in the south and warm temperate in the north, with the Florida Keys in the far south having a tropical climate. It has only two distinct seasons: the rainy season from June to September, when over half the annual rain falls, and the mostly dry season for the rest of the year. Annual rainfall throughout the state varies considerably from year to year by 100 per cent or more, e.g. from 40 to over 100 inches (the average is 54 inches). The northwest in particular experiences heavy rainfall in February and March.

Florida has the highest average temperatures of any US state, with annual temperatures ranging from the high 60s in the north to the mid-70s in the south, with a maximum of around 78 deg. F. at Key West. Summer temperatures average 82 to 84 deg. F., but can be much higher in the south. July and August are generally the warmest months in all areas, when maximum temperatures average almost 90 deg. F. on the coast and are slightly higher in inland areas. However, heat waves are rare and are more likely to occur in northern Florida. The sun shines for around two thirds of all daylight hours throughout the year, hence Florida's official nickname the 'Sunshine State' (seen on Florida vehicle license plates). The average temperature on the coast is influenced by the Gulf Stream and is warmer in winter and cooler in the summer than in inland areas. The average minimum temperatures in the coolest months (Dec to Feb) range from the mid-40s in the north to the mid-50s in the south. January is usually the coldest month with temperatures averaging between 44 and 46 deg. F. in the north and between 54 and 56 deg. F in the south. The average winter temperature in the south is 68.5 deg. F. However, cold periods can occur as far south as Miami and temperatures can drop below freezing in most areas (when crops are at risk), although cold spells rarely last for more than a few days. Frost is rare as far south as Fort Lauderdale and Naples.

In contrast to the balmy winter climate in southern Florida, the summer heat and humidity can be unmerciful, when energy levels plummet and most people just hibernate and wait the summer out (like many northerners do in winter). The humidity is due to the proximity of so much water (nowhere in Florida is more than 60 miles from salt water) and the low-lying land (a maximum 345 feet above sea level). From early June until late September, humidity ranges from around 50 to 65 per cent in the afternoons to a high of 85 to 90 per cent during the evenings and early mornings. The highest humidity is in late spring and early summer when most people find air-conditioning essential. However, the heat and humidity is relieved by sea breezes on the coasts and frequent thunderstorms, which occur on around half the days in summer, usually in the afternoon or early evening. Many areas average around 80 thunder and electrical storms a year, usually lasting one or two hours, when rain can be very heavy and temperatures drop by 10 to 20 degrees. If you're alerted to an impending storm you should batten down the hatches. Florida is the lightning capital of the US and around 10 people a year are killed by lightning strikes. Note that electrical storms can play havoc with electrical equipment and you should unplug electrical appliances and avoid using the telephone during storms.

Florida is noted for its hurricanes, which although spectacular and capable of causing widespread damage, aren't a common occurrence. The hurricane season lasts from June to November, with most occurring in September. Hurricanes are given Christian names (alternating male and female names in order to remain politically correct), which are allocated in advance in alphabetical order. Over twice as many hurricanes hit Florida as any other US state, although in the last few decades the number has dropped and with a few exceptions (e.g. Hurricane Andrew in 1992) they are less powerful than in earlier years. Hurricanes are rated on a disaster-potential scale from category 1 (winds from 74 to 95 mph, storm surge 4 to 5 feet) to category 5 (winds above 155mph, storm surge over 18 feet). Prior to 1992, the previous hurricane of category 3 (winds from 111 to 130mph, storm surge 9 to 12 feet) or above to hit Florida was in 1987 (Hurricane Floyd), which did only minimal damage in the Keys (in recent years the average has been one every five years).

The southern part of the state is more prone to hurricanes than the north, with the Atlantic coast most at risk. Most damage is done where a hurricane hits landfall and its energy usually dissipates quickly as it travels inland, although high winds and torrential rainfall can still create havoc. Although infrequent, hurricanes are never to be taken lightly. Florida has an excellent hurricane alert system and hurricane warnings are given well in advance. Safety guidelines are published for residents in vulnerable areas (also listed in telephone directories) and evacuation routes are clearly signposted in coastal areas. Building regulations require new homes to be built to withstand hurricanes and most homes should survive them relatively unscathed, providing a few precautions are taken (you can have glass areas laminated to protect against hurricanes or fit steel shutters). Florida also experiences around 10 to 15 tornadoes (most frequently in spring, although they can occur in any season), funnel clouds and waterspouts a year.

The average high and low (second line) temperatures (in Fahrenheit) for selected Florida cities are shown below:

City	Month Jan	Feb	Mar	Apr	May	Jun	Jul	Aug	Sep	Oct	Nov	Dec
Jacksonville	71/ 45	74/ 53	78/ 53	79/ 54	87/ 63	92/ 69	93/ 74	94/ 72	91/ 68	84/ 62	77/ 50	73/ 49
Key West	79/ 68	80/ 71	80/ 70	82/ 71	86/ 77	89/ 79	90/ 79	91/ 79	90/ 78	86/ 76	80/ 71	79/ 70
Miami	81/ 66	81/ 67	81/ 67	83/ 68	87/ 74	90/ 76	91/ 76	92/ 76	90/ 76	84/ 75	82/ 67	80/ 66
Orlando	77/ 54	79/ 59	81/ 58	82/ 61	90/ 69	92/ 72	92/ 74	93/ 74	92/ 72	86/ 68	79/ 59	78/ 55
Pensacola	65/ 45	68/ 50	73/ 52	76/ 56	83/ 65	91/ 72	92/ 74	95/ 73	90/ 70	81/ 59	74/ 50	67/ 48
Tallahassee	71/ 41	73/ 49	78/ 49	81/ 51	88/ 62	94/ 69	94/ 71	95/ 71	92/ 66	84/ 58	77/ 45	71/ 46
Tampa	77/ 55	79/ 60	81/ 59	83/ 61	90/ 71	92/ 74	91/ 74	93/ 75	92/ 73	87/ 68	82/ 59	78/ 56

A quick way to make a rough conversion from Fahrenheit to Centigrade is to subtract 30 and divide by two (see also **Appendix C**).

GEOGRAPHY

Florida covers an area of 58,560 square miles (94,240 square kilometers) and has the longest stretch of salt-water beaches in the continental US of around 1,350 miles (2,173 kilometers), 770 miles on the Gulf of Mexico and 580 miles on the Atlantic Ocean. Florida is the most southerly US mainland state and has borders with just two states, Alabama and Georgia. The state capital is Tallahassee in the northwestern region known as the Panhandle (named after its frying pan handle shape). Florida can be roughly divided into five major geological areas; the northern belt containing the Panhandle, consisting of rolling hills and lowland plains; the lake-dotted central ridge stretching along the spine of the state; the flat and wooded coastal plains extending inland for up to 100 miles along the Atlantic and Gulf coasts; the Everglades-Lake Okeechobee basin in the south; and the southern island chain which includes the Florida Keys (a key is an island or bank composed of coral fragments). Half the state's total land area is covered in forests, mostly in the northwest.

Florida consists largely of a peninsula extending from the southeastern corner of the North American continent separating the Gulf of Mexico and the Atlantic Ocean. On the Atlantic coast, barrier beaches (long narrow islands comprising sandy beaches and mangrove forests) enclose the Intracoastal Waterway which separates at St. Lucie Inlet. One tributary runs south to Key West and the other crosses the state to Fort Myers, where it resumes its intermittent path along the Gulf. The west coast is deeply indented with bays and coves south of the Suwannee River and becomes low and marshy as it approaches the Ten Thousand Islands in the far south. Due to its countless bays, islands and inlets, Florida has the longest tidal coast of any US state.

In the north the terrain slopes gradually from the central Panhandle into the Atlantic, where part of Georgia's Okefenokee swamp extends into Florida west of Jacksonville. The central backbone of the peninsula rises slightly in the area north of Lake Okeechobee, then dips to sea level. The highest point in the state is just 345 feet (105 meters) above sea level (in the northwest near Lakewood in Walton County) and most of the state is less than 100 feet (30 meters) above sea level. In the far south the 135-mile chain of islands known as the Florida Keys curves southwestward into the Gulf of Mexico. Along the major rivers and the west coast are the majority of the state's 27 artesian springs (with a flow rate of 100 cubic feet or more per second).

Florida contains around 30,000 lakes, ranging from small ponds to the 730 square mile (1,890 square km) Lake Okeechobee, the largest freshwater lake enclosed wholly within a US state. Southwest of Lake Okeechobee lies the Everglades National Park, the largest subtropical wilderness in the US, where the highest land is only a few feet above sea level. It consists of myriad labyrinthine waterways weaving their way through cypress and mangrove swamps, grassy hammocks and immense plains of shallow water and sawgrass.

REGIONS

Florida is divided into various geographical regions, although geographers and state officials can't seem to decide on the actual regions and which counties they contain. The regions described below are roughly the most common division and are depicted on the map in **Appendix D**.

Northwest (The Panhandle): The northwestern region stretches from the state's western border with Alabama to the banks of the Suwannee River (immortalized in Florida's official state song). The main towns are Pensacola (in the central time zone), rich in history and where Florida was ceded to the US in 1821, and Tallahassee, the state capital, a provincial Old South city of around 125,000 inhabitants, where the residents still sip mint julips on their verandas. Other major cities in the region are Panama City and Fort Walton Beach. The northwest has the longest stretches of open beaches in the state, including some of America's finest, and some of the most glorious coastal scenery in Florida (although some areas such as Panama City Beach are a nightmare of commercialism and overdevelopment). Not surprisingly the area is noted for its excellent fishing (e.g. snapper, grouper, sailfish, marlin and tuna) and seafood. The northeast coastline is easily navigable and is the only one in the state that extends east to west, eventually turning slowly southwards in an arc to the old-world tranquility of outlying Cedar Key. A coastal road (US highway 98) linked by a network of spectacular bridges hugs the coast from Pensacola to just south of Tallahassee, where it heads inland. Inland areas contain a wealth of trail systems (with relaxing walks through pine forests), hidden caverns, bubbly springs, sinkholes and the Apalachicola National Forest, the best preserved wilderness area in Florida.

The northwest contains the counties of Bay (Panama City is the county seat), Calhoun (Blountstown), Dixie (Cross City), Escambia (Pensacola), Franklin (Apalachicola), Gadsden (Quincy), Gilchrist (Trenton), Gulf (Port St. Joe), Holmes (Bonifay), Jackson (Marianna), Jefferson (Monticello), Lafayette (Mayo), Leon (Tallahassee), Levy (Bronson), Liberty (Bristol), Madison (Madison), Okaloosa (Crestview), Santa Rosa (Milton), Taylor (Perry), Wakulla (Crawfordville), Walton (DeFuniak Springs) and Washington (Chipley).

Northeast: The northeast contains a number of historic towns including St. Augustine (St. Johns County), the oldest permanent European settlement in the US, dating back to 1565. The region is dominated by Jacksonville, Florida's largest city and the city with the largest land mass in the US (covering 841 square miles), and an important gateway for the southeastern US. The northeast has a number of exclusive communities including Ponte Vedra Beach close to Jacksonville and Amelia Island

(Nassau County), a thin strip of land 13 miles long and two miles wide at the state's northernmost extremity. Another important city in the region is Gainsville (Alachua County), home of the University of Florida (Florida's oldest and largest), situated in the central area straddling interstate highway 75. The northeastern coastline borders the Atlantic Ocean and is noted for its golden beaches and dunes, and miles of points and peninsulas flanked by barrier islands. The northeast region contains the Osceola National Forest, located just south of the famous Okefenokee Swamp, which extends from Georgia into Florida. The region includes the counties of Alachua (Gainesville is the county seat), Baker (Macclenny), Bradford (Starke), Clay (Green Cove Springs), Columbia (Lake City), Duval (Jacksonville), Flagler (Bunnell), Hamilton (Jasper), Nassau (Fernandina Beach), Putnam (Palatka), St. Johns (St. Augustine), Suwannee (Live Oak) and Union (Lake Butler).

Central West: The central west region contains the cosmopolitan cities of Tampa, St. Petersburg, Clearwater and Bradenton, making it a popular destination for new arrivals and one of the fastest-growing regions in the US. Tampa is the largest metropolitan area in Florida (even larger than Miami) and Pinellas County west of Tampa, which has around 360 days sunshine a year, is the most densely populated county in the state (and one of the most expensive). The region contains almost 90 miles of beautiful, blindingly white sandy beaches (reputedly the world's whitest) on the Gulf Coast, where property is in high demand. An imposing network of bridges (including the striking Sunshine Skyway Bridge) links the scattered islands and peninsula of the region, and creates a seemingly endless shoreline, which is illuminated nightly by spectacular orange-pink sunsets over the Gulf. The northern reaches are known as the Nature Coast and are dappled with scenic, freshwater sources including Crystal River and Weeki Watchee River in Hernando County. The region contains a huge variety of rolling parks, scenic campsites and man-made attractions including Busch Gardens (a popular theme park), the Museum of Science and Industry (MOSI), the new Florida Aquarium, the Garrison Seaport Center and the Salvador Dali Museum. The central west region contains the counties of Citrus (Inverness is the county seat), Hernando (Brooksville), Hillsborough (Tampa), Manatee (Bradenton), Pasco (Dade City) and Pinellas (Clearwater).

Central: The central region is Florida's heartland and contains the highest concentration of attractions anywhere in the world including Walt Disney World (Magic Kingdom, Epcot Disney-MGM studios), Universal Studios, Blizzard Beach, Pleasure Island, Cypress Gardens, Sea World and Splendid China. The region contains the city of Orlando, one of Florida's major cities (with over 1m inhabitants) and the hub of the region's thriving tourist industry (the number one tourist destination in the US). Orlando is the county seat of Orange County, historically a major citrus-producing center. Other major cities include Lakeland, Ocala and Kissimmee. Lake County (with over 1,000 lakes) is a popular location for those seeking peace and tranquility, while at the same time being close enough to the main attractions (but not too close!). The region is a haven for nature lovers and is renowned for its lakes (and freshwater fishing), the Highland Hammock State Park and the majestic Ocala National Forest. The central region contains the counties of Highlands (Sebring is the county seat), Lake (Tavares), Marion (Ocala), Orange (Orlando), Osceola (Kissimmee), Polk (Barlow), Seminole (Sanford) and Sumter (Bushnell).

Central East: The central east region is a popular holiday destination and is famous for car races (e.g. the Daytona 500), space launches and over 200 miles of sandy beaches, including the celebrated Daytona Beach (dubbed 'the world's most famous beach') and Cocoa Beach. Major cities in the region include Daytona Beach,

Melbourne, Palm Bay, Port St. Lucie, Titusville and Fort Pierce. The NASA Kennedy Space Center is among Florida's most fascinating tourist attractions; a shuttle launch is an unforgettable experience and isn't to be missed if you have the opportunity. Lake Okeechobee in the south is the second largest freshwater lake in the US (and the largest enclosed entirely within a state) and the region's biggest attraction, particularly among anglers (favorite quarry include largemouth bass, crappie, bream, catfish and speckled perch). The central east region contains the counties of Brevard (Titusville is the county seat), Indian River (Vero Beach), Martin (Stuart), Okeechobee (Okeechobee), St. Lucie (Fort Pierce) and Volusia (DeLand).

Southwest: The southwest region is crammed with fashionable and sophisticated Gulf Coast resorts such as Naples and Venice, and the islands of Sanibel, Captiva and Marco (other major cities are Sarasota, Fort Myers and Cape Coral). The region offers a wealth of sports and leisure pursuits including excellent sport fishing, boating (waterfront homes abound) and a wealth of golf courses. Naples has 41 miles of public beaches and is a mecca for retirees and 'snowbirds', and one of the Gulf coast's most expensive towns (Collier County is said to be home to more millionaires than any county in the US). In fact the whole Gulf Coast, from St. Petersburg in the north to Marco Island in the south, contains some of the most expensive and desirable real estate in Florida. Naples and Sarasota are havens for artists and writers and are among the most renowned arts' centers in Florida. Embracing a jumble of Gulf Coast islands, the region winds along the edge of the Gulf of Mexico from Sarasota to Collier County, with its famous patchwork of 10,000 islands. The southwest region contains the counties of Charlotte (Punta Gorda is the county seat), Collier (Naples), De Soto (Arcadia), Hardee (Wauchula), Hendry (LaBelle) Lee (Fort Myers) and Sarasota (Sarasota).

Southeast: The southeast region stretches from Palm Beach to the Florida Keys and is the winter playground of the world's jet-set, where movie and pop stars, luxurious homes, millionaire yachts and fashionable night-spots abound (not surprisingly the area is also called the Gold Coast). The main cities in the area are Miami, Hialeah, Fort Lauderdale, West Palm Beach, Boca Raton and Key West. Miami is Florida's second largest city in population (to Jacksonville) and one of America's great cities, and the most exciting and sophisticated city in Florida (it also has the highest crime rate). Miami has the largest number of native Spanish-speaking residents (around 1m people, mostly Cubans and Nicaraguans) of any US city and it also has a large Haitian population. It's made up of 26 distinctly different municipalities, from colorful ethnic enclaves to exclusive 'millionaire' neighborhoods which include Coconut Grove, Coral Gables (the first planned community in the US), Key Biscayne and Miami Beach (famous for its fashionable art deco apartment buildings in the South Beach Art Deco district).

The Florida Keys, stretching for over 100 miles from Key Largo south to Key West (one of the wackiest cities in America), are one of Florida's major attractions and are connected by the aptly named Overseas Highway encompassing 42 bridges (part of US highway 1). The Keys contain North America's only living coral reef system and is a popular area for snorkeling and scuba diving, besides being one of the best places in Florida to witness spectacular sunsets. Despite its large metropolitan areas, the southeast also contains vast tracts of protected wilderness (including the Biscayne National Park, the nation's largest marine park), freshwater lakes and rivers, and lush parks. The crowning glory of the region is the imposing and majestic subtropical beauty of the Everglades National Park, encompassing some 1.5m acres and home to a number of rare and endangered species including the Florida panther. The southeast region contains the counties of Broward (Fort Lauderdale is the county seat), Dade (Miami), Glades (Moore Haven), Monroe (Key West) and Palm Beach (West Palm Beach).

Profiles of all counties are published by the Florida Department of Commerce, Division of Economic Development, Bureau of Economic Analysis, Tallahassee, FL 32399-2000 (tel. 904/487-2971) and available at public libraries.

HEALTH

One of the most important aspects of living in Florida (or anywhere else for that matter) is maintaining good health. American hospitals are jam-packed with the latest high-tech equipment and highly trained and motivated staff; a total of around 2.5m surgeons, physicians, nurses and dentists (although somewhat surprisingly, there's a chronic shortage of nurses). The US leads the world in high-tech surgery such as transplants and heart and brain surgery. There's an abundance of health-care facilities in most areas of Florida, although some counties have a shortage of doctors and even fewer hospitals, and dentists are also thin on the ground in some areas. Before deciding where to live, you should compare the availability of local physicians, specialists and hospitals, particularly if you have a history of health problems. Provision for the handicapped and wheelchair access to buildings and public transport (such as it is) is generally good in Florida.

The US has the most expensive health care in the world, consuming around 15 per cent of GDP (equal to over 1,000 billion dollars!) and costing around twice as much as in Britain, Germany and Japan. Before arriving in America, even for a short stay, it's essential to ensure that you have adequate health insurance (see page 54), generally considered to be a minimum of $500,000. The US has no reciprocal health care agreements with other countries and only emergency patients are treated without prior payment and treatment may be refused without evidence of insurance or a large deposit.

Common Health Problems in Florida: Generally Florida is a healthy place to live, providing you have health insurance (and avoid inner cities after dark!). Apart from the dangers to your health posed by your fellow man, your main health problems are likely to be associated with Florida's affluent life-style including stress (expatriate stress is a recognized mental condition), over-eating, too much alcohol, lack of exercise, obesity (some 80 per cent of American adults are overweight) and drugs. The major health issues in the US (apart from health insurance) include AIDS, drug addiction, alcoholism, abortion and care for the elderly. The leading causes of death are heart and blood diseases, which are responsible for almost half of all deaths or almost as many as cancer, pneumonia, influenza, AIDS, accidents, murders and all other causes combined.

Bugs: Bugs are one of the biggest aggravations of life in Florida and include mosquitos, biting gnats and midges (sand flies), deer or yellow flies, fleas, love bugs, cockroaches and spiders. Mosquitos (of which there are some 70 different varieties in Florida) can be a problem in some areas, particularly around wetlands. You should avoid stagnant water, which is the mosquitos' breeding ground and ensure that there isn't any around your home. If you want to avoid mosquitos as much as possible, buy a home in a county with a well-funded mosquito-control program (some have no program at all). It's advisable to wear a long-sleeved shirt, use insect repellent and limit night-time activity when mosquitos are active.

Sunshine & Heat: If you aren't used to the hot sun, you should limit your exposure and avoid it altogether during the hottest part of the day (between 11am and 2pm), wear protective clothing (including sunglasses, a wide-brimmed hat and a long-sleeved shirt) and use a sunscreen with a high skin protection factor (e.g. 15 or higher). Too much sun and too little protection will dry your skin and cause premature aging, to say nothing of the dangers of sunburn, heat exhaustion, sunstroke and skin cancer. Care should also be taken to replace the natural oils lost from too many hours in the sun, and the elderly should take particular care not to exert themselves during hot weather (when air-conditioning should be used). It's also important to drink plenty of fluids (but not alcohol) to prevent dehydration (water fountains are provided in popular tourist areas). On the other hand, Florida's balmy winter climate is therapeutic, particularly for sufferers of rheumatism and arthritis, and those prone to bronchitis, colds and pneumonia. The climate and lifestyle in any country has a noticeable effect on mental health and people living in hot climates are generally happier and more relaxed than those living in cold, wet climates (such as northern Europe).

Pre-Departure Check: If you're planning to take up residence in Florida, even if only for six months of the year, it's advisable to have a health check (medical or screening, eyes, teeth, etc.) before your arrival, particularly if you have a record of poor health or are elderly. If you've been putting off elective medical or dental treatment, it's likely to be far less expensive to have it done overseas than in Florida. If you're already taking regular medication, you should note that the brand names of drugs and medicines vary from country to country and should ask your doctor for the generic name. If you wish to match medication prescribed abroad, you will need a current prescription with the medication's trade name, the manufacturer's name, the chemical name and the dosage. Most drugs have an equivalent in other countries, although particular brands may be difficult or impossible to obtain in Florida.

It's possible to have medication sent from abroad, when no import duty or value added tax is usually payable. If you're visiting a holiday home in Florida for a limited period, you should take sufficient medication to cover your stay. In an emergency a local doctor will write a prescription which can be filled at a local pharmacy or a hospital may refill a prescription from its own pharmacy. It's also advisable to take some of your favorite non-prescription drugs (e.g. aspirins, cold and flu remedies, creams, etc.) with you, as they may be difficult or impossible to obtain in Florida or may be much more expensive. If applicable, take a spare pair of spectacles, contact lenses, dentures or a hearing aid with you.

INSURANCE

An important aspect of owning a home in Florida is insurance, not only for your home and its contents, but also for your family when visiting Florida. If you live in Florida permanently you will require additional insurance. It's unnecessary to spend half your income insuring yourself against every eventuality from the common cold to being sued for your last dime, but it's important to insure against any event that could precipitate a major financial disaster, such as a serious accident or your house being demolished by a hurricane. **The cost of being uninsured or under-insured in the US can be astronomical.**

As with anything connected with finance, it's important to shop around when buying insurance. Simply collecting a few brochures from insurance agents or making a few telephone calls could save you a lot of money. Note, however, that not all insurance companies are equally reliable or have the same financial stability, and it may be better to insure with a large international company with a good reputation than with a small local company, even if this means paying a higher premium. Read all insurance contracts carefully and make sure that you understand the terms and the cover provided before signing them. Some insurance companies will do almost anything to avoid paying out on claims and will use any available legal loophole, therefore it pays to deal only with reputable companies (not that this provides a foolproof guarantee). Policies often contain traps and legal loopholes in the small print and it's therefore advisable to obtain legal advice before signing a contract.

In all matters regarding insurance, you're responsible for ensuring that you and your family are legally insured in Florida. Regrettably you can't insure yourself against being uninsured or sue your insurance agent for giving you bad advice! Bear in mind that if you wish to make a claim on an insurance policy, you may be required to report an incident to the police within 24 hours (this may also be a legal requirement). The law in Florida may differ considerably from that in your home country or your previous country of residence, so therefore you should *never* assume that it's the same. If you're unsure of your rights, you're advised to obtain legal advice for anything other than a minor claim.

This section contains information about health insurance, homeowner's insurance (i.e. building & household insurance), third party liability insurance and travel insurance. See also **Car Insurance** on page 36.

Health Insurance

With the exception of the very poor, persons aged over 65 and the disabled, there's no national system of free health care or inexpensive health insurance in the US (as there is in every other western country). There's also no free treatment for visitors who fall ill there. The health insurance cover required when visiting most other countries is totally inadequate in America, where the recommended minimum cover is $500,000. Long stay visitors should have travel or long stay health insurance or an international health policy (see **Health Insurance for Visitors** on page 58). When traveling in the US, you should always have proof of your health insurance with you.

If you're visiting, living or working in Florida, it's extremely risky not to have health insurance for your family, as if you're uninsured or under-insured you could be faced with astronomical medical bills. When deciding on the type and extent of health insurance, make sure that it covers *all* your family's present and future health requirements in the US, **before you receive a large bill.** A health insurance policy should cover you for *all* essential health care whatever the reason, including accidents (e.g. sports accidents) and injuries, whether they occur in your home, at your place of work or while traveling. **Don't take anything for granted, but check in advance. Note that it can be difficult for new arrivals to obtain health insurance as American insurance companies are often reluctant to take on clients without knowing their medical history.** In this case you must have an international 'expatriate' health policy.

The Florida Department of Insurance publishes a consumer guide to health insurance available from them at The Capitol, Lower level 25, Tallahassee, Florida 32399-0030 (tel. 904/488-0030). You can also check the *A.M. Best Life and Health Insurance* rating book available at US public libraries.

Health Insurance for Residents

The majority of Americans have health insurance which is paid partly or wholly by their employers (see below). This is, however, voluntary on the part of the employer and employees have no right to it. Note that while health care for the wealthy and securely-employed in the US is among the best in the world, it's sparse to non-existent for the poor and unemployed. Astonishingly for a first world nation, some 40m Americans (2.5m in Florida), or around 15 per cent of the population, have no health insurance and a further 65m have inadequate insurance. Publicly-funded health schemes are provided for the over 65s and the disabled (Medicare), and the very poor (Medicaid), although most people without private insurance must pay for their own medical treatment. Most uninsured people simply can't afford doctors' visits (which cost between $50 and $75) and drugs (which are expensive), and therefore usually go without treatment. Not surprisingly most Americans are extremely health conscious and are terrified of an accident or long illness which could bankrupt them and leave them (or their survivors) paying off the debt for many years afterwards.

Company Plans: Most American companies who can afford to do so provide their employees with voluntary basic health insurance (around 60 per cent of Americans have health insurance paid partly or wholly by their employers). Most large and medium sized companies have a group insurance plan in which all employees and their families are enroled from their first day of employment (although there may be a qualifying period for some benefits). Group cover is usually provided without an individual medical examination. Large multinationals and the US government provide employees and their families with free comprehensive health insurance, although most companies pay a percentage of premiums only, e.g. 50 to 90 per cent. Only some 10 per cent of American employers pay the entire cost of traditional fee-for-service medical coverage. Employers have been battling for years to reduce health care costs and many small firms simply can't afford to insure their employees or their families (over 80 per cent of the total number of uninsured persons are workers or their dependants). Less than 20 per cent of employers provide health insurance for their employees' dependants and some 40 per cent of children aren't covered by employer-based insurance plans.

HMOs & PPOs: An increasing number of employers are replacing traditional fee-for-service or indemnity plans (such as provided by Blue Cross and Blue Shield) with less expensive group practice plans, known as Health Maintenance Organizations (HMOs) and Preferred Provider Organizations (PPOs), which combine fee-for-service insurance with the group practice concept. Under HMO plans there are less likely to be restrictions on the number of days' hospital care, no dollar maximums on benefits, and no required payments by individuals. HMOs nearly always include cover for hearing care, physical examinations, well-baby care, and immunization and inoculations (required under the HMO Act), which aren't usually covered by fee-for-service plans.

Employee Contributions: The average employee contribution is around $50 per month for individuals and over $100 per month for families, and the average employee deductible is $500 a year per family member ($1,500 maximum per family). The trend is for employers to shift more of the cost of health insurance to employees. To reduce costs, many employers pay only 50 per cent of their employees' health insurance, where they previously paid 90 or 100 per cent. If you're an employee and are required to pay a percentage of your health insurance, it's automatically deducted from your salary in equal instalments throughout the year.

Restrictions: Some employers impose a health insurance surcharge on smokers and a few even refuse to hire smokers on the grounds that their habit may lead to costlier health insurance and more lost working days due to sickness. Being overweight or a heavy drinker may also increase your health insurance costs. Some companies even prohibit employees from indulging in 'hazardous activities and pursuits', although many US states have passed legislation prohibiting employers from curtailing their employees' legal out-of-hours activities.   Some employers offer health insurance discounts to non-smoking employees or those who take regular exercise.

Extent of Cover: The extent of health cover varies considerably depending on the company and the individual policy.   Some policies offer 'no-frills' insurance for basic medical expenses, while others are comprehensive plans (although few cover all medical expenses). Most insurance plans offer a range of medical 'packages', e.g. basic protection and major medical, plus optional or supplemental packages such as dental, optical, maternity and disability insurance.

Major Medical: The usual health insurance policy is called major medical and includes physician's, surgeon's and anaesthetist's fees; out-of-hospital prescription drugs; consultations with specialists; hospital accommodations and meals; any operation or other treatment necessary (e.g. physiotherapy, radiotherapy and chemotherapy); X-Rays and diagnostic tests; maternity care (after a 12-month qualification period); drugs, X-rays and dressings while in hospital; physical and mental health conditions; substance abuse treatment; home nursing; and extended care facilities.

Options: All health plans offer options or supplements, which vary from policy to policy.   Options that aren't usually included in a basic health plan (particularly a direct-pay plan) include dental care; maternity and well-baby care; routine physical examinations; eye and ear examinations; hospice care for the terminally ill; intensive care; disability; and organ transplants.   A basic plan also usually excludes extras for hospital in-patients such as a telephone, TV or visitors' meals. Well-baby care, routine physical examinations, dental care, and eye and ear examinations are usually included in an HMO or PPO plan.   Treatment of any medical condition for which you've already received medical attention or which existed prior to the start of the policy (called 'pre-existing'), may not be covered.   Health insurance doesn't cover childbirth if you were pregnant when you took out health insurance; however, comprehensive medical insurance usually covers complications associated with childbirth, such as a Caesarean section.   If possible, verify before a pregnancy that regular maternity charges are covered as 'any illness'.   Some health insurance policies don't cover childbirth in a hospital, but usually cover the cost of a birthing center.

Families: Insurance provided by an employer often covers an employee only and *not* his family.   Some company insurance plans aren't open to foreign employees until they have been resident in the US for six months.   In this case you should be covered by an individual health policy.   Children over 18 may not be included in a family policy. Few employers offer free comprehensive cover (i.e. pay all medical bills) for employees and their families, although there are a few exceptions such as companies who transfer foreign employees to the US.   **If you're offered a job in the US, carefully check the health insurance cover provided.**

Students: Full-time students in Florida colleges or universities may be able to pay a college infirmary fee entitling them to receive infirmary treatment.   Students' families aren't covered by students' college infirmary fees and must be covered privately. Students can also buy additional low cost accident insurance, which is recommended and may be compulsory.   All American colleges and universities provide foreign students with information about compulsory and recommended health insurance before their arrival in the US.

Treatment Abroad: If you do a lot of overseas traveling, ensure that your health plan covers you outside the US (most do).   Note that all bills, particularly those received for treatment outside the US, must include precise details of all treatment and prescriptions received.   Terms such as 'Dental Treatment' or 'Consultation' are insufficient. It's also helpful if bills are written in English, although this obviously isn't possible in all countries.

Premiums & Payments: Health insurance in the US is *very* expensive, with a typical policy for a family of four costing $thousands a year ($500 to $1,000 per month is typical). Before buying health insurance, shop around among different agents and companies and ask your colleagues, friends and neighbors for their recommendations. **Note that there are some 450 companies selling health insurance in Florida and premiums can vary by as much as 200 or 300 per cent for similar policies!** The major American health insurance companies include Blue Cross, Blue Shield, Major Medical, Prudential, Group Health Insurance and Aetna.

Premiums for men are usually lower than for women, although the highest premiums are usually for babies under two years old. Some policies levy deductibles on a variety of services, e.g. $10 for each routine visit to a physician, 20 per cent of ambulance costs, and 20 per cent or $1,000 per hospital admission (as an in-patient). Under an HMO or PPO plan, members usually pay a co-payment of $5 to $20 for each service rendered. Most policies have an annual deductible, typically $100 to $250 for an individual and $500 to $1,000 for a family. This is the amount you must pay towards your total medical bills in any year *before* your insurance company starts paying. Consider taking a higher deductible (e.g. $1,000) rather than paying higher premiums if you're young or in good health and avoid buying excess cover (i.e. more than you need or something you don't need). There may be a maximum limit on the amount an insurer will pay in any one year, e.g. $50,000, and a lifetime maximum such as $1m. Many insurers require a second opinion or a pre-admission review on non-emergency surgery and may penalize you (e.g. up to $1,000) if you don't follow the rules. File all claims promptly as some insurers reject claims that aren't filed within a limited period.

Unemployed & Self-Employed: If you're unemployed, self-employed or your employer doesn't provide a group insurance plan, you must purchase private health insurance or a direct-pay plan for your family. You may qualify for low-cost group insurance through a professional association or another organization, and you may also be able to obtain inexpensive insurance through an HMO or PPO. The self-employed can obtain information and insurance through the National Association of Self-Employed (NASE), PO Box 612067, DFW Airport, TX 75261-2067 (tel. 1-800-232-NASE). If you don't qualify for a reduced group rate, your premiums will be much higher (possibly even higher than your mortgage!). However, never assume that a group rate is lower than a direct-pay plan, as some organizations charge huge commissions and are a rip off. Retirees can obtain a low-cost policy from the American Association of Retired Persons (AARP), 601 E. Street, NW, Washington, DC 20049 (tel. 202/434-2277).

With some plans, the more claims you make, the more your insurance premiums will increase. If you have a long term illness or a poor medical history, you may be unable to obtain health insurance at any price. If you or a member of your family contracts a serious, expensive or chronic disease (such as AIDS), you may find that your health insurance is canceled or that your premiums skyrocket (it isn't uncommon for American insurance companies to cancel the policies of its sickest patients!). You may be required to pay your own medical bills and receive reimbursement from your insurance company later (less the percentage for which you're liable, if applicable). On the other hand, your insurance company may settle bills directly with physicians or hospitals and send you a bill for your contribution. Always obtain itemized medical bills, check them thoroughly and query anything you don't understand.

Changing Employers or Insurance Companies: When changing employers or leaving America, you should ensure that you have continuous health insurance. If you and your family are covered by a company health plan, your insurance will probably cease after your last official day of employment. **If you're planning to change your health insurance plan, ensure that no important benefits are lost, e.g. existing medical conditions usually won't be covered.** When changing health insurance companies, it's advisable to inform your old company if you have any outstanding bills for which they are liable.

Health Insurance for Visitors

Visitors spending short periods in Florida (e.g. up to a month) should have a travel health insurance policy (see page 64), particularly if they aren't covered by an international health policy. If you plan to spend up to six months in Florida you should either take out a travel policy (see page 64), a special long stay policy or an international health policy, which should cover you in your home country and when traveling in other countries. Note that prices can vary considerably and it's imperative to shop around. Most international health policies include repatriation or evacuation (although it may be optional), which may also include shipment (by air) of the body of a person who dies abroad to his home country for burial. Note that an international policy also allows you to choose to have non-urgent medical treatment in the country of your choice.

Most international insurance companies offer health policies for different areas, e.g. Europe, worldwide excluding North America, and worldwide including North America. **Note that a policy for Florida must provide unlimited cover in North America, which is the most expensive option.** Most companies offer different levels of cover, for example basic, standard, comprehensive and prestige levels of cover. There's always an annual limit on the total annual medical costs, which should be at least $500,000 (although many provide cover of up to $1.5m) and some companies also limit the charges for specific treatment or care such as specialist's fees, operations and hospital accommodations. A medical examination isn't usually required for international health policies, although pre-existing health problems are excluded for a period, e.g. one or two years.

Claims are usually settled in all major currencies and large claims are usually settled directly by insurance companies (although your choice of hospitals may be limited). Always check whether an insurance company will settle large medical bills directly, as if you're required to pay bills and claim reimbursement from an insurance company, it can take several months before you receive your money (some companies are slow to pay). It isn't usually necessary to translate bills into English or another language, although you should check a company's policy. Most international health insurance companies provide emergency telephone assistance.

The cost of international health insurance varies considerably depending on your age and the extent of cover. Note that with most international insurance policies, you must enrol before you reach a certain age, e.g. between 60 and 80, to be guaranteed continuous cover in your old age. Premiums can sometimes be paid monthly, quarterly or annually, although some companies insist on payment annually in advance. When comparing policies, always carefully check the extent of cover and exactly what's included and excluded from a policy (often indicated only in the *very* small print), in addition to premiums and excess charges. In some countries, premium increases are limited by law, although this may apply only to residents in the country where a company is registered and not to overseas policy holders. Although there may be significant differences in premiums, generally you get what you pay for and can tailor premiums to your requirements. The most important questions to ask yourself are does the policy provide the cover required and is it good value for money? If you're in good health and are able to pay for your own out-patient treatment, such as visits to your family doctor and prescriptions, then the best value may be a policy covering specialist and hospital treatment only.

Homeowner's Insurance

A homeowner's insurance policy usually consists of two types of insurance; casualty and liability protection. Casualty insurance (see below) covers losses that you suffer yourself, either man-made or from natural causes, and includes loss or damage to your home *and* your personal possessions (unlike in many other countries, where buildings and personal possessions are usually insured separately). Liability insurance (see page 63) covers you against financial responsibility for injuries to third parties on your property or accidents directly attributed to something connected with your property.

If you're buying your home with a mortgage, your lender will usually insist that it's covered by a homeowner's insurance policy. When the mortgage is paid off, it's unnecessary to have homeowner's insurance, although it's always advisable as many people have their homes damaged or destroyed each year in Florida by natural disasters such as fires, floods and hurricanes. Some 5 per cent of US owners don't carry any homeowner's insurance and it's estimated by the Insurance Information Institute that eight out of ten homeowners have insufficient insurance for their homes and possessions. Note that the amount you should insure your home for isn't the current market value, but its replacement value, i.e. the cost of rebuilding the property should it be totally destroyed.

The following types of homeowner's insurance policies are offered in the US, although some companies don't use the standard 'HO' categories:

HO-1: Basic Policy. The basic homeowner's policy insures your home and possessions against losses caused by the 11 'common perils' (listed below under **Casualty Insurance**). The basic policy is inadequate for most homeowners.

HO-2: Broad Policy. The 'broad' homeowner's policy insures your home and possessions against losses caused by the 11 'common perils' and a further six perils (listed below under **Casualty Insurance**). An HO-2 policy is more popular than the basic HO-1 policy.

HO-3: All-Risk or Special Policy. An all-risk or special policy protects your home against all the perils included in an HO-2 policy, plus any other perils not specifically *excluded* in the policy. Your possessions, however, have the same cover as the HO-2 policy. This is the most popular form of homeowner's policy.

HO-4: Renter's Policy. A renter's policy provides the same protection as an HO-2 policy for the personal possessions and home improvements made by someone who's renting a property. The building itself isn't insured.

HO-5: Comprehensive Policy. A comprehensive policy covers everything, including your personal possessions, on an all-risk basis, with the exception of any exclusions listed in the policy. It's the Cadillac of policies and the most expensive.

HO-6: Condominium & Co-op Policy. This policy is for owners of condos and co-op dwellings. It covers personal possessions and improvements, but excludes the dwelling itself (which is insured by the condominium or co-op association).

HO-8: Older Homes Policy. An older homes policy is similar to a basic HO-1 policy and is specifically for older homes which would be prohibitively expensive to replace.

It insures that an older home is returned to serviceable condition, but not necessarily to the same state as previously.

Casualty Insurance

Casualty insurance is usually offered as part of a homeowner's insurance policy (see above) and includes insurance for your home *and* possessions. The other part of a homeowner's insurance policy is liability insurance (see page 63). A basic homeowner's policy (called HO-1) insures your home and possessions against losses caused by the 11 so-called 'common perils' or 'hazards' (hence 'hazard insurance') of fire or lightning; windstorm or hail; explosion; riot or civil commotion; aircraft; vehicles; smoke; vandalism or malicious mischief; theft; glass (that constitutes part of the building) breakage; and volcanic eruption.

Some homeowner's policies include the following additional six perils (making 17 in total) covering falling objects; weight of ice, snow or sleet; sudden or accidental tearing apart, cracking, burning, or bulging of a steam or hot water heating system, an air-conditioning or automatic fire protective sprinkler system, or an appliance for heating water; accidental discharge or overflow of water or steam from within a plumbing, heating or air-conditioning system, or automatic fire protective sprinkler system, or an appliance for heating water; freezing of plumbing, heating or air-conditioning systems, or automatic fire protective sprinkler system, or of a household appliance; and sudden and accidental damage from an 'artificially generated electrical current' created by appliances, devices, fixtures and wiring.

A homeowner's policy including all of the above is usually referred to as an HO-2 (broad) or an HO-4 (renter's) policy. An HO-3 (all-risk) or HO-5 (comprehensive) policy provides the most extensive protection and includes everything except flood, earthquake, war, nuclear accident and certain other risks specified in your policy. An HO-3 and most other homeowner's policies also provides protection for loss of use, i.e. when your home becomes uninhabitable and you're required to find alternative accommodations and incur additional living expenses. An HO-6 policy is for owners of a condominium or co-op dwelling and covers personal possessions and improvements. However, it excludes the dwelling itself which is insured by the condominium or co-op association. An HO-8 policy is for older homes and is similar to a basic HO-1 policy.

Extra Risks: You can insure against extra risks such as floods (see below), earthquakes and hurricanes, although in high risk areas cover is expensive, the cost usually depending on the exact location of a home. Rates are higher for wood-frame homes (because of the higher risk of fire) than masonry homes, e.g. a house built with concrete blocks. Homes located in areas susceptible to storms (e.g. hurricane) and wind damage are more expensive to insure and in rural areas you may need to pay increased fire insurance. **It's advisable to investigate the occurrence of natural disasters in an area where you're planning to buy a home and the cost of homeowner's insurance, which can be prohibitive.**

Extent of Cover: All homeowner's insurance policies include your personal possessions, such as furniture, clothing, electrical and electronic equipment, and household appliances. If you don't own your home, you can take out a renter's policy (HO-4), covering your personal possessions and, most importantly, damage caused by you to the property you're renting. When insuring your possessions, don't buy more insurance than you need, as unless you have valuable possessions the insurance may cost more than replacing them. You may be better off just insuring a few valuable items, rather than everything. Note that in America, possessions aren't usually insured for their replacement value (new for old), but their 'actual cash value' (cost minus depreciation). You can, however, buy replacement-cost insurance, although policies often include limits and are more expensive.

To calculate the amount of insurance you require, make a complete inventory of your possessions containing a description, purchase price and date, and their location in your home. Some insurance companies use a formula based on the insurance cover on your home, although this is no more than a 'guesstimate'. Keep the list and all receipts in a safe place (such as a safety deposit box). Add new purchases to your list and make adjustments to your insurance cover when necessary. There are maximum limits (listed in contracts) on cover for individual items in a standard homeowner's policy.

Valuables: High-value possessions (called 'scheduled property') such as works of art, furs and jewelry, aren't fully covered by a standard policy, and must be insured separately for their full value or through a basic policy 'rider'. You need to purchase extra insurance for these items called a *floater*, which can be either an endorsement to a standard policy or a separate policy. The cost of floaters varies considerably depending on the area and the local crime rate. A 'floater' policy may also insure your personal property if it's stolen from somewhere other than your home, e.g. a car or an hotel room. The value of high-value items must be certified by a receipt or a professional appraiser's report. It's advisable to make a video or photographic record of the contents of your home and keep receipts for all expensive items. A copy of the photographic record, the original receipts and an up-to-date inventory should be kept in a safe place, e.g. a safety deposit box (in case of a fire in your home).

Note that a basic contents policy may not include such items as credit cards (and their fraudulent use), cash, musical instruments, jewelry, valuables, sports equipment and bicycles, for which you may need to take out extra cover. A basic policy *doesn't* usually include accidental damage caused by you or members of your family to your own property (e.g. 'accidentally' putting your foot through the TV during a political broadcast) or your home freezer contents (in the event of a breakdown or power failure).

Amount of Cover: Some policies are index-linked and the amount of cover is automatically increased each year based on the federal Consumer Price Index (CPI) or a state CPI (sometimes called an 'inflation guard' provision). Even with an index-linked policy, you should review your policy regularly, e.g. annually. Homeowner's insurance must usually be renewed each year and insurance companies are continually updating their policies, therefore you must ensure that a policy still provides the cover you require when you receive the renewal notice (although sometimes the cost is simply added to your monthly mortgage payments). It's your responsibility to ensure that your level of cover is adequate, particularly if you carry out home improvements that substantially increase the value of your home.

All agents and insurance companies provide information and free advice, and will usually inspect your home to assess your insurance needs. Note, however, that an assessment should be performed by a professional appraiser, e.g. a Member of the Appraisal Institute (MAI), and the cost varies considerably. Many insurers insist that you insure your home for at least 80 per cent of the replacement cost. If you insure for less than 80 per cent of the replacement cost, you will receive a pro rata settlement of any claim, however small. For example, if you insure for 50 per cent of the replacement cost, you will receive only 50 per cent of the value of a claim.

Premiums: The cost of homeowner's insurance varies widely depending on the value of your home, its location, whether it's constructed of bricks/concrete or wood (wood-frame homes are dearer to insure) and how far it is from a fire hydrant (homes in wooded rural areas are often more expensive to insure because of the fire risk). Most policies have a deductible (excess), which is the amount of the loss you must pay. You can reduce your premium by accepting a higher deductible, e.g. $250 (or even $1,000) instead of $100. In the wake of hurricane Andrew some insurers have imposed a minimum $500 deductible. If you have extra security, such as high security door and window locks, an alarm system, fire extinguishers or sprinklers, you may receive a discount. You may also receive a discount if you're over 55 or when you buy your auto insurance from the same company.

Rates for the same level of cover from different companies can vary by as much as 100 per cent, so shop around and get at least three estimates. However, make sure that all quotes are for the same level of cover. As a *rough* guide, a $75,000 casualty policy with $100,000 liability cover and a $250 deductible costs between $250 and $400 for a masonry home in Florida and around 25 per cent more for a wood-frame home *in a low to medium risk area*. Homeowner's insurance has rocketed in recent years and has doubled or trebled in high risk areas. After hurricane Andrew in 1992 many insurers went bust (had it hit Fort Lauderdale claims would have reached $50 billion and would have wiped out all insurers), pulled out of the market or canceled the policies of thousands of customers living in high risk coastal areas. Insurance for a three bedroom, two bathroom home with a swimming pool (value circa $125,000) in a high risk area can be as high as $800 or $900 a year. The highest level of cover usually includes damage to glass (windows, patio doors, etc.) and porcelain (bath, washbasins, etc.), although you may have to pay extra for accidental damage, e.g. when your son blasts a baseball ball through a window. Always ask your insurer what isn't covered and what it will cost to include it (if required).

Flood & Subsidence Insurance: Owners of houses vulnerable to subsidence (e.g. those built on clay) and those living in flood-prone areas (such as near a coast or river) are likely to have to pay much higher premiums. If a home in Florida is below the flood plain (i.e. anywhere near the coastline) you will need flood insurance (costing some $400 a year extra for an average home). A survey and elevation may be required to determine the exact height of a property above sea level and whether flood insurance is necessary. You can insure against flood risks through the National Flood Insurance Program, operating in over 18,000 American communities and backed by the federal government (tel. 1-800-638-6620 for information). If you live in a flood plain you should have a sump pump and should call the fire department if you have a flood.

Holiday Homes: Insurance for holiday homes is higher in some areas due to their higher vulnerability to claims, particularly for theft, and many insurance companies reduce or suspend cover when a home is unoccupied for more than 30 or 60 days. It's usually possible to negotiate cover for periods of absence for a hefty surcharge, although valuable items may be excluded. Note that an insurance may not pay out on a claim for theft when there's no sign of forced entry. **If you rent a home short term you require a special 'short term rental dwelling' policy (if you rent short term with an 'ordinary' policy, it will be void). You must read all small print in policies regarding absence and rentals.**

Claims: If you wish to make a claim you must usually inform your insurance company in writing (by registered letter) within two to seven days of the incident or 24 hours in the case of theft. Thefts should also be reported to the local police within 24 hours, as the police statement (of which you receive a copy for your insurance company) constitutes 'irrefutable' evidence of your claim. Check whether you're covered for damage or thefts that occur when you're away from the property and are therefore unable to inform the insurance company immediately. Bear in mind that if you make a claim you may need to wait months for it to be settled. Generally the larger the claim, the longer you will have to wait for your money, although in an emergency some companies make an interim payment. If you aren't satisfied with the amount offered, don't accept it and try to negotiate a higher figure. If you still can't reach agreement on the amount or the time taken to settle a claim, you may be able to take your claim to an independent industry organization for arbitration. **Note that some insurance companies will do their utmost to find a loophole which makes you negligent and relieves them of liability.**

Liability Insurance

Liability insurance is usually offered as part of a homeowner's policy (see page 59), but can also be purchased separately. It's the second most important insurance to have in the US (after health insurance), where suing is a national sport (baseball is also popular but not nearly so rewarding). People sue each other at the drop of a hat in the US for the most trivial and ludicrous reasons, irrespective of who (or whether anyone) was at fault. Even more astounding, many of the most bizarre cases (most of which would be laughed out of court in other countries) actually make it into court *and* plaintiffs are awarded $millions in damages, often out of all proportion to the incident. For example, a burglar successfully sued for injuries sustained while breaking into a house and a couple sued a hospital for $4m for distressing and permanent emotional damage when their baby was harmlessly and temporarily dyed blue (unwisely referred to as a 'smurfette' by a nurse).

The practice of dragging your spouse, friends, neighbors, host, employer or physician into court at the drop of a hat, is to many foreigners one of the most appalling aspects of the American way of life. If someone falls down on your sidewalk, slips on your carpet, or trips over your vacuum cleaner lead, they may sue you for $millions. The system is designed to keep litigation lawyers (of which there are zillions in America) and insurance companies in luxury. They are aided and abetted by the courts and judges, who seem to take it for granted that people have liability insurance with which to pay the farcical 'damages' awarded. If you don't have personal liability insurance, you could find yourself in serious financial trouble.

A homeowner's insurance policy (see page 59) usually includes liability insurance of $100,000 or more for liability for bodily injury and property damage. Most companies offer optional extra cover, e.g. cover of $300,000 for an extra $10 a year. Considering the low cost of liability insurance and the high cost of law suits, most experts recommend $300,000 to be the *minimum* cover necessary. Liability insurance covers you against claims from third parties due to injury or property damage, medical bills, loss of earnings, and pain and suffering as a result of an accident on your property (or something on your property, e.g. if a branch falls off a tree and injures someone on the sidewalk or your dog bites someone through your fence). Work related losses aren't covered by a standard homeowner's policy, for example injury and damages incurred by clients, customers, business associates or domestic employees working for you on your property. If you use your home as an office or work place you must take out additional liability cover or a separate policy (including malpractice insurance). Damage or injuries caused by your children while working on someone else's property also aren't covered, but can be included for a small additional fee.

Many people take out a personal liability 'umbrella' policy to extend the cover of their homeowner's and automobile policies, which usually includes protection against claims arising from business activities and other claims, such as slander. An umbrella policy provides excess liability cover over and above the amount in your basic policies and isn't a replacement for these policies. For example, increasing the liability cover included in a basic homeowner's policy from $100,000 to $1m could be done with an umbrella policy and is usually cheaper.

Holiday & Travel Insurance

Holiday and travel insurance is recommended for all who don't wish to risk having their holiday or travel ruined by financial problems or to arrive home broke. As you probably know, anything can and often does go wrong with a holiday, sometimes before you even get started (particularly when you *don't* have insurance). The following information applies equally to both residents and non-residents, whether they are traveling to or from the US or within the continental US. **Nobody should visit Florida without travel (and health) insurance!**

Travel insurance is available from many sources including travel agents, insurance companies and brokers, banks, automobile clubs and transport companies (airline, rail and bus). Package holiday companies and tour operators also offer insurance polices, some of which are compulsory, too expensive **and don't provide adequate cover.** You can also buy 24-hour accident and flight insurance at major airports, although it's expensive and doesn't offer the best cover. Before taking out travel insurance, carefully consider the range and level of cover you require and compare policies. Short term holiday and travel insurance policies may include cover for holiday cancelation or interruption; missed flights; departure delay at both the start *and* end of a holiday (a common occurrence); delayed, lost or damaged baggage; personal effects and money; medical expenses and accidents (including evacuation home); flight insurance; personal liability and legal expenses; and default or bankruptcy insurance, e.g. a tour operator or airline going bust.

Health Cover: Medical expenses are an important aspect of travel insurance and you shouldn't rely on insurance provided by charge and credit card companies, household policies or private medical insurance (unless it's an international policy that specifically includes North America), none of which usually provide adequate cover for Florida. However, you should take advantage of what they have to offer. The minimum medical expenses cover recommended by most experts is $500,000 for North America (many policies have limits of between $3m and $7.5m). If applicable, check whether pregnancy related claims are covered and whether there are any restrictions for those over a certain age, e.g. 65 or 70 (travel insurance is becoming increasingly more expensive for those aged over 65). Personal liability cover should be $1.5m to $3m in North America. Always check any exclusion clauses in contracts by obtaining a copy of the full policy document, as not all relevant information will be included in an insurance leaflet. High risk sports and pursuits should be specifically covered and *listed* in a policy (there's usually an additional premium).

Visitors: Travel insurance for visitors to Florida should include personal liability and repatriation expenses. If your travel insurance expires while you're visiting Florida, you can buy further insurance from an insurance agent, although this won't include repatriation expenses. Flight insurance and comprehensive travel insurance is available from insurance desks at most airports, including travel accident, personal accident, world-wide medical expenses and in-transit baggage.

Cost: The cost of travel insurance varies considerably, depending on where you buy it, how long you intend to stay in Florida and your age. Generally the longer the period covered, the cheaper the daily cost, although the maximum period covered is usually limited, e.g. six months. With some policies a deductible (excess) must be paid for each claim. As a rough guide, travel insurance for two weeks costs around $100 to $150 for a family of four (two adults and two children under 16).

Annual Policies: For people who travel abroad frequently, whether on business or pleasure, an annual travel policy usually provides the best value, but always check carefully exactly what it includes. Many insurance companies offer annual travel policies for a premium of from around $150 for an individual (the equivalent of around three months insurance with a standard travel insurance policy), which are excellent value for frequent travelers. Some insurance companies also offer an 'emergency travel policy' for holiday home owners who need to travel abroad at short notice to inspect a property, e.g. after a severe storm. The cost of an annual policy may depend on the area covered, e.g. Europe, worldwide (excluding North America) and worldwide (including North America), although it doesn't usually cover travel within your country of residence. There's also a limit on the number of trips a year and the duration of each trip, e.g. 90 or 120 days. An annual policy is usually a good choice for owners of a holiday home in Florida who travel there frequently for relatively short periods. **However, always carefully check exactly what is covered (or omitted) as an annual policy may not provide adequate cover.**

Claims: If you need to make a claim, you should provide as much documentary evidence as possible in support. Travel insurance companies gladly take your money, but they aren't always so keen to pay claims and you may have to persevere before they pay up. Always be persistent and make a claim *irrespective* of any small print, as this may be unreasonable and therefore invalid in law. Insurance companies usually require you to report a loss (or any incident for which you intend to make a claim) to the local police or carriers within 24 hours and obtain a written report. Failure to do so may mean that a claim won't be considered.

SHOPPING

The US is the ultimate consumer society, with annual consumer spending totaling over $4 trillion (or $4,000,000,000,000!). The US is jam-packed with bustling shopping malls, vast department stores, colorful markets, bargain discount stores, chic boutiques and numerous specialty stores. One of the delights of owning a home in Florida is the huge variety of shopping malls on your doorstep, enough to satisfy even the most ardent and discerning shoppers. In Florida you can buy anything and everything at almost any time of day or night, and will enjoy the most competitive prices and widest choice of goods available anywhere in the world. Americans believe in abundant choice and everything is available in every size, color and flavor imaginable. In the US shopping is all things to all men and women and is variously a sport, pastime, entertainment, game, business, amusement, love, all consuming passion and the Meaning of Life.

Not surprisingly, the US is the world's major importer of famous and exclusive international labels and branded goods, which can often be purchased there for less than in their country of origin. Designer products (perfection at double the price) are much in vogue and include coffee, beer, ice cream, health foods, clothes and numerous other items. Most consumer goods in the US are inexpensive (never ask for something 'cheap' in America, which is synonymous with trash or poor quality) compared with other countries including electronic goods, cameras, computer hardware and software, stereo systems, CDs, videos, sports equipment, and clothes (particularly jeans and casual clothes), all of which offer excellent value for money.

Bargains: What matters most to Americans is value for money and low prices (which aren't always the same) and hardly anyone pays top dollar for anything in the US (many stores will meet any advertised price). If you're an avid bargain hunter it's important to 'comparison shop 'til you drop' as suggested retail prices are almost extinct in America. Avoid stores that don't display their prices, as if you have to ask the price it usually means you can't afford it! Most people save their spending sprees or major purchases for the sales or shop at discount and factory outlets (see below), where huge savings can be made. Note that prices in stores are always shown exclusive of sales tax (see page 117).

Payment: Most stores accept all major credit cards, although you may be required to make a minimum purchase. Many will only accept a personal check if your bank is located in the same city and you show at least two forms of identification. In some stores you may have to go to a special desk and have a check approved before going to the checkout and some stores will accept personal checks only from customers to whom they have previously issued an ID card. Almost all retailers accept $US travelers' checks and most give change. You'll be pleased to know that most places also accept cash (or even insist on it, e.g. some restaurants and gas stations). If you run out of the folding stuff, many stores, supermarkets and malls have automated teller machines (ATMs) which accept most cash and credit cards.

Discount Coupons: Most American retailers (particularly supermarkets) regularly offer discount coupons, which are found in local newspapers and magazines, particularly at weekends. Shopping with coupons is a way of life for most Americans and it's a rare shopper who never uses them. If you don't use coupons you will simply pay too much, as prices are set with the expectation that most customers will use them. In order not to lose business to their rivals, many stores and businesses also accept coupons issued by their competitors.

Customer Relations: In the US the customer is always, but always right! Most retailers, particularly department and chain stores, will exchange goods or give refunds without question. Americans enjoy a high degree of consumer protection and almost any complaint is dealt with promptly and favorably (particularly if you threaten to sue!). If you pay by credit card, you can have a charge removed from your bill if you don't receive goods or services or a sale was obtained through fraud or misrepresentation. If you have any questions about your rights as a consumer, contact your local consumer protection agency or better business bureau. You can also call the free consumer complaints line (tel. 1-800-435-7352).

Many stores, particularly department and chain stores, provide free catalogs at various times throughout the year (catalogs are delivered to homes with other junk mail) and free shopping guides are published in all areas. If you're looking for a particular item or anything unusual, you'll find that the Yellow Pages will save you time, trouble and shoe leather. For those who aren't accustomed to buying goods with American measures and sizes, a list of comparative weights and measures is included in **Appendix C**.

On a negative note, always keep a firm grip on your belongings when shopping in crowded towns and cities, as pickpockets and bag-snatchers are an integral part of the American free enterprise system.

Sales, Factory Outlets & Warehouse Clubs

Although dickering and haggling (bargaining or bartering) isn't a way of life in the US (except in Congress), you should never be shy about asking for a discount, particularly when buying an expensive item or a large quantity of goods. Although prices are fixed in supermarkets, department and chain stores, many stores will match any genuinely advertised price. In the tough trading times experienced in recent years, retailers have discovered that the only thing that attracts shoppers is discounts and low prices, which has put the shopper firmly in the driving seat. If you're planning to buy an expensive item, for example a TV, computer or camera (the US is a mecca for hi-tech freaks), always compare prices in advertisements in local newspapers (particularly Sunday editions) and consumer magazines or call several local stores before buying. **However, when comparing prices, make sure that you're comparing the same or similar goods and services, as anyone can 'save' money by purchasing inferior products!** Don't forget to ask your friends, neighbors and colleagues for their advice in addition to doing your own research. Be wary of bargains that seem too good to be true, as they probably will be.

The best bargains can be found at warehouse clubs, factory outlets, and discount malls and centers (shopping malls comprised entirely of off-price, discount and factory-outlet stores). Discount stores and factory outlets are able to offer lower prices on branded goods because profit margins and overheads are cut to the bone and the middleman is excluded. Factory outlet malls (such as Belz in Orlando) usually have rules stating that tenants *must* discount merchandise a minimum of 10 per cent less than any local discount store or offer at least one third off regular retail prices.

Warehouse clubs and discount stores operate on the 'pile high and sell low' principle, with no fancy displays or customer areas, usually no demonstrations, and little customer or after-sales service; just rock-bottom prices. You should know exactly what you want when shopping at discount stores as staff don't waste time discussing products and are likely to employ the hard sell if you're undecided. When shopping with a special offer voucher it isn't advisable to tell the clerk until you have verified that he has the goods in stock, otherwise if he knows you have a discount voucher you may find the store is suddenly out of stock (your discount usually comes out of his commission). Warehouse clubs (including Costco, Pace Membership Warehouse, Price Club and Sam's Warehouse) were ostensibly created to supply businesses, but it isn't difficult for retail customers to obtain membership. You must buy in bulk but the savings are substantial, with prices as much as 25 per cent lower than supermarkets.

Most stores hold sales at various times of the year, the largest of which are held in January and July or August when bargains abound, particularly in major cities. Top department stores usually have pre-season fashion sales, e.g. fall/winter clothes are on sale for a limited period in August or September. Sales are also common on federal and local holidays such as the Presidents' Day and Veterans' Day weekends. Traditionally sales start after Thanksgiving in November (the day after thanksgiving is the biggest shopping day of the year). Most Americans have an eye for a bargain and many shop for luxury or expensive items only when they're on sale. It also pays to stock up on non-perishable, everyday items during sales as this can save you $hundreds over a year.

Factory outlets, owned and operated by manufacturers, abound throughout the US. Although they may sell obsolete or overstocked items, most factory outlets don't sell poor quality goods or 'seconds' (flawed or damaged goods), but sell quality products at bargain prices. Ask your friends and neighbors if there are any in your area and look out for them on your travels. Designer clothes can also be purchased from factory outlets in cities. Note that factory outlets frequently accept cash only. In most cities there are also huge warehouse stores specializing in selling remainders, leftover stock, overruns and canceled orders at reduced prices, typically 25 to 75 per cent below normal retail prices.

If you're a keen bargain hunter, a multitude of outlet guides are published including the *Joy of Outlet Shopping* (Outlet Consumer Report, Box 7867, St. Petersburg, FL 33734), the *Guide to the Nations Best Outlets* (Outletbound, PO Box 1255, Orange, CT 06477, tel. 1-800-33-OUTLET) listing over 4,500 outlets nationwide, *Fabulous Finds* by Iris Ellis (Writer's Digest Books) and *Outlet Bound: Guide to the Nation's Best Outlets* (Outlet Marketing Group). Several regional factory outlet guides are published by Globe Pequot Press, Affiliated Publishing, PO Box Q, Chester, CT 06412 (tel. 203/526-9571).

Shopping by Mail-Order & Telephone

Mail-order Shoppingand telephone shopping is widespread in America, where mail-order business generates over $200 billion in annual sales from some 13 billion catalogs. Over half of all Americans shop by telephone or mail and almost anything can be bought by mail (even firearms) and delivered overnight (although you pay extra for this service). One of the advantages of catalog purchases is that they're exempt from sales tax (except in states where the supplier has an office). Despite increased competition from stores, mail-order remains big business and you will regularly receive unsolicited catalogs in your mail. American mail-order firms don't use agents, but deal directly with customers, which helps reduce overheads and keep down prices. Note that mail-order in the US doesn't usually mean buying on the instalment plan (credit terms), as in some other countries.

Many American manufacturers sell their products by mail-order only, both to corporate and private customers. Many specialist companies such as Sears, JC Penney, Orvis, Spiegel, Lane Bryant and Montgomery Ward produce comprehensive and elaborate catalogs. Sears of Chicago produces the most famous and largest mail-order catalog in the world, containing over 1,600 pages and some 250,000 items. The top American mail-order companies include J.C. Penney, Fingerhut, Spiegel, Land's End and L.L. Bean, while the best companies for mail-order clothing include L.L. Bean, Patagonia, Land's End, REI and Cabela's. Orders can usually be placed by telephone (toll-free) at local retail outlets and delivery can be made to your home or office. Catalogs are free or cost around $5 and often come with free gifts and/or discount coupons.

There's generally little risk when buying goods by mail-order in the US, as there are strict federal consumer-protection laws governing mail-order sales. If you have any doubts about a company's reputation, you can check with the US Postal Service, your state or local consumer protection agency, or a Better Business Bureau before ordering. Keep a copy of the advertisement or offer and a record of your order, including the company's name, address and telephone number, the price of items ordered, any handling or other charges, the date you mailed or telephoned your order, and your method of payment. Also keep copies of all canceled checks and statements. Before committing yourself to buying anything by mail, always make sure you know what you're signing and don't send cash through the mail or pay for anything in advance unless it's absolutely necessary. It's foolish to send advance payment by mail in response to an ad (or to anyone) unless you're sure that the company is reputable and offers a foolproof money-back guarantee.

Telephone Shopping: Shopping by telephone has increased dramatically in recent years, particularly with the proliferation of charge, credit and debit cards. One of the most popular methods of telephone shopping is via TV through companies such as the Home Shopping Club, QVC and Prodigy. Cable TV shopping shows offer goods at seemingly bargain prices, some even providing a 24-hour service for insomniac shoppers. Orders are placed by telephone and goods are mailed to you. Payment can be made by credit card, personal check or money order. However, before placing an order, check that an item isn't available cheaper in local discount stores and set a spending limit before switching on the box! In-flight shopping is also possible via SkyMall catalogs found on most American airlines. Orders are placed on toll-free numbers via Airfones and charged to credit cards. The latest method of shopping is via computer, which is set to boom in the next few years with the introduction of virtual reality programs.

Furniture & Furnishings

Furniture is usually good value for money in Florida and is often less expensive than in many other countries. There's a huge choice of both traditional and contemporary designs in every price range, although as with most things the quality is usually reflected in the price. Exclusive modern designs, both American and imported, are available, usually with matching exclusive prices. The best value-for-money imports include quality leather suites and a wide range of cane furniture from the Far East. Most furniture stores have personal designers and decorators whose services may be provided free to high-spending customers.

A number of manufacturers sell directly to the public, although you shouldn't assume that this will result in large savings and should always compare prices *and* quality before buying (the least expensive furniture may be poor value for money if you want something that will last). If you plan to rent your Florida home you will need sturdy, hard-wearing furniture and furnishings. There are also stores specializing in beds, leather, reproduction and antique furniture, and companies that both manufacture and install fitted bedrooms and kitchens. If you want reasonably priced, good quality, modern furniture, there are a number of companies selling furniture for home assembly which helps keep down prices. All large furniture retailers publish catalogs, which are generally distributed free to homes.

Furniture and home furnishings is a competitive business in the US and you can often reduce the price by some judicious haggling, particularly when you're spending a large amount. Another way to save money is to wait for the sales, when prices are slashed. If you can't wait and don't want or can't afford to pay cash, you may be able to find an interest-free credit deal. Check the advertisements in local newspapers (particularly 'home' or 'habitat' magazine sections) and national home and design magazines. If you're buying a new home, most builders offer furnishing packages (see page 140) which include everything from furniture and major appliances down to a corkscrew. However, they may not offer savings over selective buying of individual items and are mainly intended for owners wishing to rent their properties. Check other homes that builders have furnished and comparison shop before committing yourself. Many stores offer 'rooms-to-go', where you can buy a complete roomful of furnishings in one go. Secondhand furniture can be bought from charity stores, through ads in local newspapers, and yard, garage and estate sales. Furniture rental is also fairly common in the US, although it isn't cost-effective in the long term.

Household Goods

The electricity supply in Florida is 110/120 volts AC with a frequency of 60 hertz (cycles) and therefore imported electrical equipment made for a 220/240V 50 cycle supply won't function unless it has a 'dual voltage' switch or is used with a transformer (see page 171). It isn't worthwhile bringing electrical equipment to the US as a wide range of American-made and imported items are available at reasonable prices. Don't bring a TV made for a different market (e.g. Europe) to the US as it won't work (see page 72). Note that most new homes come complete with major appliances such as a range (cooker) and dishwasher, and may also include a microwave, refrigerator and washer.

Practically nobody brings large household appliances to the US, particularly as the standard American width isn't the same as in other countries. American refrigerators are huge and usually have the capacity to store a year's supply of dairy products for a family of 14 (and a dog). Small appliances such as vacuum cleaners, grills, toasters and electric irons are inexpensive in the US. Always shop around when buying large appliances and be prepared to haggle over prices, even when goods are on sale. Look for 0 per cent interest deals, but also make sure that the price is competitive. Note that some inexpensive deals don't include delivery and installation, so always compare inclusive prices. If you plan to export appliances later to a country with a 240v 50 cycle electricity supply, always ensure that they have a voltage and frequency selector and operate on 50/60 cycles.

If you want kitchen measuring equipment and can't cope with American measures, you will need to provide your own measuring scales, thermometers jugs, cups (e.g. American and British 'recipe' cups *aren't* the same size). See also **Appendix C**. Note that American beds (sheets), pillows and comforters (quilts) aren't the same size or shape as in most other countries. See also **Electricity** on page 171.

PETS

All animals imported into the US are subject to health, quarantine, agriculture, wildlife and customs requirements and prohibitions, as are pets taken out of the US and returned. Pets must be examined at the first port of entry for possible evidence of disease that can be transmitted to humans and those excluded from entry must be exported or destroyed. Dogs, cats and turtles may be imported free of duty, although duty may be payable on other pets, the value of which can be included in your customs exemption if they accompany you and aren't for resale.

Dogs must be vaccinated against rabies at least 30 days prior to entry into the US. Exceptions are puppies less than three months old and dogs originating or located for six months or longer in areas designated by the Public Health Service as being rabies free. Domestic cats must be free of evidence of diseases communicable to man when examined at the port of entry (vaccination against rabies isn't required). Birds must be quarantined at the owner's expense upon arrival for at least 30 days in a facility operated by the US Department of Agriculture (USDA). For regulations concerning the importation of other animals, contact your local US embassy or consulate or write to the US Public Health Service, Center for Disease Control, Foreign Quarantine Program, Atlanta, Georgia 30333 (tel. 404/639-2574). A leaflet entitled *Pets, Wildlife: US*

Customs is available from the US Customs Service, Office of Public Information, 1301 Constitution Avenue, PO Box 7407, NW, Washington, DC 20229 (tel. 202/566-8195).

You can take your dog or cat to a veterinary surgeon (vet) for a course of vaccinations, some of which, such as rabies, are mandatory. Some municipalities provide free rabies shots for cats and dogs. After vaccination your pet must wear a rabies tag attached to its collar. If you live in a rabies area, don't allow your pets to run free and don't let your children play with or approach strange or wild animals, as they could have rabies. If a child is bitten by an unknown animal, he may require a series of anti-rabies injections. Vets also perform spaying or neutering, which is recommended by the ASPCA (see below), the cost of which varies depending on the region and the particular vet. Always shop around and compare veterinarian fees. It's possible to take out health insurance for your pets to reduce veterinary bills.

Many Americans aren't content with just keeping a cat or a dog like 'normal' people, but keep exotic pets such as leopards, cougars or boa constrictors. Although most states have strict regulations regarding the keeping of wild animals as pets, many Americans keep them illegally, particularly in Florida, one of the main gateways for the importation of illegal animals. Note also the following:

- Many municipalities and cities require cats and dogs to have a license, usually costing around $10 a year (possibly less if an animal has been neutered). Licensing may depend on a pet's age. Proof of a rabies' vaccination is required to obtain a license. Check with your local tax collector's office or city clerk.

- In the US it's illegal not to clear up after your dog, for which you can be fined. Take a 'poop-scoop' and a plastic bag with you when walking your dog. Dog 'mess' is called 'doodie' or 'doo-doo' in polite circles.

- With the exception of Seeing Eye and hearing-guide dogs (which may travel on trains and buses free of charge), dogs aren't allowed on public transport or in most restaurants and shopping malls.

- Many towns have strict leash laws and pets may not be permitted on beaches (or must be kept on a leash).

- Many condos and co-op developments have regulations forbidding the keeping of dogs and other animals (although cats are usually okay), and finding accommodations that accept dogs is difficult in most cities. The number of cats and dogs per residence may also be limited and large animals such as horses may be prohibited (particularly in condos).

- Most cities and large towns have animal hospitals and clinics, and individuals and organizations in many areas operate sanctuaries for injured or orphaned wild animals and abandoned pets. Note, however, that using an animal hospital may be much more expensive than going to a local vet. Many cities have animal shelters where you can obtain a stray dog free of charge.

- Your vet will arrange to collect and cremate the body of a dead pet (for a fee), although you can bury a dead pet in your yard in some areas. There are many commercial pet cemeteries in America, where the pets of the rich and famous are given a send off befitting their pampered position in life.

Animal lovers can join the American Society for the Prevention of Cruelty to Animals (ASPCA, Education Department, 441 East 92nd St., New York, NY 10128, tel. 212/876-7700), which campaigns vigorously against the killing of wildlife and the destruction of their habitats and publishes a wealth of information for pet owners.

TELEVISION & RADIO

Although many people complain endlessly about the poor quality of television (TV) programs in their home countries, many find they can't live without a TV when they are abroad. Unfortunately, everything you've heard about American TV (the tube) is true, only it's far worse. In the US, TV is a catchall for the banality and senselessness of much American culture, and many people blame TV for destroying the fabric of American society. In many homes, TV rivals family and religion as the dispenser of values, and is often referred to as the 'plug-in drug' or the 'third parent'. The average American family watches over seven hours TV a day and the average person around 30 hours per week (equal to 65 24-hour days a year!). Some 'couch potatoes' (people who spend all their time passively watching TV) leave their TVs on all day and even overnight. Prime time viewing (from around 7 to 11pm) attracts an average 85m viewers. Even the most modest motel or hotel boasts a color TV in every room, airports and bus stations have coin-operated TVs built into the arms of chairs, and bars, clubs, dance halls and even laundromats have banks of TVs (often showing live ballgames).

Quality: Most foreigners have little idea just how bad American TV can be. The American programs sold around the world are actually the *best* stuff they produce and much of the home market sap is simply appalling. Most programs are targeted at viewers with an IQ of below 50, many of whom have an attention span of around five microseconds. If something electrifying doesn't happen during that time (such as a graphic and gruesome murder or someone winning a jackpot prize), they're off zapping through the remaining 40 to 50 channels. American TV can be condescending, boring, total rubbish and an insult to the intelligence (nobody ever lost money in the US by *underestimating* public intelligence), its sole purpose being to make money, rather than entertain, educate or inform.

Advertising: The main role of American TV is as a medium for advertisers, some of whom spend over $500m a year on TV advertising. TV programs are advertised incessantly in much the same way as soap powder (although soap powder ads are usually more interesting) and programs are even advertised during other programs, as well as every few minutes in commercial breaks (you can't say you weren't warned!). Often it's difficult to tell where a program breaks and the ads start, as there's usually (deliberately) no warning that ads are about to start or have started (ads are also designed to look like program promos). Advertising on American TV is blatant, loud, amazingly frequent (often as much as 15 minutes an hour) and usually not funny (with certain hilarious exceptions). Even sports are interrupted every few minutes for a 'message from our sponsors' and if there aren't enough natural breaks the rules are changed to create more. Advertising during sports programs is unbelievable and makes some sports unwatchable (e.g. golf).

Guides: TV programs (broadcast and cable) are listed in daily newspapers, many of which also provide free weekly programs. There are free TV guides in most areas (good for coupons) and many others are available on news stands, including the best-selling *TV Guide* (over 5m copies sold weekly).

Standards: The standards for TV reception in the US **aren't the same as in other countries**. The American transmission standard is NTSC (never the same color!), which is broadcast on 525 lines rather than the 625-line PAL standard employed in most of Europe. TVs and video recorders that aren't manufactured for the NTSC standard won't function in the US (although dual-standard TVs are available). If you import a TV you may get a picture or sound, but not both. Video recorders manufactured for foreign (non-US) markets can't be used to record or play back NTSC-standard videos (however, PAL-standard video recorders and TVs are useful for playing PAL-standard videos in the US).

Locating a particular station on a strange TV (e.g. in an hotel) is often a lottery, as there's usually no relationship between the channel number selected and the channel number shown in the *TV Guide* or major newspapers. There are no national standards across the country and therefore ABC, CBS, NBC and Fox network stations may be found on any channel. In addition to the main network and cable TV stations, there are dozens of local TV stations in Florida. In apartments there's no need to fit a private antenna (aerial), as all large buildings have a master antenna on the roof. If you have cable TV (see below) you will receive all your stations via the cable link, which although it provides better reception than a roof antenna, can be affected by power cuts and extreme weather conditions. Reception is poor in many remote areas, with snowy and fuzzy pictures the norm rather than the exception (and that's if you're lucky enough to be located close to a transmitter or have cable TV).

Cable TV: Cable TV is available in around 60 per cent of American households and all metropolitan areas. Most cable stations broadcast 24-hours a day and in the larger cities there's an average of 35 cable channels in addition to the national networks and Public Broadcasting System (PBS) stations, although many cable subscribers receive over 50 stations. Although there are some general entertainment cable TV channels, many channels are dedicated to a particular topic including movies, sports, religion (an endless tirade of sin and salvation), comics, pornography, local events, news, financial news, shopping (worth over $1 billion a year), children's programs, weather, health, music (rock, country) and foreign-language programs (e.g. Spanish). Cable TV isn't subject to the same federal laws as broadcast TV and therefore channels may show programs (such as pornographic movies) that aren't permitted on network TV. The cable channels available in a city or locality depend on the franchise agreement with the local municipality, although the most popular channels are usually available throughout the country. Cable companies provide a basic cable service for a flat fee of $15 to $25 a month, plus premium subscription stations, with the average subscriber paying around $30 a month. Some companies provide a preferred or plus service, which is an expanded basic service. You can also subscribe to an FM stereo service (around $5 a month) in most areas, which improves FM reception on a stereo (radio) receiver.

Satellite TV: There are over 20 TV satellites serving North America, each with the capacity to transmit up to 24 channels. The so-called independent superstations utilize the power of both cable and satellites to program nationwide. Most satellite transmissions are broadcast exclusively for local cable TV companies, who pass the satellite signal through their cable network to subscribers. Every hotel, bar and club has a huge satellite dish (often 8 to 10 feet in diameter), which is mainly used to receive sports events, many of which show a number of live ballgames simultaneously on different TVs.

A growing number of people are buying satellite dishes to receive transmissions, particularly in remote rural areas where homes can't be connected to a cable system. Satellite systems with an 8 to 10ft dish cost from $2,000 to $5,000 and can receive TV stations from around the world. Low-power KU-Band systems are also available requiring much less expensive 3-foot dishes, e.g. $500 to $1,000, although they mostly receive pay-per-view stations only. Note that zoning boards are strict about the placement of satellite dishes and unless you have somewhere to hide it, you're unlikely to obtain permission to install one if you live in a metropolitan area. Satellite TV viewers may be interested in the annual *World Radio and TV Handbook* (Billboard), containing over 600 pages of information and the frequencies of all major TV (and radio) stations worldwide.

Radio: Radio flourishes in the US and has a huge audience, despite the competition from TV, cinema and videos. Radio reception is excellent in most parts of Florida (which has no mountains), including stereo reception. The US has over 10,000 local radio stations and in major cities you generally have a choice of 50 to 100 local stations, although in remote areas you may be able to receive a few stations only. Like TV stations, many radio stations are affiliated to national networks such as ABC, CBS, and NBC. There are also over 100 regional radio networks. Although most stations are commercial, advertising on radio is a lot less obtrusive than on TV. Many radio stations are highly specialized and include a variety of foreign language stations and non-commercial stations operated by colleges, universities and public authorities.

American mainstream commercial radio (like commercial TV) is of little interest if you're looking for serious discussion or education, but excellent if you're into music, news or religion. Stations are classified as news, talk, music or a combination. As a general rule, news and talk stations broadcast on AM and music stations on FM (in stereo). There are lots of zany talk or chat shows where hosts are employed for their amazing ability to ramble on and on (and on and on) about nothing in particular for hours and hours. Music stations are highly specialized, the most common of which are categorized as adult contemporary, country, contemporary hits, easy listening, or middle of the road (MOR). There are also stations specializing in top 40 hits, golden oldies or classic rock, urban contemporary (black music), adult oriented rock (AOR), lite rock, jazz, blues, bluegrass, R&B, progressive, gospel, reggae and classical.

If you're looking for serious radio, then you need to tune into National Public Radio (NPR), which like TV's Public Broadcasting Service is non-commercial and specializes in news and public affairs. American Public Radio (APR) is also non-commercial and specializes in entertainment. Both NPR and APR survive on grants and sponsorship from large corporations and donations from individuals. Like PBS TV, NPR is considered highbrow, although it's usually the only choice if you want to listen to drama, serious talks, current affairs or world news (taken from the British Broadcasting Corporation). NPR and APR stations also broadcast live and recorded major classical concerts, sponsored by large corporations, which are transmitted via satellite to around 5m listeners through over 300 affiliated stations across America. Homes with cable TV can also subscribe to an FM stereo service in most areas, which provides improved FM reception on your stereo receiver.

BBC: The BBC World Service is broadcast on short wave on several frequencies simultaneously and you can usually receive a good signal on one of them. The signal strength varies depending on the region, the time of day and year, the power and positioning of your receiver, and atmospheric conditions. For a free BBC World Service program guide and frequency information write to BBC Worldwide, BBC World Service, PO Box 76, Bush House, Strand, London WC2B 4PH, UK (tel. 0171-752 5040). The BBC publish a monthly magazine, *BBC Worldwide*, containing comprehensive information about BBC World Service radio and TV programs. It's available on subscription from the above address for £30 (US$48) a year.

Other International Radio Stations: There are many other international radio stations that can be received on the short wave band including Radio Australia, Radio France Internationale, Radio *Deutsche Welle*, Radio Nederland, Radio Sweden and many more. The *World Radio and TV Handbook* (Billboard) contains the frequencies of radio stations worldwide.

CRIME

No doubt you have already heard about Florida's high crime rate (unless you live on the Moon) and may be anxious about your safety there. Despite the appalling crime statistics, you should keep in mind that the odds against you becoming a victim of a violent crime in Florida are astronomical and outside the main urban centers serious crime is relatively rare (crime figures in Florida are distorted by Miami's high level of crime). **However, if you come from a country with a low crime rate, you should note that the ground rules aren't the same in Florida or elsewhere in the US. If you follow the rules (see 'Crime Prevention & Safety' below) your chances of becoming a victim are as low as in most other countries (e.g. in western Europe), but break the rules and they rise dramatically.**

One of the most pressing problems facing the authorities in Florida is convincing tourists and potential foreign homeowners that they will be safe. The Florida authorities and the travel industry are extremely sensitive about crime figures and in the past were loathe to inform visitors of the risks of crime in certain areas of Florida, partly because they didn't want to alarm them unnecessarily, but largely because they feared discouraging visitors. However, the widely publicized murders of a number of tourists in the last few years badly affected tourism and led to the formation of a Task Force on Tourist Safety and increased policing and illumination at night in tourist areas.

More column inches in US newspapers and magazines and TV air-time is devoted to crime than any other topic in the US. The American media delights in providing blow-by-blow accounts of gory crimes, with TV beaming the latest carnage into living rooms each evening in glorious technicolor. TV crime reporting has become so graphic and horrifying that hotels in some cities (including Miami) censor the crime news so as not to distress visitors (dead tourists are bad for business, which isn't helped by T-shirts with slogans such as 'Shoot Me, I'm European'!).

Between 1983 and 1992 Florida's crime rate was the highest in the US (with the exception of Washington DC), although it has fallen in the last few years. The most common causes of violence are the drug epidemic (some 80 per cent of crime is drug-related); gang violence (often also drug related); the easy availability of guns (Florida is noted for its liberal gun laws); homelessness and unemployment; and the growing impoverishment of inner-city ghettos. Car crime and muggings are the most widespread crime problems in Florida, although rape statistics are also high and school crime is causing increasing concern. Note that major metropolitan areas average around 30 per cent more crimes than small cities and towns.

Black-on-black crime is the biggest problem in the US and white America has largely ignored the urban warfare raging in black inner-city areas. Most whites live in communities in suburbs and rural areas that are hermetically sealed off from the trigger-happy chaos of US urban life (although there are increasing signs that the horror of the US romance with the gun is spreading to small town white America). Murder is the main cause of death among America's gun-toting youths, particularly in urban black and Hispanic ghettos. The US murder rate (per head of population) is 10 times that of Japan and 15 times that of Britain.

One of the biggest problems is the American gun culture and the the easy availability of guns. Americans own over 200 million guns, including some 75m handguns. Some two million handguns are sold every year (or around 300 an hour) and one is produced every 20 seconds. Rapid-fire combat weapons, such as sub-machine guns firing 500 rounds a minute, are easily obtainable and there are over 500,000 semi-automatic machine guns in private hands (although their sale is now banned).

Crime Prevention & Safety

Staying safe in Florida is largely a matter of common sense, although you need to develop survival skills in cities and urban areas. Most areas are safe most of the time, particularly during daylight hours and when there are a lot of people about. However, parents should warn their children about the dangers of American 'street life', especially if they're used to living in a country where it's taken for granted that a person can safely go almost anywhere at any time of day or night. It may be necessary to totally re-educate your family regarding all aspects of public life. Wherever you live and whatever the age of your children, you should warn them against taking unnecessary risks and discourage them from frequenting remote or high risk areas, talking to strangers and attracting unwanted attention.

At night, always keep to brightly lit main streets and avoid secluded areas. Always avoid parks at night and keep to a park's main paths or where there are other people during the day. Best of all take a taxi and get the driver to drop you in a well lit area as close as possible to your destination. If you need to wait for a train or bus at night, do so in the main waiting room, a well lit area, or where there's a guard or policeman. If possible, avoid using public transport in the late evening or after midnight. All major cities have 'no-go' areas at night and some have areas that are to be avoided at any time, e.g. Miami. When you're in an unfamiliar region, ask a policeman, taxi driver or local person if there are any unsafe neighborhoods — and avoid them! Lone women should take particular care and should never hitchhike alone (rape statistics in Florida are high).

Beware of pickpockets and bag-snatchers in cities and always remain vigilant at tourist attractions, in queues and on public transport. *Never* tempt fate with an exposed wallet or purse or by flashing your money around and hang on tight to your shoulder bag. One of the most effective methods of protecting your passport, money, travelers' checks and credit cards is with an old-fashioned money belt. You should also beware of bag-snatchers in airport and other car parks and should wear shoulder bags diagonally across your chest, although it's better not to carry a bag at all (the strap can be cut) and wear a wrist pouch or money belt. Never wear valuable jewelry and watches in high-risk areas. Don't leave cash or valuables unattended when swimming or leave your bags, cameras or jackets lying around on chairs in cafés or bars (*always* keep an eye on your belongings in public places).

Never keep your passport, driver's license and other important documents in your wallet or purse where they can be stolen. Some experts advise you to keep your cash in at least two separate places and to split your cash and credit cards. It's advisable to carry the bare minimum of cash, e.g. $20 to $50, often referred to as 'mugger's money'. This is because in the event that you're mugged, it's usually sufficient to satisfy a mugger and prevent him becoming violent or searching further.

You should never resist a mugger. It's far better to lose your wallet and jewelry than your life. **Many muggers are desperate and irrational people (often officially classified as 'emotionally disturbed persons' or EDPs), possibly under the influence of drugs, who can turn violent if resisted.** Anaesthetic sprays sold in drugstores or ordinary hair or insect sprays are carried by some people to deter assailants (as are mace and pepper sprays, which are legal in Florida). These are, however, of little use against an armed assailant and may increase the likelihood of violence.

Robbery is a constant threat in American cities and something many Americans have experienced at first hand. Don't leave cash, checks, credit cards, passports, jewelry and other 'valuables' lying around or even hidden in your home (the crooks know all the hiding places). Store valuables in a home safe or in a safety deposit box at a local bank. High quality door and window locks and an alarm will help, but may not deter a determined thief (see page 168). In cities, triple door locks, metal bars and steel gratings on windows are standard equipment. Often apartment buildings are fitted with a security system so that you can speak to visitors before allowing them access to a building, and luxury apartments often have armed guards in the lobby with closed-circuit TV and voice identification security systems.

Most apartments have a peephole and security chain on front doors, so that you can check a caller's identity before opening the door. Be careful who you allow into your home and always check the identity of anyone claiming to be an official inspector or a utility company employee. Ask for ID and confirm it with their office *before* opening the door. **Note that if a person renting your home is attacked there, you could be sued for damages.** You should be wary of anyone hanging around outside your home and have your keys ready to enter as quickly as possible. Hotel room robberies are fairly commonplace (often inside jobs) and valuables should be stored in the hotel safe and you shouldn't let anyone into your room unless you're certain of their identity (crooks sometimes pose as staff).

Store anything of value in a home safe or a bank safety deposit box and always make sure that you have adequate insurance (see page 59). Don't make it obvious that nobody is at home by leaving tell-tale signs such as a pile of newspapers or mail. Many people leave lights, a radio or a TV on (possibly activated by random timers) when they're out and ask neighbors to keep an eye on their homes when they're away. Many towns have 'crime watch' areas, where residents keep a look out for suspicious characters and report them to the local police. Many communities are fenced and gated with security lighting and 24-hour security guards and patrols.

Driving: When driving you should keep to main highways and avoid high-risk areas. Never drive with your windows open or your doors unlocked in towns or with valuables (such as handbags or wallets) on the seats (motorcycle thieves sometimes smash car windows at traffic lights to steal articles left on seats). Take extra care at night in car parks and when returning to your car and *never* sleep in a car. If you have an accident in a dangerous or hostile area, police usually advise you not to stop but to drive to the nearest police station to report it. Be careful where you stop, keep your doors locked and the windows closed, use a reliable map, and never stray off 'safe' routes. If you get lost, seek help from a police station, service station or a business in a well lit area. Drivers of rental cars have been targeted by muggers in Florida, although after a spate of attacks rental cars are now indistinguishable from privately-owned vehicles (previously they had license plates with a 'Y' or 'Z' prefix or 'LEASE').

Highway Piracy: Highway piracy is an increasing problem in some areas, where accidents are staged to rob unsuspecting drivers (called highway hold-ups) or cars are deliberately bumped to get drivers to stop (don't stop but drive to the nearest police station). A driver may also pose as a plain clothes policeman and try to get you to stop by flashing a bogus 'badge'. If you stop at an accident in a remote area or are flagged down at a road block, keep the engine running and in gear and your doors locked, and open your window only a fraction to speak to someone, while remaining ready to drive off if you're threatened or are suspicious. See also **Car Crime** on page 37.

Summary: Although the foregoing catalog of crime paints a bleak and depressing picture of life in Florida, the vast majority of Floridians manage to get through the day without being molested, mugged, knifed or shot, and most live to a ripe old age and die natural deaths. The crime rate varies considerably from neighborhood to neighborhood and anyone buying a home in Florida should choose a low-crime, middle class community and avoid 'high-crime' areas at all times if at all possible. Wherever you live in America, if you take care of your personal property and take simple precautions against crime, your chances of becoming a victim are greatly reduced. Police forces, the federal government, local communities and security companies all provide information and advice about crime prevention, and your local police department will usually carry out a free home security check.

Although crime and violence are among the most disturbing aspects of life in Florida, it's important to maintain a sense of perspective, as heightened anxiety or paranoia about crime can be just as bad or worse than being a victim, and is a complete waste of time and effort. **In most suburbs and rural communities, violent crime is rare and people go about their daily business without giving a thought to being assaulted or robbed.**

LEGAL SYSTEM

The American legal system is based on federal law, augmented by laws enacted by state legislatures and local laws passed by counties and cities. American law and the US constitution apply to everyone in America, irrespective of citizenship or immigration status, and even illegal immigrants have the same basic legal rights as a US citizen. Under the US constitution, each state has the power to establish its own system of criminal and civil laws, resulting in 50 different state legal systems, each supported by its own laws, prisons, police forces, and county and city courts. There's a wide variation in state and local laws, making life difficult for people moving between states. For example, Florida has state laws against dropping litter, an obscene bumper sticker law, a law against carrying open alcohol containers in vehicles, and liquor laws controlling the sale and consumption of alcohol (you must be 21 to consume alcohol in a public place). **Never assume that the law is the same in different US states (conflict of laws is a popular course in American law schools).**

There's a clear separation and distinction between civil courts, which settle disputes between people (such as property division after a divorce) and criminal courts that prosecute those who break the law. In the US crimes are categorized as misdemeanors (minor offenses) or felonies (more serious violations of the law). Misdemeanors include offenses such as dropping litter, illegal parking or jay-walking (crossing the road on a red light or anywhere except at an intersection), and are usually dealt with by a fine without a court appearance. Felonies, which include robbery and other serious offenses, are tried in a court of law. In many counties and cities there are often bizarre local laws (usually misdemeanors rather than felonies), although unsuspecting foreigners who violate local by-laws may be let off with a warning.

People who commit misdemeanors may be issued a summons, while anyone committing a felony is arrested. An arrest almost always involves being 'frisked' for concealed weapons, handcuffed and being read your rights. You must be advised of your constitutional (Miranda) rights when arrested. These include the right to remain silent, the right to have a lawyer present during questioning, and the right to have a free court-appointed lawyer if you can't afford one. You will be asked if you wish to waive your rights. This isn't advisable as any statement you make can be used against you in a court of law. It's better to retain your rights and say nothing until you have spoken with a lawyer.

At the police department you will be charged and have the right to make one telephone call. This should be to your embassy or a local consulate, a lawyer or the local legal aid office, or (if necessary) to someone who will stand bail for you. You will then be put into a cell until your case comes before a judge, usually the same or the next day, who will either release you (if there's no case to answer) or set bail. Bail may be a cash sum or the equivalent property value. For minor offenses you may be released on your 'personal recognizance'. In serious cases a judge may oppose bail. Automobile clubs such as the AAA provide bail bonds for members, which are useful when you're traveling in other US states (bail procedures differ from state to state).

In many areas, lawyer (or attorney) referral services are maintained by local (e.g. county) bar associations, whose members provide legal representation for a 'reasonable' fee. Before retaining a lawyer, always ask *exactly* what legal representation will cost, including fees for additional services such as medical experts, transcripts and court fees. Most importantly, always hire a lawyer who's a specialist and experienced in handling your type of case. If you can't afford a lawyer and your case goes to court, a court-appointed lawyer will represent you.

Litigation is an American tradition and national sport, and every American has a right to his day in court. There are 15 to 20 million civil suits a year in America, which leads to a huge backlog of cases in all states and even the Supreme Court. One of the most unusual aspects of American law is that lawyers are permitted to work on a contingency-fee basis, whereby they accept cases on a 'no-win, no-fee' basis. If they win their fee is usually at least 50 per cent of any damages. If you need to hire a lawyer on a non-contingency basis, the cost is usually outrageous. Many people believe this system helps pervert the cause of justice, as a lawyer hired on a contingency basis is concerned only with winning a case, often irrespective of any ethical standards. The contingency-fee system is responsible for the proliferation of litigation cases, which lawyers are happy to pursue due to the absurdly high awards made by American courts. Recent awards include $7.1m for sexual harassment and $2.9m to a woman who was burnt by a cup of coffee, which was apparently too hot (later reduced on appeal to a measly $640,000)!

The litigation system is primarily designed to make lawyers rich, while ensuring almost everyone else ends up as losers. Not only must individuals have liability insurance to protect against being sued, but everyone from doctors to plumbers must have expensive malpractice insurance to protect themselves against litigious clients. The whole American economy and legal system is underpinned by litigation (in which it seems half the population are directly employed and the other half are plaintiffs or defendants!). Everyone (except lawyers) agrees that litigation is out of control and is seriously undermining America's competitiveness. Nobody, however, seems to know what to do about it. Meanwhile, lawyers spend their time dreaming up new and lucrative areas of litigation.

Not surprisingly there are a great many lawyers in the US (over 500,000) and one for every 500 inhabitants (compared, for example, with one for every 10,000 people in Japan). The chief role of lawyers is to make themselves (very) rich and to make business as difficult as possible for everyone else. Never forget that lawyers are in business for themselves and nobody else, and although they may be representing you, their brief never strays far from the bottom line (how much they will get paid). If you have a dispute with a person, company or government agency involving a sum of from $100 to $5,000 (depending on the state), you can use the small claims court, which doesn't require a lawyer (hurrah!).

Many social service agencies provide free legal assistance to immigrants (both legal and illegal), although some may serve the nationals of a particular country or members of a certain religion only. There are help lines and agencies offering free legal advice in most towns and cities, many with legal aid societies (offering free advice and referral on legal matters), better business bureaux (dealing with consumer-related complaints, shopping services, etc.) and departments of consumer affairs (who also handle consumer complaints).

EDUCATION

The US has the most diversified education system in the world, with public (state) and private schools ('school' usually refers to everything from kindergarten to university) at all levels flourishing alongside one another. Around 80 per cent of students complete high school and the US also has a higher percentage of college graduates than any other country. Many American universities and other higher education institutions are internationally renowned and their student bodies include thousands of foreign students from all corners of the globe. Formal education in the US comprises three levels, elementary, secondary and higher education. Vocational training, adult education, and special schools or classes (e.g. for gifted and handicapped children) also form part of the education program in most states.

Full-time education is compulsory in all states and includes the children of foreigners permanently or temporarily resident in the US for a minimum of one year. However, admission to a public school for foreign children is dependent on the type and duration of the visa granted to their parents, and attendance may not be possible. Schooling in Florida is compulsory between the ages of 6 and 16 (children must be five years old before 1st September to begin kindergarten). There's no federal education system in the US, where education is the responsibility of individual states and districts, and consequently education standards and requirements vary considerably from state to state and district to district. No fees are payable in public (state) primary and secondary schools, which are attended by around 90 per cent of students (schoolchildren of all ages are usually referred to as students in America).

Florida Public Schools: According to the US department of Education, Florida has one of the worst state public education records in the US, although state officials claim that it isn't as black as it's painted. For example, federal statistics don't take into account the state's large migrant population and the method of testing used for high school graduation. However, it's true that the Florida school dropout rate is among the nation's highest, the high school graduation rate is among the lowest, and college entrance examination (ACT and SAT) results are among the worst in the US. The failings of the education system are starkly reflected in the state's high crime rate. However, the state has made some improvements in recent years, particularly with regard to higher education. Florida has nine universities: Boca Raton, Gainsville, Jacksonville, Miami, Orlando, Pensacola, Tallahassee (two) and Tampa. Most public schools (pre-school, elementary and high) are co-educational (mixed) day schools.

Private Education: In recent years, many parents concerned about the decline in public education have turned to private fee-paying schools (attended by around 10 per cent of students), most of which are church-sponsored (often Roman Catholic) parochial schools. Private schools include both day and boarding schools and are mostly co-educational (often abbreviated as 'coed', which confusingly also refers to female college students), although some are single sex. Despite the high cost of private education, many parents consider it an acceptable price to pay, particularly if the outcome is a bachelor's or master's degree from a prestigious university. Note that education for its own sake or the love of learning is rare in the US, where education and qualifications are judged primarily on their earning power.

Choosing a Public School: For most American parents, one of the most important (if not *the* most important) criteria when buying a home is the reputation of the local public schools. **Even if your family has no need or plans to use local public schools, the value of your home will be greatly influenced by the quality of local schools.** A property located close to a good school will usually sell quickly for a premium price and you may even be able to sell it privately. Many communities take pride in the quality of their local public school system, which is crucial in maintaining property values.

If you plan to send your child to a public school in Florida, you should make enquiries about the quality of local schools before deciding where to live. Generally the more expensive property is in a community, the better the local public schools. Because public education is largely locally funded (from property taxes), schools in wealthy areas are much better funded than schools in poor areas, e.g. inner-city and rural farming communities. Often you can estimate the quality of a neighborhood's schools simply by driving around town or checking the cost of real estate in the local papers. The equipment available in affluent schools often includes educational TV, electronic and portable language laboratories, slides and viewers, and expensive computer systems. Schools in poorer areas often have a lack of basic supplies and equipment such as desks, lockers, books, general supplies, cafeteria facilities or gym equipment. In the worst inner city schools, drugs and violence are commonplace and arguments and fights are likely to be decided by knives or even guns (violence against teachers and staff is also commonplace).

The quality of public schools is measured variously by the dropout rate, the high school graduation rate, results in college entrance examinations (ACT and SAT), and the number of students who gain entrance to famous American colleges. Note, however, that it's often difficult to access the quality of public education in a particular school or county, and statistics don't tell the whole story and can be easily distorted or manipulated. Relocation guides are published by Chambers of Commerce in all towns and counties, and usually include profiles of local schools and comparative scores for different grades. If your children don't speak English fluently, you should enquire whether English as a Second Language (ESL) classes are available or whether study is available in other languages.

LEISURE & SPORTS

Florida offers a huge variety of leisure and sports facilities, as you would expect from a state that earns most of its income from tourism. The central region of Florida contains the highest concentration of attractions anywhere in the world and is the number one tourist destination in the US. Its major attractions include Walt Disney World (Magic Kingdom, Epcot and Disney-MGM studios), the world's largest and most popular tourist attraction, Universal Studios, Sea World, Busch Gardens, Cypress Gardens and the NASA Kennedy Space Center/Spaceport USA.

Walt Disney World: Not surprisingly, the attraction which draws the most visitors and which put Florida on the international tourist map is Walt Disney World, encompassing a vast area of 28,000 acres. Walt Disney World opened in 1971 and today comprises three theme parks: The Magic Kingdom, EPCOT Center and Disney-MGM Studios. There are also smaller and cheaper Disney theme parks (including Discovery Island, River County and Typhoon Lagoon water park), plus Pleasure Island, a sprawling 6-acre conglomeration of shops, restaurants, bars and themed nightclubs. The **Magic Kingdom** contains seven 'lands' comprising around 45 shows and rides. The **Epcot (Experimental Prototype Community of Tomorrow) Center** opened in 1982 and comprises two major areas: Future World (distinguished by its 180-foot high silver geosphere) and the World Staircase. Epcot is a large sprawling complex that involves a lot of walking and is more for adults than children (it can be particularly boring for young children). **Disney-MGM** studios opened in 1989 and provides a behind-the-scenes look at the production of movies and TV shows. It's suitable for all ages and provides some fascinating special effects and visits to real working studios.

Walt Disney World is so vast that it takes four or five days to explore, therefore it's wise to read up on it beforehand and identify the things you most want to see and do. It isn't advisable to tackle more than one park a day. The busiest periods are from mid-February to August and the slowest from September to January, excluding the Christmas Day and New Year holidays. Each park is open daily from 9am until 11pm between February and August and from 9am until 9pm at other times. It's best to arrive early (e.g. 8am) or late (e.g. 5 or 6pm) and avoid the mid-afternoon crush (lines are also shorter for food early and late in the day). Fridays and Sundays are the least crowded days and Tuesday the busiest. If at all possible, it's advisable to avoid peak periods such as weekends and federal holidays, when crowds of 100,000 a day visit the parks. It's advisable to make for the most popular rides with the longest queues first. Waiting times for shows and rides are shown on notice boards and are often up to an hour, although 10 minutes is more usual.

The cost of visiting Disney World may come as something of a shock. A one-day ticket costs $37 for adults and $30 for children under 10 (10-year-olds are classified as adults in Florida), with children under three years free. A day ticket is valid for one park only, with unlimited passouts. A four-day 'Park-Hopper' pass for the Magic Kingdom, Epcot and Disney MGM Studios costs $137 (children $109) and a five-day 'World-Hopper' pass includes entrance to the above parks for five days plus entrance to all other Disney attractions for seven days. It costs $186 (children $148) and includes free use of shuttle buses and the monorail between parks. Visitors can buy an annual pass for $209 (children $179), which is excellent value if you make a number of trips to the parks a year. Sales tax of 6 per cent must be added to all prices. Reduced-price tickets are available from authorized ticket agents throughout Florida and also save time lining up to buy tickets. **Florida residents can take advantage of special offers (e.g. $10 off a one-day ticket allowing you to visit all three Disney parks on the same day — not that it's possible), but you must be able to prove that you live there (usually a property tax or utility bill is sufficient, although a Florida ID card or driver's license is better).** Annual seasonal passes are also available to residents for $139 (children $118), allowing free access at any time outside the peak summer, Christmas/New Year and Easter periods.

Disney World is nothing if not expensive and there's even a charge of $5 a day for parking (don't forget where you parked as lots are gigantic and it can take a long time to find a 'lost' car). Picnics are banned to increase profits at the restaurants and fast-food outlets (no alcohol is served except in Pleasure Island), and bags are sometimes searched for illicit sandwiches (you can always stuff your pockets full of choc bars and drink from free fountains). A family of four can easily spend $200 a day including meals. Despite its huge success in bringing visitors and jobs to Florida, not everybody loves Disney World, particularly many old-time Orlando natives (who dub Mickey 'the mouse that ate Orlando'), who reckon that Florida sold its soul for a fast buck. However, it offers a spotlessly clean (litter is whisked away before it hits the ground) and crime-fee environment, and some of the best escapism short of taking part in a moonshot.

There are numerous Disney World guides including *Orlando and Disney World* by Bob Martin (Teakwood Press), Birnbaum's *Walt Disney World: The Official Guide* and *Walt Disney World for Adults* by Rita Devo (Fodor's). Disney information is also available in Florida by telephone (tel. 407/824-4321).

Universal Studios: Opened in 1990, Universal studios provides direct competition to Disney-MGM Studios and styles itself 'the No. 1 movie studio and theme park in the world'. Note that it takes two days to take in everything, unless you're extremely energetic. Universal Studios are open from 9am to 7pm (extended during the peak season) and entrance costs $37 for adults and $30 for children aged 3-9 (two-day pass $55/$44). Together, Universal and Disney-MGM studios provide increasingly vigorous competition to Hollywood and many people expect Florida to become the US movie-making capital in the next century.

Sea World: While it isn't the only aquarium or marine park in Florida, Seaworld is the biggest and best (you need to allow a whole day to see everything). Exhibits and shows include 'Terrors of the Deep'; 'Manatees: The Last Generation?'; 'Wild Arctic'; 'Penguin Encounter'; the new 'Key West at Sea World'; and the highlight, 'Shamu: World Focus', the celebrated performing killer whale show. Sea World is open from 9am until 7pm (extended during the peak season) and entrance costs $35.95 for adults and $30.95 for children aged 3-9. Other popular aquariums include the Florida Aquarium (Tampa), Marineland of Florida (near St. Augustine) and the Miami Seaquarium.

Busch Gardens: Located on the west side of Tampa, the 300-acre Busch Gardens is one of Florida's oldest (1959) theme parks and one of the state's most popular attractions. Its theme is a re-creation of late 19th-century colonial Africa, hence the garden's subtitle 'The Dark Continent' (which doesn't go down at all well with African Americans). It's a combination of theme, roller-coaster park and zoo, and a masterpiece of kitsch and bad taste (hence its popularity with Americans). Busch Gardens is open from 9.30am until 7pm (extended during the peak season) and entrance costs $34.60 for adults and $28.20 for children aged 3-9.

Cypress Gardens: Cypress Gardens is located east of Winter Haven around 40 minutes south of Disney World. Its main attractions are its water-ski show (it calls itself 'the water ski capital of the world') and 208-acre botanical gardens containing 8,000 varieties of plants and flowers, plus alligator, snake and bird exhibitions. The garden's prime attraction is its relative tranquility, particularly when compared with the frenetic world of Florida's theme parks. The gardens are open from 9am until 5.30pm and the entrance fee is $27.95 for adults (over 55s $22.95) and $17.95 for children aged 3-9.

NASA Kennedy Space Center/Spaceport USA: Located on the east coast (Brevard County) around an hour from Orlando, the Kennedy Space Center is the nucleus of the US space program. Spaceport USA houses the museum, Rocket Gardens and the IMAX film theater and is open from 9am until sunset. Arrive early to avoid the crowds, which are smaller on weekends and during May and September. The Space Center is one of Florida's few bargains, with the narrated bus tour costing just $7 (children aged 3-11 $4) and the film $4 (children aged 3-11 $2). However, the best free entertainment in Florida is a shuttle launch, which can be witnessed from within a 40-mile radius of the Space Center (tel. 1-800-SHUTTLE or 407/452-2121 for information).

Water Parks: Water parks, where all rides and activities are water-based, are not surprisingly extremely popular in Florida. Attractions include giant tidal wave pools, rapids for tubing, slides that shoot down from great heights, jet slides, wind and rain tunnels, whirlpools and wavepools, helical rides on water mats, and surf lagoons with four-foot waves. A typical water park is Wet 'n Wild (Orlando), where a one day pass costs $21.95 for adults (over 54 $11) and $17.95 for children aged 3-9.

Other Attractions: Other popular Florida attractions include Splendid China, Medieval Time, Silver Springs, Church Street Station, Fantasy of Flight, Miracle Strip Amusement Park, Miami Metrozoo, (where the visitors are caged and the animals roam free), Gaterland Zoo, the Edison Winter Home, and St. Augustine, America's oldest permanent European settlement. There are also numerous other attractions and parks throughout the state. Discount coupons for many amusement parks are contained in local tourist guides and brochures, and discounted tickets are available from ticket agents in local hotels and restaurants. Members of the American Automobile Association and other American organizations receive discounts of 10 to 20 per cent at many attractions. **Note that ticket prices increase constantly and by the time you read this they will have increased again!**

Arts, Theater, Music and Dance: Florida is noted for its wealth of excellent performing arts centers including theaters, ballet, opera and symphony concert halls (the state has over 40 symphony orchestras). For the connoisseur of fine arts, Florida also has much to offer and all major cities have an abundance of museums, galleries and arts centers. A few deserving a special mention include the Salvador Dali Museum (St. Petersburg, housing the best collection of his works in the world), the Museum of Science and Industry (two miles east of Busch Gardens), and Great Explorations (St. Petersburg), the last two of which house a wealth of fascinating hands-on exhibits for kids and adults (grown up kids). Florida is also host to a multitude of festivals and celebrations each year including art, food, music and sports festivals. Tickets for music, theater and sports events are available from Ticketmaster outlets and can be purchased by telephone with a credit card.

Parks and Forests: Getting away from it all isn't difficult in Florida, which has an abundance of natural areas including over 7,500 lakes of 10 or more acres; around 1,700 rivers, canals and streams; over 1,000 miles of excellent beaches; and millions of acres of wilderness, many of which are protected within the state's 105 state parks and reserves, seven national parks and three national forests. The most famous parks include Apalachicola National Forest, Ocala National Forest, Osceola National Forest and the celebrated Everglades National Park, the largest subtropical wilderness in the US encompassing some 1.5m acres.

Sports Facilities: Florida offers a huge variety and quantity of sports facilities including over 1,000 golf courses, some 10,000 tennis courts, almost 1,000 miles of hiking trails; numerous public swimming pools and 1,000 miles of sandy beaches (among the safest in the world, although unguarded beaches should be avoided), plus enough water (inland and coastal) to satisfy the most ardent water sports' enthusiast. Popular water sports include boating, canoeing, wind-surfing, water-skiing, snorkeling, scuba diving, jet-skiing, para-sailing and surfing. The Florida Keys offer some of the best snorkeling and scuba diving in the world (Key Largo claims to be the diving capital of the world), while surfers head for the area between Sebastian inlet and Cocoa Beach just south of the Kennedy Space Center. Florida also offers some of the best saltwater sport fishing in the world (e.g. marlin, tuna, barracuda, shark, dolphin, cobia, grouper, wahoo, sailfish, amberjack and tarpon) and an abundance of inland fresh-water fishing areas where catfish, bass, carp, crappie and perch are among the most common species. Note that a license is required for both salt and freshwater fishing.

Florida is a golfer's paradise and boasts the largest number of courses of any US state and some of the best in the world. Property ownership in many communities includes membership of a golf club or you can become a member of a private golf club (monthly and annual membership is usually available) or play at a public golf course. Many community properties (see page 144) have communal swimming pools and tennis courts, plus a variety of other sports facilities, which can be used free or for a nominal fee by homeowners. On a more general note, almost any sport can be enjoyed in Florida and most are accessible (and affordable) by everybody, rather than just the privileged or wealthy few as in many other countries.

Like the rest of the US, Florida is also crazy about spectator sports, although somewhat surprisingly collegiate sports attract more attention than the professional teams, most of which were established only in recent years. Major league sports include baseball (Florida Marlins, established in 1993), basketball (Miami Heat, Orlando Magic) and American football (Miami Dolphins, Tampa Bay Buccaneers). Florida is the winter home to most US professional baseball teams during their 'spring training season'. Motor sports are also popular in Florida where the most important races include the celebrated Daytona 500, the Miami grand prix and the 12 hours of Sebring.

Leisure and sports information is widely available in local newspapers and magazines, plus a wealth of guide books (see **Appendix B**).

3.

FINANCE

O ne of the most important aspects of buying a home in Florida and living there (even for relatively brief periods) is finance, which includes everything from transferring and changing money to mortgages and taxes. If you're planning to invest in a property or a business in Florida financed with imported funds, it's important to consider both the present and possible future exchange rates. On the other hand, if you live and work in Florida and are paid in US$ this may affect your financial commitments abroad. **Bear in mind that if your income is received in a currency other than US$ it can be exposed to risks beyond your control when you live in Florida, particularly regarding inflation and exchange rate fluctuations.**

If you own a home in Florida it's advisable to employ a local professional, e.g. an accountant or tax adviser, as your representative to look after your local financial affairs and declare and pay your taxes. You can also have your representative receive your bank statements, ensure that your bank is paying your standing orders (e.g. for utilities and taxes), and that you have sufficient funds to pay them. If you rent a home in Florida through a local company, they will usually perform the above tasks as part of their services (for a fee).

Note that it's essential to have at least one and preferably a number of credit or charge cards in Florida (Mastercard and Visa are the most widely accepted). Even if you don't like plastic money and shun any form of credit, credit cards do have their uses and anyone in the US without a number of them is considered financially untrustworthy. They can be used to pay many people who don't usually accept credit cards in other countries such as doctors, dentists or hospitals, post offices, taxis, movie theaters, parking lots, fast-food restaurants and telephone companies. Other benefits include no deposits on rental cars, no pre-paying hotel bills (plus guaranteed bookings), obtaining cash, simple telephone and mail-order payments, safety and security (compared to carrying large amounts of cash), and above all, convenience. Note, however, that not all businesses and professionals accept cards.

This section includes information on importing and exporting money; credit rating; banking; mortgages; taxes (property, income, capital gains, inheritance, gift and sales); wills; and the cost of living.

US CURRENCY

Unless you've just arrived from another planet, you will be aware that the American unit of currency is the US dollar ($US). The $US is everyone's favorite currency (particularly counterfeiters) and it's the world's leading international currency. It's used for most international trading and practically all international lending and borrowing transactions. Consequently US interest rates are of major concern to foreign debtor nations. In many countries, particularly in South America, Asia and eastern Europe, the $US acts as an unofficial second currency and is often preferred to local currency (which may not be accepted at all by some people). The US dollar has been highly volatile in recent years, during which it has fallen in value against most major currencies (hitting record lows against the Japanese yen). This has created instability in world trade markets, where fluctuations in foreign currency rates and the prices of stocks and precious metals are due in part to the dollar's relative weakness.

The dollar is divided into 100 cents and American coins are minted in 1¢ (penny), 5¢ (nickel), 10¢ (dime), 25¢ (quarter) 50¢ (half-dollar) and $1 or silver dollars (which naturally aren't made of real silver and are rarely found in circulation). Two bits is slang for a quarter (25¢), although the names given to American coins shown above are official names used by everybody and aren't colloquial terms. With the exception of the penny (copper), all coins are silver in color (an amalgam of silver and copper). The nickel and quarter are similar in size and easily confused, except that the quarter has a serrated edge. The dime is the smallest of all coins. Half-dollar (JFK) and dollar (Susan B. Anthony) coins are rare and found almost exclusively in gambling cities such as Atlanta and Las Vegas, where they are used in slot machines. There's been talk of phasing out the penny as it's worth so little and is more valuable as scrap metal than currency (although if you have a few million . . .). The quarter is the most useful coin and you should always carry some with you for parking meters, bus and subway fares, road tolls, payphones, baggage lockers, vending machines, tips, etc.

Just to confuse everybody (especially foreigners), all American bills (banknotes) are the same shade of green (hence 'greenbacks'), the same size and have similar designs, although a different president (noted below) is depicted on the front. American bills are printed in denominations of $1 (Washington), $5 (Lincoln), $10 (Hamilton), $20 (Jackson), $50 (Grant), $100 (Franklin), $500, $1,000 and $10,000. The $2 (Jefferson) and $500 bills are no longer printed (although still legal tender) and along with $1,000 and $10,000 bills, they aren't in general circulation. The US dollar has a number of slang names including buck and greenback; a fin is a $5 bill and a sawbuck a $10 bill.

If you're unfamiliar with US bills, you should stick to low denominations (up to $20) and check them carefully to avoid errors, both when receiving bills in change and when spending them. Bills above $20 are often treated suspiciously as they are a favorite target of counterfeiters the world over. They may not be accepted by some stores, although this depends on what you're buying. US bills are the most counterfeited in the world and incredibly the design of the $1 dollar bill hasn't changed since 1929. There's an estimated $240 billion in circulation worldwide, not counting $billions in counterfeit bills. New bills with additional security features have been introduced in recent years to combat counterfeiters. It's advisable to obtain some US bills before arriving in the US and to familiarize yourself and your family with them. You should have some US dollars in cash (e.g. a total of $50 to $100 in small bills) when you arrive, which will save you having to line up (queue) to change money on arrival at a US airport (where you often get a poor exchange rate). However, you should avoid carrying a lot of cash.

IMPORTING & EXPORTING MONEY

The US has no currency restrictions and there's no limit to the amount of money you may bring in or take out of the country. However, any amount over $10,000 in monetary instruments including US or foreign coins or currency, travelers' checks, money orders, and negotiable instruments or investment securities in bearer form, must be declared to customs on arrival in or departure from the US. US Customs Form 4790 must be completed by the person who directly or indirectly imports the funds and financial institutions must keep records and file reports for any cash transactions above $10,000. Disclosure forms are usually completed by the professional doing the transaction, although a property buyer has ultimate responsibility for meeting the filing requirements. There are fines and penalties for failure to comply. The importation of gold coins or small amounts of gold must be declared on arrival.

Note that most stores and businesses in the US *don't* accept foreign currency or travelers' checks in foreign currencies, **and it's best to avoid bringing them to America.** It can even be difficult to find a bank or other financial institution that will exchange foreign currency or travelers' checks in foreign currencies, particularly in small towns. You usually receive an unfavorable exchange rate or pay a high commission when changing money at an hotel or a bureau de change. When changing foreign money or travelers' checks in foreign currencies, you should always try to do it in large cities, where increased competition usually ensures a better exchange rate (although still worse than you would obtain abroad). You may be asked for ID when changing foreign bills at a bank.

The most widely recognized and accepted travelers' checks are issued by American Express, followed by those of Visa and Thomas Cook (which, if lost, can be replaced at any Hertz car rental office). The normal fee charged when buying travelers' checks worldwide is 1 per cent of their value, although this may be waived when travel arrangements are made with the company issuing the checks (e.g. American Express or Thomas Cook). The commission on American Express checks is usually higher when they aren't bought directly from an American Express office. Note that commission rates for travelers' checks are usually lower at US exchange bureaux such as Deak-Perera and Thomas Cook than at banks. Some US organizations such as the American Automobile Association provide members with fee-free travelers' checks. Travelers' checks can be cashed at most banks, although some levy a fee, which should be avoided if possible.

Almost all businesses and retailers (exceptions usually include taxi drivers and some small businesses) in the US readily accept $US travelers' checks and will give you change as if you had paid in cash. Dollar checks to the value of $10 and $20 are accepted almost everywhere, while larger denominations may be accepted for expensive purchases only (so don't try to pay for a coffee with a $50 check!). You may be asked for identification (ID) when cashing travelers' checks at a bank, e.g. a driver's license or credit card, and may also be asked for ID in stores. The sign 'no checks' applies to personal checks only and not to travelers' checks. Many hotels will change travelers' checks for residents, as will some stores, although they usually give a poor exchange rate.

Always keep a separate record of check numbers and note where and when they were cashed. American Express provides a free three-hour replacement service for lost or stolen travelers' checks at any of their offices worldwide, providing you know the serial numbers of the lost checks. Without the serial numbers, replacement can take up to three days. Most companies provide toll-free numbers for reporting lost or stolen travelers' checks in the US including American Express (1-800-221-7282), Diners Card (1-800-968-8300), Mastercard/Access (1-800-336-8472), Thomas Cook (1-800-223-7373) and Visa (1-800-227-6811 or 1-800-627-6811).

Most banks will also make electronic or telegraphic transfers to the US. Shop around banks and financial institutions for the best deal and don't hesitate to try another bank if the service doesn't meet your expectations. Many banks subscribe to an international electronic network to (hopefully) facilitate fast and inexpensive transfers between members. Of these, one of the best is the Interbank On-Line System (IBOS) network whose members include banks in Britain (the Royal Bank of Scotland), Belgium, Denmark, France, Italy, the Netherlands, Portugal, Spain and the USA (First Fidelity Bank Corporation and Chase Manhattan). The Eurogiro electronic payment system also provides fast and cost-effective international transfers and has members in most western European countries (e.g. Girobank in Britain) and the Chase Manhattan Bank and US Postal Service in the US. **If you plan to send a large amount of money to the US, e.g. to buy a business or property, you should ensure you receive the commercial rate of exchange rather than the tourist rate (it may pay to shop around for the best rate).**

If you have money transferred to the US by banker's draft or a letter of credit, bear in mind that it may take up to two weeks to be cleared. Note also, that in the unlikely event that it's lost or stolen, it's impossible to stop payment and you must wait six months before a new draft can be issued. You can also have money sent to you in the US by international money order (via a post office or a bank), a cashier's check or a telegraphic transfer, e.g. via Western Union (the quickest and safest method, but also the most expensive). A.telegraphic or cable transfer to the US from overseas takes 24 to 48 hours and costs around $20. Within the US, a cash wire transfer via Western Union costs a minimum of $12 (depending on the amount) and takes as little as 15 minutes. It costs $2.95 to collect transferred funds from any of Western Union's 9,000 American offices and for an additional $2.95 they will notify you by telephone when it arrives.

Transfers can also be made by airmail letter, which although it takes longer, e.g. around eight days from Europe, is much cheaper. You can have money sent to you in the US in the form of a certified check (which can be cashed at any bank) and send money within the US via a post office money order, which can be purchased or cashed at any US post office (American Express also provide money orders). Up to $2,000 can be sent from a MasterCard or Visa account via Western Union (tel. 1-800-325-4176) and American Express card-holders can transfer up to $10,000 (depending on the card holder's credit limit) by 'Moneygram', both within the US and internationally. A less expensive way to transfer funds to the US from some countries is by purchasing an international money order from a bank, for which there's a standard charge, e.g. £7 up to $2,500 and £12 up to $7,500 from Britain. The money order is made payable to yourself at the receiving American bank at face value.

You need your passport or other ID to collect money transferred from abroad or to cash a banker's draft (or other credit note). If you're sending money abroad, it's best to send it in the local currency so that the recipient doesn't have to pay conversion charges. You can send money direct from your bank to another bank via an interbank transfer. Most banks have a minimum service charge for international transfers, generally making it expensive, particularly for small sums. Overseas banks also take a cut, usually a percentage (e.g. 1 or 2 per cent) of the amount transferred.

One thing to bear in mind when traveling in the US (or anywhere) is <u>never to</u> rely on one source of funds only.

CREDIT RATING

It can be difficult for new arrivals in the US to establish a credit rating (or 'line of credit') or obtain credit without excellent references from an employer or bank. Usually you must have been employed by the same employer for at least one year and earn a minimum salary, although it can still take a number of years to establish a good credit rating. It's usually even more difficult for self-employed people to obtain credit as most credit applications are geared towards employees. It may, however, be possible to convince your bank through your income tax returns. Many foreigners find they must build up their credit rating by obtaining credit from local businesses and stores. You should pay all your bills promptly and never bounce checks, which can ruin your credit rating. Once you've established a good credit rating, you can usually obtain far more credit than is good for you (generally the more you buy on credit, the more credit-worthy you become), and banks, finance companies, credit card companies, and other financial institutions will constantly push credit at you.

In the US, everybody's credit history is maintained by private companies called credit-reporting agencies (e.g. Equifax, TransUnion and TRW). They collect information reported to them by banks, mortgage companies, stores and other creditors. Your credit record contains information such as judgments or liens against you or your property, bankruptcies or foreclosures, as well as failure to pay your debts, e.g. payments on revolving charge accounts. Even late payments may appear on your credit record. Credit companies can legally report *accurate* negative credit information for seven years and bankruptcy information for ten years. The only information in your credit report that can be changed is incorrect items and items outside the seven or ten year reporting periods.

If a company denies your request for credit because of your credit report, it must (under the Fair Credit Reporting Act) tell you so and identify the company that supplied the report. All credit reporting companies are required by law to share with you any information they have on file about you. This must be provided free if you've been denied credit within the past 30 days, otherwise you can be charged a fee, e.g. between $5 and $20. In some states credit-reporting agencies are required by law to make an investigation into complaints within 30 days, erase non-verifiable items, provide free reports once a year, and provide consumers with the credit-rating scores it gives to lenders. Employers often obtain a credit report on prospective employees, particularly when they will be in a position of trust or handling cash.

If you have a bad credit rating, avoid so-called 'credit-repair' companies like the plague. These companies charge from $50 to over $1,000 to 'fix' your credit report. In most cases they do nothing at all or nothing you can't do yourself for free or for a few dollars. Never give anyone advertising easy credit approval or low credit card interest rates your checking account number, which may be used to fraudulently withdraw money from your account. Finally, if you're refused credit, try looking on the bright side; without it you can't run up any bad debts! For further information obtain a copy of the *Consumer Handbook of Credit Protection Laws* available free from the Board of Governors of the Federal Reserve System, Washington, DC 20551.

BANKING

There are some 250 commercial banks and trust companies in Florida with a total of over 4,000 offices. The biggest Florida banks (by assets) include Barnett Bank (various counties), AmSouth Bank of Florida (Pensacola), Sun Bank (various counties), Capital Bank (Miami) and the Intercontinental Bank (Miami). Barnett Bank is by far the largest in Florida, although it operates separately in each county, where assets are held independently. Note that there are numerous small banks in the US, many of which operate in one county only. Around 1,500 privately-owned banks are required to maintain sizeable interest-free reserves with the Federal Reserve (the 'Fed'), which is composed of 12 federal reserve banks that act as the country's central bank, executing national monetary policy and setting interest rates in co-operation with the Treasury.

There are two main types of banks in the US, 'commercial' banks and 'savings' banks or savings and loan associations, known simply as 'thrifts'. Commercial banks usually offer a wider choice of services, while savings banks may offer a better rate of interest. Savings banks and savings and loan associations are granted government charters to collect deposits and make home loans, and they hold half of all American home mortgages. Since deregulation of the savings and loan industry in 1982 (intended to increase competition), hundreds of thrifts have folded. In the mid-1980s there was a crisis among savings banks, when the industry lost billions and the federal government was forced to spend taxpayers' money to support government-insured banks (the bailout of depositors in the wake of the Savings & Loan fiasco cost taxpayers tens of billions of dollars).

When selecting a bank it's advisable to choose a large (hopefully safe) bank covered by the FDIC guarantee (see below). The ten largest American banks (by assets) are Citibank, Bank of America, Chase Manhattan, Morgan Guaranty, Manufacturers Hanover, Security Pacific, Wells Fargo, Bankers Trust New York, Chemical Bank and the Bank of New York. Note, however, that you may be better served by a small bank, where you're more likely to be treated as an individual than an account number. You should also ask about such things as credit card fees and interest rates, loans, overdrafts and other services. Florida's banks compete vigorously for new customers and provide comprehensive information packages for newcomers. Most offer special deals for 'senior citizens' (e.g. generally refers to those aged over 55 or over) which may include no-fee checking accounts, no minimum balances, brokerage service commission discounts, a bank-by-mail service, free notary service, no-fee credit cards, $100,000 in free accidental death travel insurance, and free travelers' and cashier's checks.

The US invented drive-in (or drive-up) banks, where Americans (many of whom live in their cars) can obtain cash without leaving their vehicles. Some banks have auto-tellers placed at car window height while others have a complicated system of vacuum pipes, microphones and loudspeakers used to conduct business with an invisible teller. If you're unfamiliar with this method of doing business, take time to read the instructions before attempting it. You can also drive up to a window and conduct business face-to-face with a teller, as you would in any bank. Drive-in banks can also be used by motorcyclists, cyclists and even pedestrians.

In some respects, the US banking system is relatively 'primitive' in comparison with other western nations and standards vary considerably. Many banks' business is restricted to a particular city, county or state (or a number of states). Some banks have just one branch and many have just a few local branches. There are no nationwide banks with the vast branch networks and influence of, for example, major European banks. For many years, major banks have been prohibited from interstate branching to protect smaller banks from unfair competition, although a new bill passed in 1994 allows banks to open branches anywhere in the US from June 1st 1997 (when some 5,000 banks are expected to disappear as banks merge). Consequently the US banking system is far less integrated than in many other regions, e.g. Europe. There's no national check clearing system in the US, which relies mainly on bank-owned clearing houses to handle fund transfers and clear checks (the average check must clear three banks before being returned and it can take up to 10 days for an out-of-state or non-local check to clear). There are 48 Federal Reserve check processing regions (one for each state) in the continental US and a check is considered to be a 'local' check only when it's deposited in the same processing region as the bank it's drawn on.

Insured Deposits: Due to a spate of bank failures in the 1930s, the federal government established the Federal Deposit Insurance Corporation (FDIC) to guarantee deposits in the event of bank failures (there's a similar insurance for savings and loan associations called the Federal Savings and Loan Insurance Corporation). The maximum amount insured in any bank or savings association is constantly being reviewed and currently stands at $100,000 (which is more than most of us are ever likely to see, particularly struggling authors). However, deposits maintained in different rights, capacities or forms of ownership, are each separately insured for up to $100,000 (e.g. IRA funds and demand deposits). Therefore it's possible to have more than one insured account with the same insured bank, although retirement funds such as an IRA, Keogh and 401(k) plan aren't insured separately.

Always make sure that each separate deposit is not more than $100,000 and that all deposits in any financial institution are covered by the FDIC guarantee. Note that separate accounts in different branches of the same bank (e.g. checking and savings accounts) are treated as *one* account for the purposes of the FDIC insurance. **Never deposit any money in a bank that isn't covered by the FDIC (insured institutions must display an official FDIC sign).** S&Ls and banks are having to pay higher premiums for their FDIC insurance, which in turn means higher bank charges for customers. All banks publish information about FDIC insurance rules. You can verify a bank's financial standing before opening an account by contacting Veribanc (tel. 1-800-442-2657) or Weiss Research (tel. 1-800-289-9222), both of which provide instant ratings over the telephone (around $10 to $15 per bank) and detailed written reports ($25).

Checking Accounts

There are two main types of bank accounts in the US; checking accounts and savings (deposit) accounts. Most Americans are paid by check, either biweekly (every two weeks) or monthly, which they then cash or deposit in a bank account. If you want to cash a check you must take it to the branch where it was drawn or a branch of the same bank (usually banks are inundated by employees cashing their pay checks on Fridays). It's estimated that some 15 per cent of American families don't have a bank account. If you're paid by check, one of your first acts should be to open an account with a bank or a savings and loan association. You can also have your salary paid directly into your bank account by direct deposit, although most Americans prefer to be paid by check. If you want to be paid by direct deposit, give your account details to your employer.

Before opening an account, you should shop around among local banks and compare accounts, interest rates, services and fees. You should take particular note of a bank's fees (of which there are over 200!), which have increased considerably in the last few years and cause considerable outrage among customers (nowadays most bank robbers are employed by the banks!). To avoid fees you should never overdraw your account or accept checks from unreliable sources, keep a minimum balance in a checking account, use your own bank's ATMs (or other ATMs which incur no transaction fees), obtain overdraft protection (see below), and read your bank's fee-disclosure literature.

The best type of account to open initially is a checking account, which is the usual account for day-to-day financial transactions in the US. Many banks offer combined checking and savings accounts. To open an account, simply go to the bank of your choice and tell them you wish to open an account. You usually need a permanent address and a social security number (residents only), although you may be asked to provide further identification (ID) such as a state identification card, a driver's license or a passport. You may also be asked for a reference or co-signer, although many banks will waive this requirement in the ceaseless quest for new customers. A deposit of around $50 is usually required to open a standard checking or savings account. Non-resident aliens must complete a 'Certificate of Foreign Status' (W-8) form. All banks provide a range of personal and business checking accounts which usually include regular checking accounts, special or basic checking accounts, and possibly NOW (and super NOW) accounts:

Regular accounts: A regular checking account usually requires a minimum balance, e.g. $300 to $2,000. There's usually no charge for writing checks and no monthly account fees, although if the balance falls below the required minimum there's a monthly service fee, e.g. $5 to $10. This type of account may not be worthwhile unless you write at least 20 or 25 checks per month, as you will get a better rate of interest in a savings account.

Special or Basic accounts: Special or basic checking accounts don't require a minimum balance, but have a monthly service fee, e.g. $5 to $10, and/or a per check charge of 20¢ to 35¢. Some banks may levy a monthly service fee plus 75¢ for each transaction over a certain number (e.g. eight) in each statement period, irrespective of the account balance.

NOW accounts: NOW (negotiable order or withdrawal) accounts require a minimum deposit and are a combination of checking and savings accounts, with no interest rate ceiling or floor. The interest rate is calculated on a sliding scale depending on the account balance. A super NOW account requires a higher minimum balance than a standard NOW account. Some NOW accounts require a high minimum deposit, e.g. $5,000 to $10,000, and include privileges such as no bank charges, a no-fee credit card, preferred credit card interest rates, preferred CD (certificates of deposit) rates, overdraft protection, a credit line (e.g. up to $5,000), and a premium savings rate.

Many banks used to provide gifts (e.g. a toaster or blender), 'prizes' or goods at a discount when you opened an account (particularly a savings account with a large minimum deposit), although these have mostly been replaced by interest payments in recent years. Other inducements may include free checking for a number of months (or life), a free gold credit card for one year (or life), extended warranty and 90-day purchase protection, $20 off your local telephone bill, free checks (often the first 50 are free) and a new account 'bonus certificate' worth $10. Although incentives may be attractive, you shouldn't allow them to influence your choice of bank or the type of account you open (unless, of course, all other terms, fees and conditions are equal).

Most banks offer free checking or accounts free of service charges (and a range of other inducements) for customers aged under 18 and over 55 or 65, particularly when your income is paid by direct deposit. Many banks also offer low cost checking accounts, e.g. $3.50 per month and no per-check charges, and students may be offered accounts with no per-check fees or monthly service charges during the summer months. Some accounts combine checking (with an ATM card), savings and credit card accounts in one account, and may combine the balances of checking, savings, CDs and IRAs. Some banks also offer on-line banking via a home computer.

Checks aren't provided free by American banks and typically cost $10 to $20 for a box containing five pads of 20 to 25 checks. It's cheaper to buy your checks from a check printing company such as Checks in The Mail, PO Box 7802, Irwindale, CA 91706 (tel. 1-800-733-4443) and Current Checks Product Division, PO Box 19000, Colorado Springs, CO 80935-9000 (tel. 1-800-533-3973). First-time customers can order 200 single checks for around $5 in a wide variety of designs and typefaces. Most banks return canceled checks with your monthly statement, although some will ask whether you prefer an itemized statement and no checks.

Check Usage

Although most Americans have checking accounts, US banks don't issue check guarantee cards (so checks can't be guaranteed) and there's no American equivalent of eurocheques. Check theft is rife in the US and therefore checks are subject to far more scrutiny than in most other countries, and may be accepted only when drawn on a local or in-state bank or by a business where you're known personally. Most retailers have strict rules regarding the acceptance of checks and some businesses won't accept checks at all, e.g. gas stations and restaurants often have signs proclaiming 'NO CHECKS'. On the other hand, in stores where you're well-known, they may allow you to write a check for *more* than the amount of your bill and pay you the difference in cash. When paying by check in some stores, you must go to a special desk and have your check approved before going to the checkout desk, e.g. in some supermarkets. Some stores insist that customers obtain a store ID card before they will accept personal checks.

All checks must be printed with your name and address. You will also need identification (ID), usually a state driver's license and one other form of ID such as a credit card, green card, passport, or employer or college ID card. You may also be asked for personal details and your employer's name and telephone number, your social security number, and to deposit two pints of blood and your first born until the check has cleared

When writing checks, Americans write cents as a percentage, e.g. $107.42 is written as:

one hundred and seven $\dfrac{42}{100}$

When you deposit a check in a bank, most banks require you to endorse it with your signature or an endorsement stamp. This must always be written on the reverse sideways at the top left-hand end (the perforated end) of the check and not lengthwise. If you want to endorse a check payable to you so that it can be paid into another account, you must write on the back 'Pay to the order of _____ (name)' and sign it using the same form of your name entered under payee. This is called double-endorsement and a double-endorsed check may not be accepted by a bank. In some stores there are signs saying 'No Two-Party Checks', which means that double-endorsed checks aren't accepted. Note that in the US the date is written month/day/year and not day/month/year, e.g. September 12th 1996 must be written 9/12/96 and not 12/9/96.

Check bouncing (or check 'kiting'), i.e. writing a check for more than the balance of your account, is a national sport in the US, where some 400 million checks are bounced annually. Note, however, that most banks will close your account automatically after a certain number of bad checks have been written. The names of those whose accounts have been closed due to check bouncing are entered into a national ChexSystems database (containing details of over 7.5m accounts). Many banks refuse to open new accounts for listed check bouncers. **Foreigners should be aware that US banks are much stricter than foreign banks with regard to overdrawing checking accounts, which may even be illegal.** Most important of all, if you bounce a check you may damage your credit rating. All banks offer customers overdraft protection on particular accounts, thus protecting them from 'inadvertently' bouncing checks. Overdraft protection is sometimes linked to a credit card or savings account, where the additional funds are debited to the account holder's credit card or savings account.

Many US businesses have signs stating 'All checks must have ID' and there may be others stating a bounced check will cost you $10 to $20. If a check bounces the payee will want to find you to recover the money plus administrative costs and the penalty payment charged by their bank. Most banks charge customers a fee, e.g. $5 to $25 (average $15) for each bounced check. It's actually a crime to bounce checks in many states, particularly if you do it deliberately. Californian law makes the drawer of a bounced check liable to three times the face value of the check or $100, whichever is greater, plus a re-presentation fee of around $20. It's even possible to go to jail for bouncing checks (unless you're a member of Congress and use their banking facilities), e.g. in California bad checks totaling $1,500 or a record of writing bad checks can get you locked up. However, you can avoid a criminal record by making restitution on overdrawn checks, paying $40 in administrative fees (plus $25 per check) and attending a four-hour 'bad-check diversion school' (similar to traffic school).

After the foregoing catalog of restrictions, suspicion and threats to your liberty, you may wonder whether it's wise to use checks at all. They do, however, have their uses and are handy for paying bills by mail (such as utilities), shopping at local stores and paying professionals.

MORTGAGES

Mortgages (home loans)in the US are available from a large number of sources including savings and loan associations (who make around half of all home loans), commercial banks (both local and national), mortgage bankers and brokers, insurance companies, credit unions, builders and developers, government agencies and home sellers. Mortgages comprise almost 80 per cent of savings and loan business, compared with around 30 per cent of commercial banks' business. Savings and loans are, by law, required to make mortgages at least 60 per cent of their business.

Deposits & Maximum Loans: US nationals and foreigners with a green card (permanent residents) can borrow as much as 90 or 95 per cent of the cost of a property and there are also mortgages available for as little as 3 per cent down (insured by the Federal Housing Authority/FHA) for qualifying buyers who can't afford a larger down payment. Residents with a non-immigrant visa, such as an E-2 treaty investor visa, may also qualify for a low deposit mortgage, but will have to shop around. However, US lenders won't lend more than 80 per cent of the market value of a property to a non-resident buying a second home (or for a re-mortgage/re-finance) or a maximum of 70 per cent for an investment home. Non-income/no asset verification status (or 'non-qualifying') mortgages of around 65 per cent are available, which don't require proof of income or tax returns as the loan is dependent on the property having sufficient value to stand as security for the loan. Note that it's usually difficult or more expensive to raise finance abroad for a US property, so this isn't usually a viable option. If you pay less than a 20 per cent deposit, a mortgage lender will insist that you have a private mortgage insurance (PMI) policy, which pays off the outstanding balance on the mortgage should you die before it's paid off. However, you should be able to stop paying PMI when your equity in a property reaches 20 per cent (check with your lender).

Lending Criteria: US banks have tightened their lending criteria in the last few years, during which the numbers of mortgage defaulters has been running at record levels, particularly in Florida. Many overseas buyers thought that they could meet mortgage payments and running costs from rental income, which is highly unlikely in most areas of Florida. Lenders will evaluate a property to confirm its value and check your credit rating (see page 91), employment history, income, assets, residence and liabilities. It's advisable to check your own credit rating before applying for a mortgage to ensure that it doesn't contain anything that could adversely affect your application (your credit rating must usually be perfect to qualify for a home loan). Note also that most lenders require overseas buyers to make a deposit equal to three to six months' mortgage (principal and interest), insurance and tax payments, which is held in an interest-bearing certificate of deposit (CD) or other type of account.

Documentation: US lenders usually require overseas second home buyers to provide comprehensive documentation which may include the following (the actual requirements vary depending on the lender):

- Proof of income for the last two or three years. Official tax forms showing annual income usually suffice, although in some cases a lender may require a letter from an employer confirming the figures. The last three months' pay slips are also required.

- The latest mortgage statement relating to your current home (if applicable), showing the amount outstanding, the monthly repayment and that there are no arrears. Statements for the previous one or two years may also be required.

- Copies of credit card statements for the last six months for as many credit cards as possible, ideally three or four.

- Copies of statements for any hire purchase or similar agreements in existence now or during the last three years.

- Copies of bank statements relating to US or overseas bank accounts.

- Evidence that the cash deposit required is available and has not been borrowed. A photocopy of a bank deposit account statement or passbook for three to four months should suffice.

- Evidence of any other material assets together with proof of any income arising therefrom, e.g. investment properties, stocks and shares, deposit, investment and savings accounts.

- Copies of income tax returns for the past two years.

- If you're self-employed you require copies of any accounts submitted to the tax authorities in your home country for the past two years.

- Evidence of a bank account in the US containing sufficient funds for the down payment.

Income Requirements: The maximum amount a bank will lend you depends on your income. Most lenders limit a mortgage to no more than three times your annual salary or limit monthly repayments to a maximum of around 30 per cent of your gross monthly income, although buyers with no debt may be able to make repayments of up to 40 per cent of their gross income. Mortgages are subject to status not age, which is rarely a factor in the US because the property is the lender's collateral. There's usually a minimum mortgage of around $40,000. When calculating how large a mortgage you can afford, you should take into account all closing costs, which average around 5 per cent of the sale price of a property and depend on location, cost and other factors. Note that you must add taxes and insurance to your monthly mortgage payments, the sum of which is called PITI (principal, interest, taxes and insurance). It's possible to have the cost of a pool included in the mortgage, although it may be cheaper to have it built separately (furniture packages can't generally be included in a mortgage). You can buy a Mortgage Payment or Mortgage Calculator Guide in a stationery or book store, which will tell you exactly what a mortgage for a given interest rate and amount will cost each month.

Loan Applications: Most lenders charge a mortgage application fee of around $500 (includes the credit report fee of $150 to $200), which is non-refundable if a mortgage is rejected, although no profit is made on the fee and any unused funds are refunded. To confirm your eligibility you can complete a mortgage assessment form and obtain pre-qualification ('conditional' approval or a 'commitment letter') for a mortgage, which shows sellers that you're a serious buyer and accelerates approval when you have found a property you wish to buy. It usually takes 30 to 45 days to arrange a mortgage (although some lenders claim to close in one week), depending on its complexity, although it can take up to 90 days for overseas buyers.

Points: The sort of mortgage deal you're able to negotiate will depend on a number of factors, not least the state of the housing and money markets. Lenders usually charge a fee for granting a mortgage, expressed as a number of points, each of which is equal to 1 per cent of the loan amount. In a competitive market you may be offered a mortgage with no points, although you may pay a slightly higher interest rate. However, when there's a glut of buyers looking for loans, you will be charged a fee of one to four points, which can increase the cost of your mortgage considerably. However, a charge of more than two points is generally considered excessive, although it may reflect a below average interest rate. The better offer may depend on how long you plan to keep the mortgage.

Shopping Around: To attract new customers, lenders may offer inducements such as below-market interest rates (or interest-free for the first year), exceptional long term loans, discounts, rebates and giveaways (gifts), most of which don't provide real savings or long term advantages. In early 1996, the interest rate for a typical 30-year, fixed-rate mortgage was around 7 per cent (or 6.5 per cent for a 15-year, fixed-rate mortgage). Shop around and obtain some independent quotes, but make sure that they're binding and inclusive of closing services and all costs (the latest mortgage rates and offers are usually published in the property section of local newspapers). Your real estate broker or builder may recommend a particular mortgage company or may arrange mortgages as part of his services. Note, however, that this is because he obtains a commission and it may not be in your best interests (sometimes builders have a financial interest in mortgage companies, which don't usually offer the best deals).

Mortgage Search Companies: The easiest way to find the best mortgage deal may be to employ a licensed, independent mortgage broker. You can employ a mortgage search company which uses a computerized network to find the best mortgage deal. A similar service is provided by *Money* magazine's 'Mortgage Match' service (tel. 1-800-243-8474) for around $30, which includes a weekly-updated list of area lenders with loan rates, points, fees, indexes, margins, caps, commitment periods, rate locks, plus other necessary information to enable you to find the best deal. The Florida Banking Commission hotline (tel. 1-800-848-3792) also provides details of the latest rates. **When comparing mortgage deals, always make sure that you're comparing like with like and that you fully understand the differences.**

Types of Mortgages

It's important to carefully consider the mortgage options available before taking out a mortgage, taking into account your present and probable future income. Note, however, that although salaries generally increase, a larger income can easily be swallowed up by a larger family, inflation and higher interest rates. Generally the more money you can put down, the more choice you will have. Note that it can be expensive to change your lender or type of mortgage, although after paying your mortgage regularly for a year or two, you can usually change your mortgage lender to take advantage of lower interest rates or better terms. There are many different types of mortgages available in the US, although most are variations of two basic types: fixed-rate mortgages and adjustable-rate mortgages (ARMs). You will receive an annual mortgage status report (usually in January), which you should carefully check for errors, which are commonplace (you can even employ a mortgage monitoring company to do this for you).

Fixed-Rate Mortgage: This is the traditional US mortgage where the interest rate is fixed, irrespective of whether interest rates go up or down, and can be repaid over 10, 15, 20 or 30 years, although the most common terms are 15 and 30 years. It's paid off in equal monthly payments comprising principal and interest (called amortization), until the debt is paid in full. A fixed-rate mortgage offers stability and long term tax advantages, although interest rates are initially higher than an adjustable-rate mortgage. A fixed-rate mortgage may be assumable (or assignable), i.e. a buyer can take over the seller's original (possibly) below-market, fixed-rate mortgage, although most lenders no longer allow this. If your income is fixed or rises slowly, you're generally better off with a fixed-rate mortgage, although some people don't qualify because their income is too low. A repayment table for 10 to 30-year fixed rate mortgages is shown below:

Monthly Payment Per $1,000 Borrowed*

Interest Rate (%)	Term (Years)/Payment per $10,000				
	10	15	20	25	30
5	10.61	7.91	6.60	5.85	5.37
5.25	10.73	8.04	6.74	5.99	5.52
5.5	10.85	8.17	6.88	6.14	5.68
5.75	10.98	8.30	7.02	6.29	5.84
6	11.10	8.44	7.16	6.44	6.00
6.25	11.23	8.57	7.31	6.60	6.16
6.5	11.35	8.71	7.46	6.75	6.32
6.75	11.48	8.85	7.60	6.91	6.49
7	11.61	8.99	7.75	7.07	6.65
7.25	11.74	9.13	7.90	7.23	6.82
7.5	11.87	9.27	8.06	7.39	6.99
7.75	12.00	9.41	8.21	7.55	7.16
8	12.13	9.56	8.36	7.72	7.34
8.25	12.27	9.70	8.52	7.88	7.51
8.5	12.40	9.85	8.68	8.05	7.69
8.75	12.53	9.99	8.84	8.22	7.87
9	12.67	10.14	9.00	8.39	8.05
9.25	12.80	10.29	9.16	8.56	8.23
9.5	12.94	10.44	9.32	8.74	8.41
9.75	13.08	10.59	9.49	8.91	8.59
10	13.22	10.75	9.65	9.09	8.78

* To calculate your monthly mortgage repayments simply locate the figure in the table corresponding to the term and interest rate and multiply it by the amount to be borrowed. For example, if you borrow $75,000 over 30 years at 7 per cent, the monthly repayments will be $6.65 x 75 = $498.75.

Adjustable-Rate Mortgage (ARM): With an ARM, the interest rate is adjusted over the life of the mortgage, resulting in changes in monthly repayments, the loan term and/or the principal. Payments usually change periodically (usually every one to five years) depending on changes in interest rates based on a specified index, such as US treasury bills or state and national inflation indices. Because it involves greater risk, an ARM is initially available at a lower interest rate than a fixed-rate mortgage, e.g. 2 per cent. You should choose an ARM with a ceiling or cap on the rate of interest that can be charged (regardless of how high the index goes). Caps limit the total amount your debt can increase and can be annual or lifetime, i.e. over the full period of the mortgage. Generally the interest rate can't rise more than 2 per cent a year or 6 per cent over the full term (life) of a loan.

An ARM can also have a payment cap, which prevents wide fluctuations in payments, although this may cause negative amortization (where the balance on the loan increases instead of reduces, despite the fact that you're making maximum monthly payments). An ARM is a good choice for someone who expects his future income to rise sufficiently to offset the likely higher repayments or someone who plans to move house after a 'few' years. When comparing the cost of an ARM with a fixed-rate mortgage, bear in mind that an increase of just 1 per cent in the interest rate, e.g. from 6 to 7 per cent, costs $65 a month on a $100,000 mortgage or around $23,500 over 30 years. Most ARMs can be converted to fixed-rate mortgages if interest rates rise significantly.

An ARM generally has a low fixed interest rate during the early years, e.g. one (1/1) to seven years (7/1), although it's important to be aware of the volatility of interest rates. Many 30-year ARMs are two-step mortgages, where the rate adjusts once only, for example after five or seven years (written as 5/25 or 7/23), with the initial rate being 0.5 to 0.75 of a point lower than a fixed 30-year loan. The fixed rate period is called the 'lock-in period' (LIP). These are convenient for someone planning to move house within five or seven years. After the fixed rate period, rates are adjusted every year. The safest way to determine whether you should have an ARM is to assume that the payments will increase each year by the maximum until the cap is reached and decide whether you could still meet the payments. If not, then an ARM may not be the best choice.

Biweekly Mortgage: The normal repayment frequency for mortgages is monthly. However, one of the most popular forms of mortgage in recent years has been the biweekly (meaning every two weeks in the US and not twice a week!) mortgage, where payments are made every two weeks. The big advantage of a biweekly mortgage is that a loan that usually takes 30 years to amortize, is paid off in 19 to 21 years when paid on a biweekly basis. The reason is that biweekly payments (26 a year) are equivalent to 13 monthly payments, meaning the loan is paid off much faster resulting in significant interest savings. The biweekly mortgage (for all its financial benefits) costs around one additional monthly payment a year more than a monthly fixed-rate mortgage, and because the extra payments are distributed throughout the year they are less of a financial burden.

Interest rates for biweekly mortgages are usually similar to those for standard 30-year, fixed-rate mortgages. Because repayments of a biweekly mortgage are slightly higher than for a 30-year, fixed-rate mortgage, income requirements are also higher. Mortgage payments for a biweekly mortgage are made directly from your bank account, so if you're paid biweekly your payments will correspond to the deposit of your paycheck (if you're paid monthly it may not be so convenient).

Other Mortgages: There are various other types of mortgages including a balloon (usually used for short term financing because although the loan is amortized over 30 years, the full loan balance becomes due after the balloon period, e.g. five years); renegotiable rate (roll-over); graduated-payment (where payments start low and increase each year until payments are high enough for amortization over the full term); purchase money; shared-appreciation; shared-equity; assumable; seller take-back; wraparound; growing-equity; land contract; buy-down; reverse-annuity; convertible and rent with option (where a renter has the option to buy at a specified time and price). Most of these are 'creative financing' mortgages which are usually offered in times of high interest rates and tight money, and they may not be offered when mortgages are readily available. The term 'jumbo' mortgage simply refers to a large mortgage, e.g. over $200,000, for which there's usually a lower interest rate.

Mortgage Period: The traditional US mortgage period is 30-years, although lenders also offer 10 or 15-year fixed-rate mortgages, requiring either a higher down payment and/or higher monthly repayments than a 30-year mortgage. If you can afford the repayments, a 10 to 25-year mortgage can save you a considerable amount in interest compared with a 30-year mortgage. For example, monthly repayments on a 15-year, $100,000 mortgage at 7 per cent would be $898.83 compared with $665.30 over a 30-year period, a saving of $233.53 a month. However, the 15-year mortgage would result in interest savings of $77,718.60 over the period of the loan at a flat 7 per cent. A 15-year mortgage is usually offered at a slightly lower interest rate (e.g. a 0.5 per cent reduction) than a 30-year mortgage, meaning you will make even greater savings. Note, however, that with a 15-year mortgage (unlike a 30-year mortgage), you can't usually reduce your monthly repayments if you have payment problems.

Low Deposit Mortgages: The Federal National Mortgage Association (popularly known as Fannie Mae) is a government-created corporation whose purpose is to make home loans available to low and moderate-income families. Note, however, that these are only available to permanent residents for the purchase of their principal residence. It doesn't lend money to consumers, but buys mortgages from a national network of 4,000 approved lenders, and specializes in 15-year mortgages. A 20 per cent down payment is required or private mortgage insurance covering up to 20 per cent of a property's value (although loans with a 3 per cent deposit are available to low-income families). Fannie Mae publishes a free booklet, *A Mortgage You Can Bank On: How a 15-year Mortgage Can Help You Save For The Future*, available from Fannie Mae, 3900 Wisconsin Avenue, NW, Washington, DC 20016.

Re-Mortgaging/Refinancing: With the plunge in interest rates in the early 1990s, many lenders rushed to refinance their home loans. Refinancing is generally worthwhile only when the interest rate on your mortgage is at least 2 per cent higher than the prevailing market rate and depends on the size of your mortgage. Bear in mind that it can take at least two months to refinance a home loan and you must consider changing interest rates and all associated fees and other payments. Refinancing costs usually range from 3 per cent of your mortgage value or about the same as a new loan, so it takes a number of years to recover the remortgage costs.

Foreign Currency Loans: It's generally recognized that you should take out a mortgage in the currency in which your income is paid or in the currency of the country where a property is situated (i.e. $US in Florida). However, it's possible to obtain a foreign currency mortgage in major currencies such as £sterling, Deutschmarks, Dutch guilders, Swiss francs or even ECUs. In recent years high interest rates in many countries meant that a foreign currency mortgage was a good deal for many foreigners. **However, you should be extremely wary of taking out a foreign currency mortgage**

as interest rate gains can be wiped out overnight by currency swings and devaluations. Few foreign lenders will lend against the security of a US property. The advantage of having a mortgage in the currency in which your income is paid is that if the currency is devalued against the $US you will have the consolation of knowing that the value of your home in Florida will (theoretically) have increased by the same percentage when converted back into your 'income' currency. When choosing between various currencies, you should take into account the costs, fees, interest rates and possible currency fluctuations. Regardless of how you finance the purchase of a home in Florida, you should always obtain expert professional advice. Note that if you have a foreign currency mortgage, you must usually pay commission charges each time you transfer currency to pay your mortgage or remit money to the US. If you rent a home in Florida, you may be able to offset the interest on your mortgage against rental income, but pro rata only. If you raise a mortgage outside your home country or in a foreign currency, you should be aware of any impact this may have on your tax allowances or liabilities.

Assumable Mortgages & Owner Financing: Owners of homes sometimes offer owner financing (although it's more common when selling a business) at better terms than banks, although the agreement must be drafted by a lawyer. It's also possible to assume (take over) a mortgage from a seller, which means that you usually need to make a small down payment only and will also save on mortgage costs. Some assumable mortgages are 'non-qualifying', which means you won't need to prove your income or undergo a US credit check. Note, however, that a buyer who assumes a mortgage must usually pay a higher interest rate if the market rate is higher than the existing mortgage rate. It's also possible to obtain a lease option, whereby the seller agrees to lease you the house at a fair market rent for a number of years, with an option to buy the house at any time during the term of the lease for a fixed price. The terms and conditions of the purchase must be clearly set out in the lease option, which may provide that all or part of the lease payments will be credited toward the purchase price.

Closing Costs: A lender will provide a 'good faith estimate' of closing costs which may include a loan application fee; a loan origination fee or a transfer fee for an existing mortgage; loan discount points (see page 99); an appraisal fee; a credit report fee; document preparation fees; title insurance; government recording and transfer charges; survey, condition and termite inspection fees; one year's homeowner's insurance premiums; advance interest and other insurance premiums; and reserves such as property taxes, additional insurance and condominium association fees. Intangible tax is payable at the closing on the principal amount of the mortgage at a rate of two mills (or $2 per $1,000 mortgage), e.g. $200 on a $100,000 mortgage.

The total settlement costs are usually around 5 per cent of the purchase price, which includes mortgage fees of around 3 per cent of the loan amount. When you buy a new property most mortgage fees are paid by the builder and the buyer's contribution usually amounts to no more than around 1 per cent of the purchase price. When a mortgage isn't required many builders offer a cash discount of around 2 per cent, which is the amount saved on closing costs. Private mortgage insurance is required if a mortgage is over 80 per cent of the purchase price, for which the average premium is equal to 2.5 per cent of the mortgage amount.

Mortgage Clauses: Mortgages always contain a plethora of clauses and conditions, some of which are more important than others. Things you should be aware of include limitations on your right to sell without the lender's consent; the required maintenance of insurance for the mortgage company; collateral rights to borrow from other sources; limitations on the use of a property; and your lender's rights to change interest rates if you assume an existing mortgage or if you obtain an adjustable rate mortgage. Other points you should check include late payment charges and early payment penalties; whether assumption is permitted when a property is sold (if so it should release you from personal liability); and whether it's possible to borrow against the mortgage after you have paid off part of the loan.

Payment Problems: If you're unable to meet your mortgage payments, most lenders are willing to renegotiate mortgages so that payments are repaid over a longer period, thus allowing you to make lower payments. A mortgage can often be assumed (taken over) by a new owner when a property is sold, which can be advantageous for a buyer. Payments are usually due on the 1st of the month and many lenders allow a two-week grace period (i.e. until the 15th), after which they charge a late-payment fee. However, you should note that if you're persistently late paying your mortgage your lender could accelerate the loan (force you to pay it back earlier) and it could also damage your credit rating. If you stop paying your mortgage, your lender will foreclose on your property (usually after around three months) and could sell it at public auction (usually at well below its market value) to pay off the loan. This should obviously be avoided at all costs as you will not only have no home, but could also be left with a large debt.

Tax Relief: Note that residents in many countries receive tax relief on mortgages, which may include both capital and interest repayments (so it may pay you to have a mortgage when living abroad even when you can afford to pay cash). Some countries (e.g. Britain) allow taxpayers to deduct mortgage interest on a mortgage on an overseas second home from their taxable income.

INCOME TAX

In the US, you must usually pay two forms of income tax, federal (see page 105) and state, plus local income tax in some cities or counties. Florida is one of the few states that levies no state personal income tax (the others are Alaska, Nevada, South Dakota, Texas, Washington and Wyoming), which is prohibited under the state constitution. However, it compensates in a large part by imposing a variety of state and local taxes (many targeted at visitors, who don't get to vote in tax referendums, etc.). In fiscal year 1994, total per capita state and local taxes in Florida averaged $1,073, ranking it the 11th lowest state in the US.

Eligibility: If you earn income from the US, you may have to file a US income tax return even if you're only visiting the country. If you're a non-resident alien (foreigner) and you work or are engaged in a trade or business in the US, you must file a tax return (form 1040NR) regardless of the amount of income or whether it's exempt from US tax. Some tax laws that apply to non-residents are different from those applying to resident aliens. Generally non-residents are taxed only on income received from US sources. You're classified as a non-resident alien if you aren't a US citizen and you don't meet either the 'Alien Registration Card (green card) test' or the 'substantial presence test'.

Green Card & Substantial Presence Tests: Under the 'green card' test you're a lawful permanent resident of the US for tax purposes if you had a green card at any time during the previous tax year. Under the substantial presence test, you're eligible to pay US income tax if you spend over 31 days there during the current year *and* a total of 183 days (six months) during the current calendar year plus the two previous calendar years. However, only a third of the number of days spent in the first previous calendar year are included and a sixth of the number of days in the second previous calendar year. For example, if you spent 90 days in the current year, e.g. 1996, these are counted in full. In the previous year, i.e. 1995, you spent 120 days in the country, a third of which is 40; in the preceding year of 1994 (or second previous calendar year), you spent 60 days in the US, a sixth of which is 10. The sum for 1994 to 1996 would therefore be 10+40+90, a total of 140 days, or 43 days less than the necessary 183 days. A presence of 122 days in each of three consecutive years will satisfy the substantial presence test. **Note, however, that under double taxation treaties (see below) residents of certain countries (e.g. Britain) are considered to be US residents only if they spend 183 days or more there in a <u>calendar year</u> or can't show that they have a tax home in a foreign country and have a closer connection to that country than the US.**

The Internal Revenue Service (IRS), the bureau of the US Treasury Department agency responsible for the administration of federal tax laws and the collection of taxes, may use 'intention' as a yardstick for establishing your country of domicile and therefore who gets your taxes. For example, the possession of a tax home in a particular country and a closer connection to that country than the US. During the year you arrive in or depart from the US, you may have dual status and be both a non-resident alien and a resident alien, when special rules apply. This subject is described at length in the IRS publication 519 *US Tax Guide for Aliens*, available free from any IRS office.

Double Taxation Treaties: The US has tax treaties with many countries to prevent people paying double taxes. Under tax treaties, certain categories of people are exempt from paying US tax or qualifying benefits. Treaties cover short stay visitors; teachers and professors; employees of foreign governments; trainees, students and apprentices; and capital gains. If part of your income is taxed abroad in a country with a treaty with the US, you won't usually have to pay US tax on that income. Contact your nearest IRS district office for information about your US tax obligations. Even if you aren't liable for US taxes, you may have to complete a tax return, e.g. a non-resident alien income tax return (form 1040NR).

Information: The IRS provides a toll-free hotline (tel. 1-800-829-1040 or 1-800-424-1040), a mail 'Problem Resolution Program' and walk-in tax assistance at IRS offices throughout the country. You can also call Tele-Tax (in most areas tel. 1-800-829-4477) which provides recorded information on around 140 topics of tax information (you should note, however, that even the IRS answers many questions incorrectly!). The IRS has a variety of video and audio tapes that can be borrowed by individuals and professional or civic organizations.

In addition to US taxes, you may also be liable for taxes in your home country, although citizens of most countries are exempt from paying taxes in their home country when they spend a minimum period abroad, e.g. one year. If you're in doubt about your tax liability in your home country or country of domicile, check with your country's embassy in the US.

Federal Income Tax

The US has five rates of federal income tax, 15, 28, 31, 36 and 39.6 per cent and one of the lowest top rates of income tax in the industrial world (although state and local taxes must be added in most states). With the reduction in top taxes during the '80s, the tax burden was shifted from corporations and the rich to the middle class. At the other end of the scale, over 6m people with incomes below the poverty level pay no tax at all. Despite the relatively low higher tax rates in the US, the top-earning 10 per cent of taxpayers pay over 50 per cent of the federal income tax bill. The tax system was supposed to have been simplified and rationalized under the 1986 Tax Reform Act, which introduced the most sweeping tax overhaul in history, but changes have been frustrated by a multitude of special-interest lobbies. One yardstick used to compare the average US citizen's tax burden with previous years is 'tax freedom day' (6th May in 1995), the day of the year on which the average person has earned sufficient income to pay his federal taxes.

US federal income tax is levied on the worldwide income of US citizens and resident aliens and on certain kinds of US income for non-resident aliens. If you're employed in the US, your employer is responsible for deducting income tax from your salary (called withholding) and paying it to the IRS. The rate of withholding tax depends on your income and the information you give your employer on form W-4 *Employee's Withholding Allowance Certificate*. The amount withheld is credited against the tax owed when you file your US tax return (see page 109). The withholding tax should equal 90 per cent of your tax liability for the year in question or 100 per cent of the amount paid in the previous year. If your tax withholding amounts to less than 90 per cent of your tax liability, you must usually compensate by making quarterly estimated tax payments. If you have income from self-employment, you *must* make estimated tax payments, as no tax is withheld at source.

The US tax system is based on self-assessment, which although it requires a smaller bureaucracy than in many other countries, puts the onus on individual taxpayers. Although the IRS are usually helpful, they have sweeping powers at their disposal and aren't slow to use them if they suspect somebody of fraud. Tax fraud is a major crime (felony) in the US and not a misdemeanor (minor crime) as in many countries. It's estimated to cost as much as $150 billion annually. The IRS carries out random checks and can demand a full-scale inspection or audit of any taxpayer at any time and can insist on receipts or other evidence to support all tax claims for the previous three years.

Many people are fearful of the IRS and their imagined 'reign of terror', although providing you aren't a crook you have little or nothing to fear. Most 'little' people are extremely honest with their tax returns. It's the big fish who can afford expensive tax lawyers who 'legally' evade $millions in taxes each year (the latest and most drastic 'tax-avoidance scheme' is depatriation, i.e. moving abroad and renouncing American nationality!). Each year the IRS selects a percentage of tax returns for audit or examination (a million a year), and although the average chance of being selected is less than 1 in a 100, if you earn over $50,000 a year or are self-employed, the odds increase significantly (so take extra care when preparing your tax return). Among the most common abuses are IRA deposits, Keogh plans, home offices, retirement payouts and depreciation.

If your return is selected for examination, it doesn't mean that the IRS suspects you of fraud, although you have a right to be alarmed as 80 per cent of audits result in extra tax being assessed (although you may receive a refund). Most examinations are conducted by mail, the process for which is described in publication 1383, *The Correspondence Process (Income Tax Accounts)*. The IRS may notify you that an examination is to be conducted by a personal interview or you can request an interview. You can have professional representation at an interview or have someone represent you in your absence.

If you're found to owe additional tax, you must pay interest from the due date of your tax return, although when an IRS error caused a delay, you *may* be entitled to a reduction in the interest. The IRS attempts to solve tax disputes through an administrative appeals system. If you disagree with your tax bill after an audit of your tax return, you're entitled to an independent review of your case. The IRS recommend that you keep all tax documents for a particular year for at least three years after filing the return. The IRS may disclose your tax information to state tax agencies (with which it has information exchange agreements), the Department of Justice and other federal agencies, and certain foreign governments under tax treaty provisions, although there are strict guidelines.

If you're an alien US taxpayer, you must satisfy the IRS that all income tax has been paid and obtain a certificate of compliance (known as a sailing or departure permit) from the IRS before leaving the US to take up residence abroad. This is done by filing a *US Departing Alien Income Tax Return* (form 1040C) or a *US Departing Alien Income Tax Statement* (form 2063). For further information obtain a copy of *Tax Information for Visitors to the United States* (IRS Publication 513), the *US Tax Guide for Aliens* (519) and *US Tax Treaties* (901). Departure permits aren't required by representatives of foreign governments with diplomatic passports and employees of foreign governments or international organizations.

Reducing your tax burden is both a national sport and an obsession in the US, where a wealth of tax books, magazines and free advice in financial magazines and newspapers is published, particularly during the few months before April 15th (tax filing day). The best selling tax guides include Consumer Reports Books' *Guide to Income Tax Preparation*, the *Ernst & Young Tax Guide*, the *H&R Block Income Tax Guide* and J.K. Lasser's *Your Income Tax*. Cheaper magazine-style guides include the World Almanac's *Cut Your Own Taxes and Save*. All tax guides (and computer programs) are updated annually and are tax deductible. The IRS publishes over 100 free publications on a range of subjects available by calling 1-800-829-3676 or writing to the IRS Forms Distribution Center, PO Box 25666, Richmond, VA 23289.

Taxable Income & Rates

Your liability to file a tax return depends on your filing status, your adjusted gross income (AGI) and your age, as shown below (if your AGI is *below* the income shown, you don't need to file a tax return):

Filing Status (1995)	Gross Income
Single:	
Under 65	$6,400
65 or older	$7,350
Married Filing Joint Return:	
Both spouses under 65	$11,550
One spouse 65 or older	$12,300
Both spouses 65 or older	$13,050
Married Filing Separate Returns:	
All (whether 65 or older)	$2,500
Head of Household:	
Under 65	$8,250
65 or older	$9,200
Qualifying Widow(er):	
Under 65	$9,050
65 or older	$9,800

There are certain exceptions to the standard filing statuses listed above. For example, 'married filing separate returns' can't be used if either spouse is claimed as a dependant on another person's tax return, and anyone who receives earned income credit must file a tax return, irrespective of his gross income. A self-employed person must file a tax return if his net earnings from self-employment for the year are $400 or more.

Your tax rate (1995) depends on your salary and your marital status as follows:

Rate	Single	Income ($) Married (Joint*)	Married (Separate*)	Head*
15%	0-23,350	0-39,000	0-19,500	0-31,250
28%	23,351-56,550	39,001-94,250	19,501-47,125	31,251-80,750
31%	56,551-117,950	94,251-143,600	47,126-71,800	80,751-130,800
36%	117,951-256,500	143,601-256,500	71,801-128,250	130,801-256,500
39.6%	over 256,500	over 256,500	over 128,250	over 256,500

* 'Married (Joint)' is a married couple filing jointly or a qualifying widow(er), 'Married (Separate)' is a married couple filing separately and 'Head' is a head of household.

All income isn't taxable; some is fully taxable, some is tax exempt, and some is partially exempt. Taxable income includes all wages; back and severance pay; interest and dividends; alimony; net income from a business or profession; property gains; annuities; social security benefits; prizes from contests, lottery and gambling winnings, rewards and royalties; income from estates, trusts and partnerships; director's and jury duty fees; rental income (e.g. from a holiday home); state unemployment compensation; sick pay; and, believe it or not, embezzled and other forms of illegal income (the IRS want its cut of your ill-gotten gains!).

Income that *isn't* taxable includes interest on tax-free securities (municipal bonds); inheritances, life insurance proceeds and bequests; gifts (which may, however, be subject to gift tax); scholarships and grants; workers' compensation; employer child-care allowances and child support payments; pay for voluntary work; employer health insurance (or 25 per cent of premiums paid by the self-employed) and pension plan contributions; Christmas and other employer gifts with a nominal value; and employer courtesy discounts.

Deductions & Exemptions

All taxpayers can claim a number of deductions, exemptions and allowances (commonly referred to as tax breaks) in order to reduce their tax bills. If you're married, you and your spouse may file separately or you may file a joint return. Usually a couple saves money by filing a joint return, although in certain cases filing separately can save taxes. To find out the best method, calculate your taxes using both separate and joint tax returns or consult your tax adviser. The most important decision all taxpayers need to make is whether to itemize their deductions or choose the standard deductions. To decide the best method, make a rough calculation by totaling your itemized deductions and comparing them with the standard deduction (see below). If your itemized deductions are greater than the standard deduction, you will pay less tax by itemizing. If you decide to itemize, it's important to claim for *everything* that's legally deductible.

If you choose to itemize your deductions, you can make the following major deductions: state and local income and property taxes; medical and dental expenses exceeding 7.5 per cent of your AGI; interest payments and finance charges (i.e. mortgage, personal and investment interest); contributions to qualified organizations (e.g. charities); casualty and theft losses (only the amount above the $100 floor exceeding 10 per cent of your AGI); educational expenses; and miscellaneous deductions (to the extent by which they cumulatively exceed 2 per cent of your AGI). Employees may also deduct a range of business expenses (to the extent that the total exceeds 2 per cent of AGI) such as meals and entertainment; business travel; automobile expenses; and the upkeep of a home office. You may also deduct moving expenses, depreciation, losses on loans and worthless securities.

Taxpayers may choose to take the following standard deductions or to itemize their deductions:

Filing Status	Standard 1995 Deduction
Single	$4,850
Married filing jointly	$7,300
Married filing separately	$4,025
Head of Household	$6,700
Qualifying Widow(er)	$7,300

Taxpayers who are aged 65 or over or are blind, are entitled to an additional standard deduction of $950 for singles and heads of households, and $750 for married taxpayers and qualified widow(er)s. For example, a couple over 65 filing jointly receive a standard deduction of $8,800 ($7,300 plus 2 x $750). If you're single with dependants, you should consider filing as a head of household, which will give you a higher standard deduction ($6,700 instead of $4,850 in 1995).

A personal exemption or a dependant exemption for each dependant is available to all taxpayers. For 1995, taxpayers were allowed to claim $2,500 for themselves and each dependant (including their spouse if filing jointly). You can't, however, claim a personal exemption if you're claimed as a dependant on another taxpayer's return, e.g. children who are claimed as dependants on their parents' return, can't claim a personal exemption on their own returns. The social security numbers of dependants aged one year or older must be reported on forms 1040 and 1040A. The personal exemption is being phased out for higher income earners.

Home Ownership: Home ownership enjoys strong tax advantages over all other forms of investment as interest charges on a mortgage and property taxes can be deducted from your taxable income, and you can also defer paying capital gains tax (see page 115). If your principal residence is used partly for business you may be eligible for certain tax benefits. In the early years of a mortgage most of the monthly payment is interest, so almost the entire payment is deductible when you itemize deductions on your income tax return. Keep records of all home improvements, because when you sell your home the cost of improvements will increase your basis (tax cost) in the property and decrease your capital gains tax liability. If you sell your home, you must complete a special *Sale or Exchange of Principal Residence* form (2119) when completing your 1040 tax form.

Tax Return

If you're an employee and receive income that's subject to US income tax withholding, you must complete a tax return and file it by April 15th for the previous tax year (January to December). If you don't receive wages subject to US income tax withholding, your tax return for the previous year is due by 15th June (this also applies to non-resident aliens who must file form 1040NR and pay tax due by this date). In certain cases you can establish a tax year other than the calendar year. The amount of tax due is compared with the withholding (tax) you have already paid and the difference is payable or refunded. If you expect to receive a refund, don't forget to tell the IRS when you move home! Tax forms are available from libraries, government offices and IRS offices or the IRS may send you a form. Public libraries provide a variety of information resources to assist taxpayers with preparing federal, state and city tax returns. People who have difficulty reading the print on IRS documents can get large-print, newspaper-size versions (tel. 1-800-829-3676).

There are a number of different tax forms, depending on your income and the complexity of your tax affairs. The blue 1040 'long' form is the standard tax form, comprising many separate forms, although few taxpayers need to complete them all. There are also two short forms, the pink 1040A and the green 1040EZ (EZ stands for 'easy'), which the IRS estimates can be used by one-third of filers. The 1040A form can be used by both individuals and couples of any age whose taxable income after deductions and exemptions is below $50,000, and who take the standard deduction rather than itemize. It allows you a bit more flexibility than the 1040EZ form, e.g. divided income, estimated income tax payments, IRA contributions and claims for dependants. The 1040EZ is for single people aged under 65 (and not blind) who take the standard deduction, have no dependants and report less than $50,000 of taxable income. Income must be of the most straightforward type, e.g. wages, tips, and a maximum of $400 in interest earnings.

Most people can complete the 1040A and 1040EZ forms without professional help, although this shouldn't influence your decision to use either of these forms, as using them may cost you money. When using a short form, make sure that it allows you to include all your deductions. Make a rough calculation by totaling your itemized deductions and comparing them with your standard deduction (see page 109). If your itemized deductions are greater than the standard deduction, you will pay less tax by itemizing, which means you must use the 1040 long form. Anyone who itemizes deductions; reports income or losses from capital gains; deducts expenses for running a business; has sold a home; receives alimony; or earns $50,000 or more a year, *must* file the 1040 long form.

Most people find completing the 1040 long form a complicated and irksome task, and over half employ some kind of professional help, e.g. a tax preparation service, an enroled agent (an expert certified by the Treasury Department), a certified public accountant (CPA) or a tax lawyer. The best way to find a qualified professional is through a recommendation from a friend, relative or business associate. Fees vary considerably, for example the fee charged by H&R Block, the leading chain of tax preparation services is around $100, while a lawyer's fees can run into $thousands. Enroled agents' and CPA's fees average around $200. The advantage of using a CPA is that he's professionally accountable for his actions and must pass rigorous examinations. As with all professional services, the size of the fee is determined by the complexity of your return and the number of forms prepared. The most appropriate professional isn't the least expensive, but the one who best meets your tax requirements. You should be wary of using anyone other than a reputable company or professional to complete your return, as anyone can set themselves up as a tax 'expert'. Note, however, that whoever you choose, almost all tax preparers are incapable of completing totally error-free returns!

If you have a home computer, you may prefer to complete your own 1040 tax return using a program (the cost of which is tax deductible) such as Andre Tobias' *Tax Cut 1040*, J.K. Lasser's *Your Income Tax*, *Personal Tax Edge*, Timeworks' *Easy Tax*, *Turbotax* (the top seller) or *Macintax*. However, tax programs are for people who already know something about taxes or who are willing to learn. Programs are also available to handle the 1040A and 1040EZ forms, although most people find them unnecessary. Many people can file their tax returns electronically and 1040EZ filers can also file by telephone.

Tax returns are sent to taxpayers at the beginning of the year and should be completed and returned to the respective agency by April 15th. You can obtain a four-month extension (until August 15th) by submitting form 4868 *Application for Automatic Extension of Time to File US individual Income Tax Return*, sought by around 5 per cent of taxpayers or over 6m people. **However, this isn't an extension of time to pay your taxes, which should still be paid by midnight on April 15th.**

If you apply for an extension, you should estimate your tax obligations and pay the amount owed. However, if you're unable to pay by April 15th, you're no longer required to pay a late filing penalty, but must pay interest for the period from April 15th until the tax is paid and possibly a late payment penalty. If you underestimate the amount due, you must pay interest and must also pay a penalty if the unpaid amount is equal to over 10 per cent of your tax for the year. If you apply for an extension, you must use form 1040 or 1040A when you file your return (you can't use form 1040EZ). You can also apply for a second extension, although this is granted in exceptional circumstances only.

If you can't pay the full amount due by April 15th, pay as much as you can and file your tax form on time anyway. The penalty for filing late, as opposed to merely paying late, runs at 5 per cent per month and up to 25 per cent of your tax debt. It's usually better to borrow and pay your tax bill on time than delay paying it, as a delay involves paying high penalties and interest. If you can't meet the deadline for completing your tax form, file form 4868 and pay any tax due. If you're unable to pay your tax bill when you receive a balance-due notice from the IRS, you can ask to set up an instalment agreement. This is usually granted if you have a good tax payment record over the past three years and owe less than $10,000.

Before mailing your tax return, check that you have signed it (both you *and* your spouse must sign if you're filing jointly) and that your CPA or tax advisor has also signed (if applicable). **Around a million people forget to sign each year!** Check that your address and social security number is entered correctly and write your social security number on each page of your return to identify them. Double check all entries, dependants, filing status, exemptions, personal and dependant deductions, all other deductions, **and your math.** If you submit an unprocessable return, you can be fined $500. Attach all W-2 forms and necessary schedules to your return and, if you owe tax, make sure you have enclosed a (signed!) check or money order with your social security number written on the reverse. **Finally before mailing your return, make a copy of all the pages, schedules and W-2 forms and retain them for at least three years.**

If you discover you have made a mistake after filing your return (particularly one which will result in a refund!), or a mistake on a return made in the previous three years, you can file a form 1040X *Amended US Individual Income Tax return* for each year you're changing. Note that you can file a corrected return for the previous three years only, e.g. a corrected return for 1993 must be filed before 15th April 1997, or you will lose any refund.

Don't have nightmares about the IRS as the worst they can do is bankrupt you and seize your home (the 'good' news is that tax evasion doesn't yet merit the death penalty)!

Taxation of Rental Income

If you rent a property in Florida for less than 14 days a year you won't have to pay income tax on the income. However, if you rent for more than 14 days you must file a US income tax return and pay tax on the income. Non-residents are taxed on their US source income at a flat rate of 30 per cent, which includes rental income from a US property. However, you can choose to pay taxes on a 'net basis' and can offset mortgage interest, property taxes and other expenses, and be taxed at regular US rates, which should amount to around 15 per cent of income. In fact, many owners achieve a bottom line tax loss on rentals and pay no tax at all, particularly during the early years of owning a property. Note that it may pay you to have a mortgage if you will be renting a property, as interest payments can be offset against income. If you own a property through a foreign company and choose to pay taxes on the 'net basis' (see below), then rental income is liable to Federal Corporation Income Tax.

A non-resident alien taxpayer must obtain a US identification number, which can be a non-working Social Security number obtainable from any Social Security Administration office in Florida. You need to show your foreign birth certificate or passport and an alien registration card or US immigration form. The identification number is required by a property management company and if you can't provide one they are required to deduct 'back-up withholding' of 31 per cent from your rental income until you do so.

If you don't receive wages subject to US income tax withholding, your tax return for the previous year must be filed by 15th June. An extension of up to six months can be requested to file form 1040NR after the 15th June deadline. All property owners must file a return, even if they have no property income. Few foreigners complete their own tax returns, but get their Florida management company to take care of it or employ an accountant or tax return preparer. The fee (which is tax deductible) is typically between $150 and $300 depending on the amount of work involved, the company and whether one or two returns (for shared ownership) are to be completed.

Net Basis Election: The most advantageous way to pay taxes on rental income is under a process termed 'net basis election' (or 'effectively connected income/ECI'). You must make an election on your first filing of form 1040NR and must also complete form 4224 annually ('Exemption from Withholding of Tax on Income Effectively Connected with the Conduct of a Trade or Business in the United States'). These forms can be completed by a property manager or rental agent in Florida. If you don't complete form 4224, your property manager must withhold tax at 30 per cent from your gross rental income (see **FADAPI** below). When you make a 'net basis' election you can offset management and legal fees; maintenance and repair costs; cleaning fees; depreciation; property taxes; mortgage interest; utilities; insurance; tax return fees; advertising; and any other costs directly related to the renting of a property. You're then taxed at regular US rates on any profit, which is usually much less than the 30 per cent withholding tax (most owners don't pay any tax at all). If the deductions exceed your rental income, the loss can be carried forward to offset income in the following year or reduce a capital gain when the property is sold.

FADAPI: If you fail to file a form 4224 tax return your rental income is referred to as 'Fixed and/or Determinable Annual or Periodic Income (FADAPI)' and is subject to withholding tax of 30 per cent with no deduction for expenses. If you have a US property manager or rental agent, he must deduct the withholding tax at source and pay it to the IRS. If the IRS discovers that tax isn't being withheld or paid, they can place a lien (embargo) on your property preventing its sale. FADAPI is a disadvantage for almost everybody and results in a tax on gross income rather than net taxable income after all expenses have been deducted, in addition to which losses can't be carried forward to be offset against a future tax (income or capital gains) liability.

Non-resident aliens owning a US property jointly must file separate 1040NR income tax returns, on which rental income and expenses must be divided in half and reported on separate returns. There's an annual depreciation deduction for the cost of the property, furnishings, appliances, capital improvements and other 'capitalized' expenses, i.e. items with a useful life of over one year. The property itself is usually depreciated over a 27.5 year period and fixtures and furnishings over a seven year period. As with property expenses, depreciation is divided equally between joint owners and entered on separate tax returns. Further information is provided in the IRS *US Tax Guide for Aliens* (publication 519), available from tax offices. **There are stringent penalties for failing to file a tax return and tax evasion, including large fines, cancelation of your visa, and even deportation and being barred from entering the US.**

Note that you may also have to pay tax on rental income in your home country, although you can usually offset this against any US tax liability. Sales tax is levied on rental income in all counties and a 'tourist development tax' is also imposed on rental income in most counties (see **Sales Tax** on page 117). See also **Rental Income** on page 176 and **Tangible Personal Property Tax** below.

PROPERTY TAXES

There are three property-based taxes in Florida: real property tax for homeowners, a tangible tax on business assets (which includes the contents of a rental home), and an intangible tax on stocks, bonds, mutual funds and money market funds. Real estate taxes are often referred to as 'ad valorem' taxes, which simply means taxes based on the value of property.

Real Property Tax: Real property tax is a tax levied annually on property owners to finance local services such as primary and secondary education; police and fire services; libraries; public transport subsidies; waste disposal; highways and road safety; maintaining trading standards; and personal social services. The value of a property is assessed on its current market value; location; size; cost; replacement value; condition; improvements; income and net proceeds from the previous sale; and the highest and best use in the immediate future and its current use. Under Florida law the assessment of the value of real property must be equal to its full market value (and not a percentage as in many other US states). Property values are set by each county and are supposed to be reviewed by law every three years (in reality it's done less frequently) unless requested earlier by a property owner. Real property tax is based on the value of a property on the preceding 1st January. During the year of construction of a new home, owners usually pay a 'lot' tax only and not the full amount.

Property taxes are calculated by the millage rate (so much per thousand dollars), with a mill equalling one-tenth of a cent or $1 per $1,000 of the taxable value of a property. For example, if a home is valued at $100,000 and the millage rate is $15, the annual property tax bill will be $1,500. Tax varies between 1 and 3 per cent of a property's value and depends largely on the level of sales tax and other taxes in a county.

Taxes on the average Florida home vary from $75 to $175 a month, depending on the area, with the millage rate on most properties between $15 and $20 (rates range from around $12 to $26). Most counties contain municipalities with millage rates above the average (usually a few mils higher) to pay for special services. There can be 20 or more different millage rates in a single county. Taxes are lower in 'unincorporated' areas, i.e. areas that aren't incorporated within a city, where fewer services are provided. Under a new rule introduced in 1995, residents' property value assessments are limited to a maximum increase of 3 per cent a year, unless a property is sold, in which case a new assessment is made. However, this rule doesn't apply to non-residents and businesses.

If you're a resident of Florida you can claim a homestead exemption of $25,000 off your home's value. For example, if your property is valued at $100,000, the taxable value will be $75,000 after deduction of the homestead exemption. Assuming a millage rate of $15, your property tax would be 75 x $15 or $1,125. The deadline to file for homestead exemption is 1st March. There are a range of property tax exemptions for residents including senior citizens and blind and disabled persons with low incomes. The system is complicated and variable and the only way to accurately determine your tax bill is to ask the county tax collector to calculate the tax for a particular property value and area. You can visit the county property appraiser's office and obtain a copy of the tax records for a home you're planning to buy and can obtain a copy of the previous bill from the Tax Collectors' Office. Note, however, that the change of ownership of a property often results in a new appraisal, so when buying a property you shouldn't assume that the appraisal will remain the same. If you're buying a new home, the builder should be able to give you the information necessary to obtain an accurate assessment. Note that the type of construction can influence the tax to be paid, so you should check prior to purchase.

One way to reduce your property tax is to appeal against your property assessment, which can cut your local tax bill by as much as 10 per cent. Check your property record card at your local assessor's office. If you find that your assessment is based on incorrect or incomplete information, ask the assessor for a review. Tax appeal deadlines vary depending on the county and community. If you appeal against your property value, be prepared to back it up with some convincing evidence, e.g. lower assessments on many similar properties and incorrect details, particularly wrong property and land dimensions. If necessary hire a professional appraiser. Note, however, that a county assessor is permitted a margin of error of 15 per cent.

Property tax bills are sent out in the first week of November and are due for payment by March 31st. There's a discount of 4 per cent if the bill is paid in November, 3 per cent in December, 2 per cent in January and 1 per cent in February (none in March). Payment can also be made instalments. If you pay through an escrow account your bank will budget for payment by 1st November. If you have a mortgage your lender will usually establish an escrow account to pay your real property taxes and will add an appropriate amount to your monthly mortgage to pay the tax (and property insurance). You should receive an annual statement in January from your mortgage company showing the taxes and insurance premiums paid. If you fail to complete a tax form, your county may assess a percentage based on the real estate value of your property, which can be as high as 4 per cent on a condominium and 6 per cent for a single-family home. There's a penalty for late payment and late payers may be named in local newspapers. If tax isn't paid, a county can place a lien (embargo) on the sale of a property and if taxes remain unpaid for a long period the property can be seized and sold for non-payment.

There are a number of books designed to help you reduce your property taxes including *Cut Your Real Estate Taxes Down To Size: How to Win the Battle Against Spiralling Property Taxes* by Brett Jason Sinclair (Probus Publishing), *Digging for Gold in Your Own Backyard: The Complete Homeowner's Guide to Lowering Your Real Estate Taxes* by Gary Whalen (REI Press), and *How to Fight Property Taxes* published by the National Taxpayers Union (tel. 202/543-1300).

Intangible Tax: Intangible tax is a state 'wealth' tax on individuals with intangible assets above $20,000 and couples whose assets are over $40,000. Intangible assets include stocks, bonds, accounts, mutual funds and money market funds, notes and loans receivable, annuities, chattel mortgages on real estate outside Florida, and all other classes of intangible personal property. It doesn't apply to cash assets such as bank deposits, IRAs, certificates of deposit or annuities. The intangible tax rate is one mill ($1 per $1,000) of assets valued up to $100,000 and two mil ($2 per $1,000) for assets exceeding $100,000 ($200,000 for a couple). It's assessed on the value of your assets on January 1st of each year. No tax is due if your liability is less than $5, but a return (DR-601-I) must be filed. Bills are mailed during the first week of January and are payable by 30th June. There's a discount of 4 per cent if tax is paid in January or February, 3 per cent in March, 2 per cent in April and 1 per cent in May (none in June). For more information about intangible tax contact the Department of Revenue (tel. 1-800-352-3671 or 904/488-6800).

Tangible Personal Property Tax: Tangible tax is a county tax levied on business and personal property that isn't used for 'family or household comfort', including everything used in a business except vehicles and real estate. Tangible tax applies to three types of property: business equipment, attachments to mobile homes on rented land, and articles contained in properties that are rented (such as furniture, washers, dryers, stoves, refrigerators, lawnmowers, computers and fax machines, etc.). All companies, corporations and individuals who lease, manage, or have control of any tangible personal property are required to file a 'Tangible Personal Property Tax Return' (form DR-405) with the County Property Appraiser's Office by 31st March each year.

It includes anyone earning an income from property through rentals. If you own a home in Florida which you rent for profit, you should keep receipts for all major purchases of furniture, appliances and household goods. Tangible tax is usually payable on any property that's rented on January 1st, although in some counties it's based on the amount of time a property is rented out. Bills are sent out at the same time as real property tax bills (see above) and the payment schedule and discounts are also the same. There's a penalty of 10 per cent of the tax due for failure to file a return and a penalty for late filing of 5 per cent of the tax due per month up to a maximum penalty of 25 per cent. There's a certain amount of confusion over tangible tax and you're likely to receive conflicting information depending on who you ask. The best source of accurate information is your local county tax office, although you should still insist on an answer in writing. You can also call the Florida Department of Revenue for information about state taxes (tel. 1-800-488-6800).

CAPITAL GAINS TAX

Capital Gains Tax (CGT) is applicable whenever you sell or otherwise dispose of an asset (e.g. lease, exchange or lose), which broadly speaking includes everything you own and use for personal purposes, pleasure, or investment. This includes stocks and bonds held in personal accounts; a property owned and occupied by you and your family; household furnishings; a car used for pleasure or commuting; coin or stamp collections; gems, jewelry, gold, silver and any other collectibles.

Since 1991, the maximum capital gains tax rate has been 28 per cent, although the maximum marginal tax rate could exceed this depending on your income, as capital gains are generally included in gross income. This applies to individuals, estates and trusts, but not corporations. In most cases, when you buy and sell capital assets, each transaction is taxed as it's concluded. However, if you make a profit on the sale of your principal home, you can defer payment of capital gains tax by setting aside the money for the purchase of a new principal home (in the US). You must usually buy and occupy a new home within the period beginning two years before the sale of your old home and up to two years after the sale (extended to four years for Americans living overseas). Note that there's no indexation relief in the US and capital gains tax on real estate doesn't depend on how long a property has been owned.

There's no limit on the number of times you can defer capital gains on the sale of your principal residence, providing the purchase price of each new house is higher than the sale price of the old house. Even if your new home is cheaper, you're taxed only on the difference between the selling price and the purchase price. However, eventually you or your survivors will be liable for tax on the profits realized in buying and selling your principal home. If you're over 55, you can make a one-time, tax-free profit of $125,000 on the sale of your principal residence, before you're liable for capital gains tax.

In Florida (and some other states), the seller or closing agent for a sale must withhold 10 per cent of the sale price against a possible capital gains tax liability under the Foreign Investment in Real Property Tax Act (FIRPTA). This is used to pay any tax due, with the excess being refunded. It's possible to avoid or reduce the 10 per cent withholding requirement by applying for a withholding certificate prior to the sale closing date. However, you must show that the gain resulting from the sale will be less than the 10 per cent normally withheld. The IRS may then decide at its discretion to reduce the withholding tax to the amount calculated as your tax liability in your application for a withholding certificate.

US residents are required to file an information schedule *Sale or Exchange of Principal Residence* (form 2119) with their income tax return when they sell a house. A non-resident seller must file a tax return (form 1040NR) at the end of the tax year to report a capital gain or loss on a property sale. If a non-resident makes a 'net basis election' (see page 112), any gain on a property sale is automatically subject to capital gains tax. Losses made on rentals can be carried forward and offset against a capital gain when a property is sold.

You can protect yourself and your survivors from capital gains tax if you bequeath appreciated property, rather than give it away while you're alive. This is because the tax basis of the property when you owned it, i.e. the purchase price, is increased to the fair market value on your death. For example, if you bought a property for $100,000 that's worth $200,000 when you die, the recipient will be able to compute capital gains as if he had bought it at $200,000. However, such bequests may lead to a higher estate tax liability, so this should be taken into account. If you have a capital *loss* in excess of any capital gains, you're limited to a net capital loss deduction of $3,000 a year, but any capital loss above $3,000 can be carried forward to future years to offset capital gains.

ESTATE & GIFT TAX

Estate Tax: In the US, federal estate tax (called inheritance tax or death duty in some countries) is applied to the transfer of property when a person dies. If the deceased was a citizen or resident of the US at the time of his death, the value of his entire estate is subject to estate tax, regardless of where it's located. A non-resident who isn't an American citizen pays estate tax on the value of property located in the US at the time of his death, although non-residents can buy real estate through an overseas company in order to avoid US estate tax. Note that joint ownership may restrict 'estate splitting' opportunities and it's therefore important to take legal advice before buying a property in Florida.

A *United States Estate and Generation-Skipping Transfer Tax Return* (form 706NA) must be filed when the gross estate of a US citizen or resident exceeds $600,000 or the gross US estate of a non-resident is over $60,000 at the time of death. In addition to the exempt amount, the tax law allows a married person to pass an estate to a spouse without paying any federal estate tax. A US resident has a unified credit of $192,800 (equal to the $600,000 exemption mentioned above) to offset against both estate and gift taxes, although part of the credit used to offset gift taxes can't be used to offset estate taxes. A non-resident is granted a limited lifetime unified credit of $13,000, which exempts the first $60,000 of an estate from estate tax. Lifetime transfers and transfers made at the time of death are combined for estate tax rate purposes. The estate tax return should be filed nine months after the date of death, unless an extension has been granted. Estate tax is also levied by the state of Florida, although it doesn't increase the amount payable as the amount paid to the state is allowed as a credit against federal estate tax.

Gift Tax: A federal gift tax is imposed on the gratuitous transfer of property, with the person making the gift usually paying the tax. Whether the recipient is subject to a gift tax may depend on whether the person making the gift is a citizen or resident of the US. A person who isn't a citizen or resident is subject to gift tax only on gifts of property situated in the US. Under federal estate and gift tax rules, US citizens and residents who make taxable gifts during the calendar year are required to file a *United States Gift Tax Return* (form 709) by April 15 of the following year. An extension of filing of up to six months can be obtained on application, although this doesn't apply to the time allowed to pay.

Gift tax applies to a transfer by gift of real or personal property, which may be tangible or intangible. You can give away $10,000 to any individual during any calendar year without incurring gift tax and a couple can agree to treat gifts to individuals as joint gifts, and exclude up to $20,000 a year (no filing is required). There's also an unlimited exclusion from gift tax for medical expenses and school tuition fees. Gift and estate tax rates are progressive and are calculated according to a unified rate schedule from 18 to 55 per cent, which in 1995 was 18 per cent on $10,000 ($1,800), 23.8 per cent on $100,000 ($23,800) and 34.58 per cent on $1m ($345,800). Florida levies no gift tax.

SALES TAX

Prices of goods and services in the US are *always* shown and quoted exclusive of state sales tax, which accounts for some 70 per cent of state revenue. Sales tax is levied at 6 per cent in Florida, although individual counties are permitted to levy a discretionary surtax of up to 1 per cent. Four counties (Bay, Dade, Duval and Hillsborough) have a

6.5 per cent sales tax and 39 counties (Baker, Bradford, Calhoun, Charlotte, Clay, Columbia, De Soto, Dixie, Escambia, Flagler, Gadsden, Gilchrist, Glades, Hamilton, Hardee, Hendry, Highlands, Holmes, Indian River, Jackson, Jefferson, Lafayette, Lake, Leon, Levy, Liberty, Madison, Manatee, Monroe, Okaloosa, Okeechobee, Osceola, Pinellas, Santa Rosa, Sarasota, Seminole, Sumter, Suwannee, Taylor, Union, Wakulla, Walton and Washington) levy a 7 per cent sales tax. The remaining 20 states levy sales tax at 6 per cent. Note that counties levy sales tax only on the first $5,000 of the purchase price.

Sales tax must be levied on short term property rentals of less than six months' duration, whether the rental is paid for in the US in US$ or outside the US in a foreign currency. Leases for periods of six months or more aren't subject to sales tax. Certain counties also levy additional taxes on short term rentals. Most counties levy a local Optional Tourist Development Tax or Resort Tax of 2 to 4 per cent (except for Orange County, where it's 5 per cent) on property rentals, which when added to the sales tax makes a total of 11 per cent in some counties (i.e. Orange and Osceola). A few states have other taxes such as a 1 per cent Tourist Impact Tax (Monroe County) and a Convention Development Tax of 2 to 3 per cent (Dade, De Soto and Volusia). Sales tax is payable to the state of Florida, while 'tourist' and other county taxes are usually payable to the county tax collector (although in a few counties they are all collected by the state). **Note that all the above taxes and the rates at which they are levied are likely to change at short notice.**

A sales tax certificate number must be obtained before renting a property by completing an *Application for Sales and Use Tax Registration* (form DR-1), which must be sent with the registration fee ($5) to the Florida Department of Revenue. You're sent your sales tax number with a book of *Sales and Use Tax Return* forms (DR-15) on which to declare your monthly sales tax. A return must be filed by the 20th day of each month for income received in the previous month (e.g. taxes collected in January are payable by February 20th), even if you received no rental income for that month (when you file a 'zero' return). When tax is paid by the 20th of the month you receive a 2.5 per cent discount of the first $1,200 due (a maximum of $30 per return). There are penalties for late filing. If applicable, you must also file a Tourist Development Tax or other tax application with the local county. If you have a US-based property manager or rental agent, he must declare and pay sales taxes on all property income, regardless of who rents it or receives the income.

Sales tax isn't levied on all items, which vary from state to state and often appear to have been selected at random. In Florida, exemptions include groceries, drugs/pharmaceuticals, newspapers and magazines, school meals, legal and accounting services, and any other service which doesn't involve the sale of a tangible item. When you're planning to make an expensive purchase it may pay you to shop by mail-order, as there's no sales tax on mail-order purchases (except in states where the supplier has an office) and shipping costs are low within the continental US. Many people cross state lines (borders) to buy alcohol and cigarettes, as there are often wide variations in prices due to different tax levels. Note that sales tax doesn't apply only to new goods or goods sold by businesses, but also to private sales of certain used products, e.g. cars, motor homes, boats and aircraft. Sales tax is calculated on the amount paid for a used item (usually less any trade in) and is paid by the buyer.

WILLS

It's an unfortunate fact of life, but you're unable to take your worldly goods with you when you take your final bow (even if you plan to come back in a later life). Therefore it's preferable to leave them to someone or something you love, rather than to the IRS or a mess which everyone will fight over (unless that's your intention). A large number of people in the US die intestate, i.e. without making a will, meaning that their estates are distributed according to local state law rather than as they may have wished. The biggest problem of not leaving a will is often the delay in winding up an estate (while perhaps searching for a will), which can cause considerable hardship and distress at an already stressful time. Note that when someone dies, the estate's assets can't be touched until estate tax (see above) has been paid and probate (the official proving of a will) has been granted.

There are two main types of inheritance law in the US: common law (42 states) and community property law (Arizona, California, Idaho, Louisiana, Nevada, New Mexico, Texas and Washington). Under common law, which includes Florida, the estate is divided among all surviving relatives including the spouse, children, parents and others. Under community law, all assets acquired by a couple during their marriage are usually deemed to be owned jointly during their lives, with the exception of real or personal property acquired through inheritance, gifts or compensation. A valid will made in another US state is usually legal in Florida, although it's advisable for residents to make a new will under Florida law.

All adults should make a will (the minimum age is 18 in Florida) regardless of how large or small their assets. If your circumstances change dramatically, for example you get married, you must make a new will as marriage automatically revokes any existing wills. Both husbands and wives should make separate wills. Similarly, if you separate or are divorced, you should consider making a new will, but make sure you have only one valid will. You should check your will every few years to make sure it still fits your wishes and circumstances (hopefully your assets will increase dramatically in value). Many Americans make tax-free bequests to charities in their wills, which is why charities are so keen that you make a will (leaving it all to them).

If you're a foreigner resident in the US, you may be permitted to dispose of your US assets under the law of your home country, providing your will is valid under the law of that country. If you have lived in the US for a long time, it's necessary to create a legal domicile in your home country. If you don't specify in your will that the law of another country applies to your estate, it will be subject to US estate and gift laws (see above). It isn't *necessary* to have an American will for US property, although it's advisable to have a separate will for *any* country where you own property. In this case, when someone dies his assets can be dealt with immediately under local law without having to wait for the granting of probate in another country (and the administration of a foreign estate is also cheaper). Having a Florida will for your Florida assets speeds up the will's execution and delivers you from the long and complicated process of having a foreign will executed in the US. Note that if you have two or more wills, you *must* ensure that they don't contradict or invalidate each other. It's important to periodically review your will to ensure that it reflects your current financial and personal circumstances.

Once you've accepted that you're mortal (the only statistic you can rely on is that 100 per cent of all human beings eventually die), you will find that making a will isn't a complicated or lengthy process. You can draw up your own will (which is better than none), but it's advisable to obtain legal advice from an experienced estate planning and probate lawyer. If you're a US resident with assets of over $600,000 you should have your will drawn up by an attorney who specializes in estates, as you will be liable for estate tax. If you aren't domiciled in the US and want your will to be interpreted under the law of another country, you should hire a lawyer who's conversant with the law of that country.

You can obtain a fill-in-the-blanks form will costing around $2, which is designed for parents or couples with modest estates. They usually help you leave your estate to your children or a spouse, give money to one other person or charity, and usually allow you to name a guardian and an executor. Under Florida law, two witnesses are required to the signature (not the contents) of a self-proved will, who can't be either a beneficiary or your spouse, and the signing must take place before a notary or commissioner of oaths. Note that a change of state may necessitate changing your will to comply with (or take advantage of) local law. A useful publication for anyone owning a home in Florida is *How to Make a Florida Will* by Mark Warda. The American obsession with TV has led to the practice of recording wills on videos, where the deceased makes a speech to his relatives and beneficiaries. This is shown after he has departed this life and has no legal validity as a will must still be drawn up in the usual way to be legal.

You also need someone to act as the executor of your estate, which can be particularly costly for modest estates. Your bank or lawyer will usually act as the executor, but you should shop around a few banks and lawyers and compare fees. In Florida, the cost of probate is limited to 3 per cent of an estate valued at up to $1m, after which the percentage decreases gradually. An alternative to writing a will is to create a 'Living Trust', thus eliminating the lengthy (and costly in some countries) probate process. There are a number of books about living trusts including *The Living Trust Handbook* by David E. Miller and *Understanding Living Trusts* by Vickie and Jim Schumacher.

Keep a copy of your will in a safe place (e.g. a bank) and another copy with your lawyer or the executor of your estate. You should keep information regarding bank accounts and insurance policies with your will(s), but don't forget to tell someone where they are!

COST OF LIVING

No doubt you would like to know how far your US dollars will stretch and how much money (if any) you will have left after paying your bills. Americans enjoy one of the highest standards of living in the world, although it remained static for the average American family throughout most of the 1970s and 1980s. However, over 30m live below the poverty level (including a third of all blacks and 25 per cent of Hispanics). Inflation was running at around 3 per cent in 1996. The cost of living in the US varies considerably, depending on where and how you live. In Florida the cost of living varies from county to county, with the difference between the most expensive in 1995 (Dade and Monroe) and the cheapest (Calhoun and Levy) varying by over 20 per cent. Floridians spend some 37.5 per cent of their income on housing; around 20 per cent on food; 15 per cent on health, recreation and services; 20 per cent on transportation (including automobiles); and 6.5 per cent on clothing. The best way to get an idea of food costs is to check the Florida Price Level Index, which compares the cost of living in each of Florida's 67 counties with the state average.

It's difficult to calculate an average cost of living in Florida, even for people living in the same city, as it depends very much on each individual's particular circumstances and life-style. Your food bill will usually be around half the cost in most European countries and around $200 should be sufficient to feed two adults for a month in most areas (excluding alcohol, fillet steak and caviar). Apart from the cost of accommodations, goods and services, you should also take into account the level of local taxes, e.g. property, sales and other taxes.

The most expensive item for most people is their rent or mortgage payments, which can be astronomical in some cities, although if you need to pay your own health insurance, it could be more expensive than your rent or mortgage. However, even in the most expensive areas, the cost of living needn't be astronomical and most people from western countries will find that most things are cheaper. If you shop wisely, compare prices and services before buying and don't live too extravagantly, you may be pleasantly surprised at how little you can live on.

A list of the approximate **MINIMUM** monthly major expenses for an average person or family in a typical metropolitan area are shown in the table below. **Note that these are necessarily 'ball park' figures only and depend on your lifestyle, extravagance or frugality, and where you live.** One thing everyone will agree on is that they are either too low or too high!

ITEM	MONTHLY COSTS ($)		
	Single	Couple	Couple with 2 children
Housing (1)	400	500	600
Food (2)	150	200	300
Utilities (3)	150	200	250
Leisure (4)	150	150	250
Transport (5)	200	300	350
Insurance (6)	100	200	300
Clothing	50	100	200
TOTAL	**$1,200**	**$1,650**	**$2,250**

(1) Rent or mortgage payments for a modern apartment or single-family home in an average suburb. The properties envisaged are a one or two bedroom apartment for a single person (possibly shared), a two or three bedroom property for a couple, and a three or four bedroom property for a couple with two children.

(2) Doesn't include luxuries or liquid food (alcohol).

(3) Includes electricity, gas, water, telephone, cable TV, pest control, and heating and air-conditioning costs.

(4) Includes all entertainment, dining out, sports and holiday expenses, plus newspapers and magazines.

(5) Includes running costs for an average family car, plus third-party insurance, annual taxes, gas, servicing and repairs, but not depreciation or credit costs.

(6) Includes 'voluntary' insurance such as health, homeowner's, liability, travel, automobile breakdown and life insurance. It doesn't include the full cost of health insurance (which it's assumed is paid by your employer) or car insurance, included under transport costs.

4.

FINDING YOUR DREAM HOME

A fter having decided to buy a home in Florida, your next task will be to choose the area and what sort of home to buy. If you're unsure where and what to buy, the best decision is usually to rent for a period. The secret of successfully buying a home in Florida (or anywhere else for that matter) is research, research and more research (particularly before you set foot in Florida). You may be fortunate and buy the first property you see without doing any homework and live happily ever after. However, a successful purchase is much more likely if you thoroughly investigate the towns and communities in your chosen area; compare the range and prices of properties and their relative values; and study the procedure for buying property. It's a wise or lucky person who gets his choice absolutely right first time, but there's a much higher likelihood if you do your homework thoroughly.

There's an overwhelming choice of property in Florida, which is a buyers' market, so you shouldn't be in any hurry to buy. Overdevelopment in the 1980s in some counties forced the state to introduce strict regulations for new developments. However, despite a slow-down caused by the recession in the early 1990s, development continues apace and in 1995 more residential building permits were issued in Florida than in any other US state. A slice of the good life needn't cost the earth, with mobile homes available from around $15,000, apartments (condominiums) from around $30,000, and single-family (detached) homes from as little as $40,000. However, if you desire a new villa with a swimming pool you will need to spend around $100,000 and for those with the financial resources the sky's the limit, with luxury villas with swimming pools available from $150,000 up to $millions for spacious beach and waterfront properties.

This chapter is designed to help you decide what sort of home to buy and, most importantly, its location. It will also help you avoid problems and contains information about the cost, fees, new and resale properties, community properties, contracts, deposits, legal advice, location, remodeling (renovation and restoration), warranties, rental income, security, renting, garages, surveys, real estate agents and brokers, time-share (and other part ownership schemes), utilities, heating and air-conditioning, moving house, and selling a home.

AVOIDING PROBLEMS

The problems associated with buying property abroad have been highlighted in the last decade or so, during which the property market in many countries has gone from boom to bust. From a legal viewpoint, Florida (and the US in general) is one of the safest places in the world in which to buy a home. Buyers have a high degree of protection under US and Florida state law which extends to all buyers, irrespective of whether they are American citizens or foreign non-residents. However, you should take the usual precautions regarding deposits and obtaining proper title (title insurance is usually required by lenders). In many states, hiring a lawyer for a real estate transaction is standard practice, although it isn't required under Florida law. Before hiring a lawyer you should compare the fees charged by a number of practices and check that they're experienced in real estate transactions. As when buying property in any country, you should never pay any money or sign anything without first taking legal advice.

The vast majority of people buying a home in Florida don't obtain independent legal advice and most people who experience problems take no precautions whatsoever when buying property. Of those that do take legal advice, many do so only after having paid a deposit and signed a contract or, more commonly, after they have run into problems. You will find the relatively small cost (in comparison to the cost of a home) of obtaining legal advice to be excellent value for money, if only for the peace of mind it affords. Trying to cut corners to save a few dollars on legal costs is foolhardy in the extreme when a large sum of money is at stake. Note that it *isn't* advisable to rely solely on advice given by those with a financial interest in selling you a property, such as a builder or broker, although their advice may be excellent and totally unbiased.

Among the most common problems experienced by buyers in Florida are builders going broke; overcharging (particularly foreigners); selling swampland (although rare nowadays); building on coastal reclaimed land without the necessary state approvals; non-payment of furniture companies (resulting in repossession) and subcontractors by builders (resulting in owners having to pay twice); selling lots (land or plots) that aren't owned; guaranteed high rental returns (illegal); undisclosed short term rental restrictions; property management companies doing a moonlight flit with owners' money; and the loss of unprotected deposits. If you're buying a home that's under construction or which has recently been completed, you should ensure that all the costs of construction have been paid by the seller and that you're protected against any future liability. Florida has a law that protects contractors who haven't been paid in relation to the construction of homes and if the builder fails to pay them you could end up paying twice for a property.

Most experts believe that you should always have a house inspection (survey) on a resale house and a termite inspection should be considered mandatory for older homes, as Florida has a multitude of wood-boring insects. Check that all local taxes and utility bills have been paid by the previous owner as outstanding bills are usually transferred with a property. Deal only with reputable brokers who are registered in Florida. Note that foreign agents aren't bound by Florida law and some make claims and statements (particularly regarding 'guaranteed' rental income) which would be illegal in Florida. In Florida, you're afforded extra protection when you buy from a licensed and registered realtor, as they are bound by a strict code of ethics. Many people engage a buyer's brokerage or agency, which doesn't cost any more than buying direct from a builder when buying a new home. Finally, you must *never* sign anything to buy a property in Florida without going there and checking that the builder and land actually exist (people do it!). As in most countries, there are sharks (as well as alligators!) in Florida who are only too willing to prey on 'greenhorn' foreigners.

CHOOSING THE LOCATION

The first consideration when buying (or renting) a home should be its location, or as the old adage goes, the *three* most important points are location, location and location! A property in reasonable condition in a popular area is likely to be a better investment than an exceptional property in a less attractive location, and there's usually little point in buying a dream home in a terrible location. Property located in a good neighborhood will also increase in value at an above average rate and be easier to sell. **The wrong decision regarding location is one of the main causes of disenchantment among foreigners buying property in Florida and is critical if you plan to rent a property.**

Where you buy a property will depend on a range of factors including your personal preferences, your financial resources and not least, whether you're buying a holiday or a permanent home (and if so whether you plan to work or start a business). If you plan to start a business or work in Florida, the location of your home is likely to be determined by the proximity to your place of business or employment. If, on the other hand, you're looking for a holiday or retirement home, you will have the whole of Florida from which to choose. Don't be too influenced by where you have spent an enjoyable holiday or two, as a town or area that was acceptable for a short holiday may be totally unsuitable for a permanent home, particularly regarding the proximity to shops, medical services (e.g. doctors, hospitals), public transport, and sports and leisure facilities.

If you have little idea about where you wish to live, read as much as you can about the different regions of Florida (see page 49) and spend some time exploring your areas of interest. Before looking at properties it's important to have a good idea of the type of property you're looking for and the price you wish to pay, and to draw up a short list of the areas or towns of interest. If you don't do this, you're likely to be overwhelmed by the number of properties to be viewed. Real estate agents may expect serious buyers to know where they want to buy within a 20 to 30 mile (30 to 50km) radius and some expect clients to narrow their choice down to specific towns or communities.

The 'best' area in which to live depends on whether you're buying a permanent or holiday home, your individual situation and requirements, marital status and income. You may also wish to live in an area with a certain ethnic population or mix. Other considerations may include the proximity to your place of work, schools, hospitals, fire and police services, bar, religious center, country or town, stores, public transport, bar, tennis club, swimming pool and a bar. There are excellent communities and residential areas to choose from throughout Florida, most of which are within easy traveling distance of a town or shopping center (and a bar). Don't, however, always believe the travel times and distances stated in ads and real estate agents' handouts, but check them yourself. When looking for a home, bear in mind traveling times (and the cost) to your place of work, shops and schools. If you buy a rural property the distance to local amenities and services could become a problem, particularly if you plan to retire (or semi-retire) there later. Gridlock (traffic jams) is common in urban areas and many areas are hopelessly congested, particularly in the peak winter season.

If possible you should visit an area a few times over a number of weeks, both on weekdays and at weekends, morning and afternoon, to get a feel for the neighborhood (don't just drive around, but walk). You should also visit an area at different times of the year, e.g. in both summer and winter, although this may be impractical and unnecessary. In any case you should view a property a number of times before deciding to buy it. If you're unfamiliar with an area, many experts recommend that you rent for a period before deciding to buy (see **Renting** on page 130). This is particularly important if you're planning to buy a permanent home in an unfamiliar area. Many people who don't do their homework thoroughly change their minds after a period and it isn't unusual for families to move once or twice before settling down permanently.

If you will be working in Florida, obtain a map of the area where you will be working and decide the maximum distance that you would be willing to travel to work. Using this distance as the radius, you can then draw a circle with your workplace in the middle to discover which towns and communities fall within your 'catchment' area. Obtain a large scale map of the area where you're looking and mark off the places that you've seen (you can also do this using a grading system to denote your impressions). If you use an agent, he will usually drive you around and you can then return later to those you like best at your leisure (providing that you have marked them on your map!).

There are many points to consider regarding the location of a home, which can roughly be divided into the local vicinity, e.g. the immediate surroundings and neighborhood, and the general area or region. Take into account the present and future needs of all members of your family, including the following:

- For most people the climate (see page 46) is the most important factor when buying a home in Florida, particularly a holiday or retirement home. Bear in mind both the winter and summer climate, the position of the sun, the average daily sunshine, plus the rainfall and wind conditions. If you want morning or afternoon sun (or both), you must ensure that balconies, terraces and gardens are facing the right direction. Note that although the winter climate is warm and pleasant in central and southern Florida, it gets extremely hot and humid in summer where daytime activity is reduced to the absolute minimum (and air-conditioning is a necessity). This doesn't bother most foreign buyers, the majority of whom use their Florida homes in winter only, e.g. between November and April. Northern Florida is cooler in the winter, although the summers are very hot.

- Check whether an area is particularly prone to natural disasters such as floods, hurricanes, fires or civil disturbances. If a property is situated in a high-risk area it will be much more expensive to insure (see page 59), particularly against storm and hurricane damage.

- Bear in mind that if you buy a home in a popular tourist area, you will be inundated with tourists (of which you may be one) possibly all year round. They will not only jam the roads and pack the beaches and shops, but may also occupy your favorite table at your local bar or restaurant (heaven forbid!). Bear in mind that while a 'front-line' property on the beach or in a marina development sounds attractive and may be ideal for short holidays, it isn't always the best choice for permanent residents. Many beaches are hopelessly crowded in the high season, streets may be smelly from restaurants and fast food joints, parking impossible, services stretched to breaking point, and the incessant noise may drive you crazy. You may also have to tolerate water restrictions in some areas.

- Noise can be a problem in some cities and community developments. However, although you can't choose your neighbors, you can at least ensure that a property isn't located next to a busy road, industrial plant, commercial area, discotheque, night club, bar or restaurant (where revelries may continue into the early hours). Look out for objectionable neighboring properties which might be too close to the one you're considering and check whether nearby land has been zoned for commercial activities. In community developments where many properties are second homes (and short term rentals are permitted), you may have to tolerate boisterous tourists as neighbors throughout the year.

- Do you wish to live in an area with many other foreigners from your home country or as far away from them as possible? If you wish to integrate with the local community, avoid foreign 'ghettos' and choose an area or development with mainly local inhabitants. However, many people prefer to live in an area with their own kind, whether it's a national, ethnic, age or social grouping. If you're buying a permanent home, it's important to check your prospective neighbors, particularly when buying an apartment. For example, are they noisy, sociable or absent for long periods? Do you think you will get on with them? If you buy in a retirement community, the economy, leisure and sports facilities are likely to be geared to the needs of senior citizens.

- Do you wish to be in a town or do you prefer the countryside? Inland or on the coast? How about living on an island? Bear in mind that if you buy a property in a remote area you will have to tolerate poor public transport, long traveling distances to a town of any size, solitude and remoteness. You won't be able to stroll along to the local baker for some fresh rolls or bread for breakfast, drop into the local bar for a glass of your favorite tipple with the locals, or have a choice of restaurants on your doorstep. In a town the weekly market will be just around the corner, a doctor and pharmacy close at hand, and if you need help or run into any problems your neighbors are nearby. The coastal areas, particularly in the south, are the most expensive and have been subjected to intense development and population growth in the last few decades. However, many inland community developments and towns offer a relaxed and tranquil way of life.

In the country you will be closer to nature, will have more freedom (e.g. to make as much noise as you wish) and possibly complete privacy, e.g. to sunbathe or swim *au naturel*. Living in a remote area in the country will suit nature lovers looking for peace and quiet, who don't want to involve themselves in the 'hustle and bustle' of town life. If you're after a peaceful life, make sure that there isn't a busy road or railway line nearby or a local church within 'DONGING!' distance. You may also wish to avoid air force bases and airports, of which there are many in Florida. Note, however, that many people who buy a remote country home find that the peace and tranquility of the countryside palls after a time, and many yearn for the more exciting city or coastal night-life. If you have never lived in the country, it's advisable to rent first before buying. Rural locations are mostly located in the central and northern areas of Florida, where homes are available in small towns and on large lots, and farms, ranches, orange groves and other agricultural holdings are common throughout the state. Note, however, that while it's cheaper to buy in a remote or unpopular location, it's usually more difficult to find a buyer when you want to sell.

- How secure is your job or business and are you likely to move to another area in the near future? Can you find other work in the same area, if necessary? What about your partner's and children's jobs? If there's a possibility that you may need to move within a few years you should rent or at least buy a property that will be relatively easy to sell and recoup the cost (or hopefully make a profit).

- What about your children's present and future schooling? What is the quality of local public schools? Note that even if your family has no need or plans to use local schools, the value of your home will be greatly influenced by the quality and location of local schools (see **Education** on page 80). A property located close to a good school will usually sell quickly for a premium price (you may even be able to sell it privately).

- What local health and social services are provided? Are there good local doctors and dentists? How far is the nearest hospital with an emergency department?

- What shopping facilities are provided in the neighborhood? How far is it to the nearest sizeable town with good shopping facilities, e.g. a supermarket? How would you get there if your car was out of action?

- Check the population density in an area and compare it with five or ten years ago. If it's growing fast the area may well become intolerably congested in the future. On the other hand a fast-growing neighborhood may be just what you're seeking, particularly if you're planning to start a business and get in on the ground floor.

- What is the range and quality of the local leisure, sports, community and cultural facilities? What is the proximity to sports facilities such as a golf course, beach or waterway? Bear in mind that properties close to popular coastal resorts and leisure facilities (such as Disney World) are generally more expensive, although they also have the best rental potential (see also **Rental Income** on page 176). Note that marina properties can be noisy and the marina itself may be a local tourist attraction, which creates additional problems such as parking.

- Are the local county and municipality well run? What is the quality of local public services such as garbage collection, street cleaning, water and sewerage, fire service, police and social services. What are the views of other residents? Check whether there have recently been any cutbacks in services and public recreation facilities. If a municipality is efficiently run you can usually rely on good local social and sports services and facilities.

- What are the local property and other taxes in the area (see page 113)? The quality of local public services are usually reflected by the level of local property taxes; generally the higher the taxes, the better the services.

- Is the proximity to public transport, e.g. an international airport or a railway station, or access to a freeway important? What about local bus services? Don't believe all you're told about the distance or traveling times to the nearest airport, railway station, freeway, beach, town or shopping center, but check for yourself.

- If you're planning to buy in a town or city, is there adequate private or (free) on-street parking for your family and visitors? Is it safe to park in the street? Note that in some areas it's important to have secure off-street parking if you value your car. Bear in mind that an apartment or townhouse in a community development may be some distance from the nearest road or car park. How do you feel about carrying heavy shopping hundreds of yards to your home and possibly up several flights of stairs? If you're planning to buy an apartment above the ground floor, you may wish to ensure that a building has an elevator.

- What is the local crime rate? In some areas of Florida (e.g. cities and some resorts) the incidence of housebreaking and burglary is very high and is reflected in high home insurance premiums. Check the crime rate in the local area, e.g. burglaries, house-breaking, stolen cars and crimes of violence. Is crime increasing or decreasing? Note that professional crooks like isolated houses, particularly those full of expensive furniture and other belongings, that they can strip bare at their leisure. You're much less likely to be a victim of thieves if you live in a secure (gated) community where crime may be virtually unknown. Note that exclusive areas can border inner-city slums with frightening crime rates.

- Do houses sell well in the area, e.g. in less than three months? Generally you should avoid neighborhoods where houses routinely remain on the market for six months or longer.

Generally, a quality neighborhood has high property prices and taxes. These are usually reflected in turn by better local services and amenities such as schools, hospitals, libraries, police and fire services, recreational facilities, street cleaning, garbage collection, and all the other things which add up to a prestigious community. The quality of a neighborhood should be immediately evident in the appearance and upkeep of local properties, yards and gardens, business district, parks and public buildings. You should also look for a town with plenty of community involvement, which is a good indication that people care about where they live. You can obtain information about communities from real estate agents, town halls and libraries. Many families believe it's better to buy a smaller home in a superior neighborhood with good schools, than a larger home for the same price in a mediocre neighborhood with poor schools.

When assessing an area, obtain the opinions of local people including real estate agents, local businesses and residents (but get an introduction before you go knocking on doors!). A wealth of information is published by counties and local Chambers of

Commerce for prospective homebuyers and residents in Florida, and the *The Complete Guide to Life in Florida* is essential reading for anyone planning to spend more than a few weeks a year there (see also **Further Reading** on page 203).

RENTING

If you're uncertain about exactly what sort of home you want and where you wish to live, it's advisable to rent a property for a period in order to reduce the chances of making a costly error. If possible, you should rent a similar property to that which you're planning to buy, during the time of year when you plan to occupy it. If you're planning to live in Florida year round or visit during the summer, you should spend some time in Florida during the summer months to see how you handle the heat and humidity (not to mention the bugs!). Renting allows you to become familiar with the weather, the amenities and the local people; to meet other foreigners who have made their homes in Florida and ask about their experiences; and not least, to discover the real cost of living for yourself. Providing you still find Florida alluring, this also allows you plenty of time to look around for a permanent home at your leisure.

If you're looking for a rental property for a few months, e.g. three to six months, it's probably best not to rent unseen, but to rent a holiday apartment for a week or two to allow yourself time to look around for a longer term rental. Properties for rent are advertised in local newspapers and magazines, particularly expatriate publications, and can also be found through property publications in many countries (see **Appendix A** for a list). Many real estate agents also offer short term rentals and builders and developers also rent properties to potential buyers.

Long Term Unfurnished Rentals: Long term rentals in Florida usually consist of unfurnished apartments or townhouses, although it's also possible to rent single-family villas. Most rentals are for a minimum of one year, although short term leases of six months or less are possible. Rents are from around $350 a month for a studio, $400 a month for a one bedroom apartment and from around $450 a month for a two bedroom apartment. There's usually a deposit of one month's rental plus one month's rent in advance, although foreigners without a US credit record are usually required to pay in advance for rentals of up to six months. It's also possible to rent a home for a period, e.g. one or two years, with an option to buy, although you must ensure that you have a water-tight contract.

Long term rentals are almost always rented unfurnished, although furniture can also be rented for a reasonable price and it's also possible to find furnished rentals. Unfurnished properties may include communal laundry facilities; washer and dryer connections (washers and dryers usually need to be purchased or rented); screened patios or balconies; controlled access and security patrols; handicapped access; ceiling fans and central air-conditioning and heating; fireplaces; alarms; a car wash; cable TV; garages; storage units; a dry cleaning service; and landscaped gardens with lakes. Most apartment and townhouse developments are beautifully designed and landscaped, and usually offer a wide range of leisure and sports facilities which may include swimming pools, floodlit tennis courts, fitness centers, billiards, aerobics, basketball, jogging paths, racquetball, sand and water volleyball, sauna, whirlpool spa, jacuzzi, roman tubs, golf (or golf practice), fishing, and a clubhouse.

A number of free catalogs are published for those seeking long term rentals including *For Rent* Magazine (United Advertising Publications, Inc., 18943-120th Avenue NE, Suite 101, Bothell, WA 98011, tel. 900/420-0040), which is published every four weeks in regional editions covering all of Florida's most popular rental areas. Another popular rental publication is the *Apartment Guide* published by the Haas Publishing Company (tel. 1-800-551-2787). Both the above publications are distributed free throughout Florida and can also be ordered by mail in the US (costing $4 a copy, payable by credit card). Local newspapers and magazines also contain rental sections.

Short Term Furnished Rentals: There are a vast number of short term rental properties available in Florida, many of which are holiday homes owned by foreigners. Rental properties are invariably furnished to a high standard and equipped with everything you could possibly need. Short term rentals of up to six months aren't inexpensive by European standards and many areas of Florida don't really have a low season. The high season is generally from November to April, although June to August is also popular, particularly with European visitors. Rental rates vary considerably depending on the location, quality and facilities provided, with lower rates in rural areas. The rent for a two bedroom, one bathroom seafront apartment is from around $500 a week in high season and from $350 a week in low season, although many have three-month minimum stays in high season (winter) when rates range from $1,500 to $2,500 a month (low season rates are between $750 and $1,000 a month). Villa rentals cost from around $600 a week in low season for a two bedroom, two bathroom villa, to over $1,000 a week for a four bedroom, two bathroom villa in high season, although rents are lower for longer rentals. Note that short term rentals in popular resorts vary considerably depending on the season and can be astronomical.

Hotels & Motels: Hotels and motels are relatively expensive in Florida (compared with other US states) where you should expect to pay from around $30 a night in the low season and from around $50 in the high season for a double room (a third bed can usually be added for $5 to $10). Note that the US makes little concession for single travelers who usually need to pay for a double room and receive only a slightly reduced rate. Budget hotel chains include Best Western, Days Inn, Econo Lodge, Hampton Inns, Knight Inns, Red Carpet Inns and Travelodge. Many motels have efficiencies, which are motel rooms with cooking facilities, usually costing $10 to $15 a night more than a standard room. There are also condominium hotels where rooms are rented on a daily or weekly basis. Hotel rates vary depending on the time of year (generally mid-December to April is the high season), the exact location and the individual establishment, although you can often haggle over rates. Members of the American Automobile Association (AAA) and other American organizations receive discounts at most hotel chains. There are also bed & breakfast establishments (and a number of agencies) in Florida, although they aren't budget accommodations in the US and often fall into the luxury category. For real budget accommodations you need to choose a hostel.

Home Exchange: One alternative to renting is to exchange your home for a period with one in Florida. This way you can experience home living in Florida for a relatively small cost and may save yourself the expense of a long term rental. Although there's an element of risk involved in exchanging your home with another family (depending on whether your swap is made in heaven or hell!), most agencies thoroughly vet clients and many have a track record of successful swaps. There are home exchange agencies in most countries, many of which are members of the International Home Exchange Association (IHEA). One such company is Home Base Holidays, 7 Park Avenue, London N13 5PG, UK (tel. 0181-886 8752), who also market, *Trading Places*, by Bill & Mary Barbour (Rutlidge Hill Press), which provides valuable information for novice house swappers. See also **Rental Income** on page 176.

FLORIDA HOMES

American homes are generally bigger (particularly in rural areas), more luxurious and more lavishly equipped than homes in most other western countries. Homes are built in a wide range of architectural styles including Colonial, English Tudor, French Manor, Mediterranean, Queen Anne, Spanish Mission and Victorian. However, most Florida builders offer single or two-story villas, which are built in a vast range of designs and sizes and are best suited to Florida's climate. It isn't advisable to build a new home in a style that doesn't suit Florida's climate, as it won't be so popular for resale and may not keep its value. A wide range of home styles and developments are available, from city and beach apartment blocks and townhouse developments (sometimes referred to as group or cluster housing) to town and country single-family communities. Some neighborhoods consist entirely of duplexes and fourplexes, which are multiple dwelling units of two or four homes.

Florida has a vast and flourishing property market and there's a huge range and quantity of homes from which to choose, including golf and country club developments, marina and waterfront homes with private moorings, and a wide variety of inland sites with unique attractions. There are numerous exclusive and beautifully landscaped developments in Florida (some covering 1,000 or 2,000 acres) consisting of villa-style, one-family homes on individual lots and/or townhouse and apartment developments. Many developments are completely fenced and gated with security lighting and offer a wide range of community sports and leisure facilities (see **Community Properties** on page 144).

American homes are usually built to a high standard of design and construction, and include a high level of quality fixtures and fittings. Homes are made of cement, wood or brick, or a combination. Most Florida homes employ a concrete (cement) block construction on steel reinforced concrete foundations, prevalent throughout central and southern Florida and designed to withstand hurricanes and earthquakes. Steel-framed homes have many advantages over wood and are becoming more widespread as the price of wood increases. You can, however, buy timber-frame or factory manufactured homes and most custom-built homes are timber-framed. Although timber-framed houses are more expensive to build (the wood must be shipped from northern Florida or out of state), they are cheaper to run than concrete or brick-built homes. However, they are more prone to termite damage and are more likely to be damaged by hurricanes and other storms (although construction quality and design is the major factor in reducing storm damage, rather than the building materials used).

Whereas land values constitute a large part of the cost of a home in many other countries, building lots in Florida are usually relatively inexpensive and extensive prefabrication helps reduce building costs. Quarter or one-third acre lots are standard in most areas, although these are considered large in urban areas (where you can barely walk between houses), while one acre lots are common in many parts of northern Florida and inland areas. The built living area of a new single-family home in Florida is usually a minimum of 1,250 square feet (almost 116 square meters) and the average size of new single-family homes is over 2,000 square feet (185 square meters). If you plan to buy a lot separately you must ensure that the home you plan to build will receive planning permission.

Single-Family Homes: A single-family home is simply a detached property built on its own lot. They are sold freehold and there are no community fees unless a property is part of a community development with communal amenities such as a clubhouse, swimming pool or tennis courts. Note that in Florida, homeowners are required by law to keep their lawn trimmed and their house painted and presentable, and in rural areas may be responsible for the upkeep of private roads and fencing.

Ranch-Style Villas: Typical Florida villas are single or two-story buildings with two or three bedrooms and one or two bathrooms, usually with a combined living/dining room and possibly a den (study), although this usually doubles as an optional bedroom. The main room (usually the living/dining room) may be called a family room, great room or gathering room, and often has a high ceiling (e.g. cathedral, vaulted or volume). Larger homes (e.g. four bedrooms or more) may have a living/dining room and a separate family room. Interiors tend to be light and bright with walls and ceilings painted in white or pastel colors. They are built from concrete blocks with a stucco finish, often accented with brick or wood, or painted in a variety of colors, with a contrasting shingle or barrel tile roof. Large unobstructed glass windows are usually standard, often of the awning type which can be opened completely (possibly double-glazed or 'thermopane' to reduce heating and cooling costs). Open and split floor plans are common. All single-family homes have paved or covered outdoor areas which may include terraces, patios, lanais, loggias, decks and porches. A lanai is a screened-in porch or patio where you can enjoy the fresh air without the bugs. Many homes also have a Florida room, which is a lanai converted into an extra room and used to grow plants, relax, entertain and dine informally. Few Florida homes have a basement because of the risks of flooding.

Kitchens: Kitchens in modern American homes are usually large with an eat-in dining area (breakfast nook or morning area), plenty of counter space, built-in cabinets (cupboards), dishwasher, garbage disposal unit, and possibly laundry facilities, a pantry and a breakfast nook. Many homes have a separate utility (laundry) room. Kitchens in older homes are generally smaller and are a mixed bag, depending on whether they have been modernized. Most American families have a profusion of labor-saving devices, although most don't use electric kettles or jugs to heat water for tea or coffee. Ranges or stoves (cookers) don't usually have grills but broilers, which are larger than European grills and are located in or below the oven. Broilers have no temperature controls and therefore you can't bake or roast and grill at the same time, unless you have a double-oven range. Many Americans use a portable grill or toaster oven in addition to their conventional oven. American refrigerators are frost-free, huge (big enough to withstand a supermarket strike for at least a year) and usually have ice-cube dispensers on the *outside*.

Bathrooms: Most American bathrooms contain tubs (baths) and separate showers, and many homes also have a separate shower room or a shower or bathroom attached (en-suite) to the master bedroom. Most modern two or three-bedroom, single-family homes have two full bathrooms. American bathtubs may be small and uncomfortable and not very deep (most Americans prefer to shower). When Americans want to use the toilet, they usually ask for the bathroom, which is usually where the toilet is located. Bathrooms seldom contain a bidet. Americans also have what are called half-bathrooms (or a half-bath), which isn't a bath for babies, but a room *without* a bath. It usually contains a toilet and wash basin, and possibly a shower. Modern two-story homes usually have a downstairs toilet. American showers supply water in torrents, rather than the trickle that's common in many countries.

Swimming Pools, Spas, Tubs and Jacuzzis: Many single-family homes and all community developments in Florida have in-ground swimming pools (community developments may have a number), which may be screened or caged (to keep out insects) and heated. The average size of a pool is 15 by 30 feet (4.5 by 9 meters), costing around $15,000 with a deck and screening. Note that while most foreign single-family homeowners consider a pool to be essential, many Americans believe they aren't worth the expense. Most pools have a cool deck or river rock patio, which remains cool even with all-day sun exposure. Note that if you have a pool it will need a lot of attention such as filling, emptying, cleaning, filtering, chlorinating, etc., although there are many companies that will look after it for you (you can pay someone to do anything in the US). Many homes also have spas, hot tubs or jacuzzis (costing around $5,000), usually located outside the house where the climate is favorable. A hot tub consists of a large, circular, wooden tub containing hot water, the temperature of which is thermostatically controlled. They usually accommodate a number of people and are intended for relaxation rather than washing. A jacuzzi is similar to a hot tub, but more bubbly (especially if you fill it with champagne).

Weather & Insect Proofing: Most modern houses have heating and air-conditioning (see page 174) and new houses usually have thermal insulation (standards for new homes are high) and extensive ventilation. In northern areas where it's colder in winter, houses may have double glazing, which may consist of two sets of windows, the outer set of which are called 'storm' windows. These are often left open or removed altogether in summer. Windows and doors usually have screens to keep out flies, mosquitoes and other insects during summer, although storm windows may have to be removed to fit them. Due to the climate and abundant insect life in Florida, infestations of cockroaches, ants, termites and other insects are common in many areas, even in new buildings. It's usual for residents in affected areas to use do-it-yourself deterrents and periodically have homes (interiors and exteriors) fumigated by pest-control agencies ('exterminators').

COST

Property prices in Florida vary considerably depending on the region, town and exact location (an identical home in different locations can vary in price by as much as 200 or 300 per cent). Property prices in Florida remained relatively stable during the recession of the early 1990s and generally offer better value for money than equivalent homes in Europe (always depending, of course, on prevailing exchange rates) and northern US states. In recent years property prices in Florida have increased by an average of around 5 per cent annually or in line with inflation.

New ranch-style villas cost from around $55,000 for a two bedroom, two bathroom, single-family home with a one-car garage or a two bedroom, two bathroom apartment with a community pool. Three bedroom, two bathroom villas cost from around $75,000 or around $95,000 with a swimming pool. The average price for a single-family home in Florida (January 1996) was $89,200, with a low of $62,200 in Lakeland/Winter Haven to a high of $156,900 in the Naples area (figures provided by the Florida Association of Realtors). A 2,000 square feet (185 square meters) property with a pool can be bought for as little as $120,000 in Florida. Usually builders quote the living area and the total built area including patios, porches and garages. Note that although prices of new homes may be advertised as 'everything included', many buyers add options and upgrades averaging about 10 per cent of the purchase price. A wide range of quality fixtures and fittings are usually included as standard in new homes, which can be bought 'turn-key furnished' and ready to occupy.

Although the majority of foreigners buy new homes, resale homes (see page 142) are often better value for money. If you don't have a lot of spare cash or don't want a mortgage, you can buy a resale mobile home from around $15,000, a studio efficiency (with a kitchenette) from about $20,000, apartments from $30,000 and detached homes from as little as $40,000. However, it's difficult to compare the relative values of resale homes from advertisements, as the built area is rarely quoted, particularly for apartments. If you're planning to buy in a community development (see page 144) check the monthly fees as they can be very high. Rural building lots are available from as little as $5,000 for a third of an acre. The term 'custom building' differs from the traditional custom-built home and in Florida means buying a lot and having an individual, architect-designed house built entirely to your specifications. A custom-built home in the US is usually not less than 2,500 sq. ft. in size and generally costs a minimum of around $200,000 to build, usually excluding the cost of the land, which can easily double the cost for a prime lot.

Generally the further south and the closer to the coast or an inland waterway a property is situated, the higher the price. For example, property in Key West is among the most expensive in Florida and property in inland counties in northern Florida generally the least expensive. Southern and central Florida have become more expensive in recent years, particularly around Disney World (near Orlando) and on the southern Gulf coast, where you generally need to look north of Tampa to find the best value for money. The southeast coast has traditionally been the most expensive region, particularly around Miami, Fort Lauderdale and West Palm Beach. Prices are lowest in northwest Florida, although the winter climate is much cooler than central and southern Florida, and therefore it isn't a desirable region for a holiday home during the European or North American winter.

The good news is that Florida is a buyers' market and likely to remain that way for some time. There's a huge choice of property in most areas and literally tens of thousands of homes to choose from. Never be in a hurry to sign a contract and don't allow yourself to be rushed by a builder or broker, e.g. by fears of imminent price rises or assertions that someone else is interested in a lot or home. In Florida you need never worry about missing out on a bargain as there's *always* another dream home around the next corner (and the second or third dream home is often better than those that went before). It's better to miss the 'opportunity of a lifetime' than end up regretting a purchase.

Negotiating the Price: Whether you're buying a new or resale property (two out of three buyers choose a resale home), you should always haggle over the price. When buying a property it may be worthwhile obtaining an independent valuation (appraisal) to check that it's worth the asking price. The local Board of Realtors will be able to tell you the recent sale price for similar properties in the area. Most builders have a surplus of lots and buyers are often able to negotiate a price reduction, free options or at the very least get a builder to contribute towards their closing costs. However, you should ensure that a reduction is genuine and not something you would have been offered in any case. Usually you will be able to drive a harder bargain when buying a resale property, rather than a new property that hasn't been built.

It's always advisable to make an offer on a resale property as most sellers inflate the price and don't expect to receive the asking price. Even if a property is fairly priced you should still offer around 10 per cent less. If you're using an agent or broker you should ask him what to offer, although he may not tell you (and indeed shouldn't if he's also acting for the seller). Note that if you make an offer that's too low you can always raise it, but it's impossible to lower an offer once it has been accepted (if your first offer is accepted without discussion, you will never know how low you could have gone). However, if the seller changes anything substantial in the agreement, your offer will no longer be binding and you can make a lower offer or withdraw from the purchase altogether without penalty.

If an offer is rejected it may be worth waiting a week or two before making a higher offer, always depending on the market and how keen you are to buy a particular property. Timing is of the essence in the bargaining process and it's essential to find out how long a property has been on the market and (if possible) how desperate a person is to sell. Some people will tell you outright that they must sell by a certain date and that they will accept any reasonable offer. It may be cheaper to buy during the summer when the market is generally slower, particularly if a property has been on the market since the winter.

If you simply want to buy a property at the best possible price as an investment, then shopping around and buying a 'distress sale' from an owner who simply must sell is the best choice. Obviously you will be in a better position if you're a cash buyer and are able to close quickly. Note, however, that if you're seeking an investment property, it's advisable to buy in an area that's in high demand, preferably with both buyers and renters, e.g. holiday rentals. For the best resale opportunities it's usually also best to buy in an area or community (and style) that's attractive to Americans.

You should find out as much as possible about a property before making an offer. For example, when it was built; how long the owners have lived there; whether it's a permanent or holiday home; why they are selling (they may not tell you outright, but may offer clues); how keen they are to sell; how long it has been on the market; the condition of the property; the neighbors and neighborhood; the taxes and insurance; whether the asking price is reasonable; if their mortgage is assumable; and whether the owners are offering financing or a lease option.

You may be able to find out from neighbors why someone is selling, which may help you decide whether an offer would be accepted. If a property has been on the market for a long time, e.g. longer than six months in a popular area, it may be overpriced (unless it has an obvious problem). If there are a lot of properties for sale in a particular area or development that have been on the market a long time, you should find out why. Knowing what an owner paid for a property, which can be determined by checking the tax stamps affixed to the deed at the county courthouse, may strengthen your bargaining position. This information is a matter of public record and your broker or lawyer can easily obtain this information for you or you can do it yourself. For your part you must ensure that you keep any sensitive information from a seller and give the impression that you have all the time in the world (even if you must buy immediately). All this detective stuff may seem unethical, but you can be assured that if you were selling and a prospective buyer knew you were desperate and would accept a low offer, he certainly wouldn't be in a hurry to pay you any more.

If you're an overseas buyer, you must always see property for yourself and check that it exists. This may seem fundamental but, amazingly, thousands of people (out-of-state Americans and foreigners) have bought property and land in Florida without even checking whether it exists! This is particularly true when it comes to buying building lots, which may be swampland or in a conservation area where building is prohibited.

Many builders offer fly 'n' buy programs, although these aren't necessarily a good idea as you will usually be shown the properties of one or two builders only and may be pressurized to sign a contract on the spot. You should see as many developments as necessary to form an accurate opinion and ensure that each conforms as near as possible to your requirements in every way. Inspection trips usually last a week and agents may try to keep you fully occupied so that you have no time to see properties from other agents or builders. Most builders or agents will refund the cost of an hotel or property rental (usually the first seven nights or week only) during an inspection visit if you buy a property from them. Note, however, that this isn't a freebie and you can easily negotiate a discount to this value when traveling independently.

There's little point in paying for a home outright in Florida unless you're loaded. This is particularly true if you're going to rent a home, when mortgage interest payments can be offset against rental income, which will help reduce your US tax liability. The interest charges on a mortgage can generally be deducted from your taxable income, and this should be taken into account if you're in a position to choose between buying and renting (for which there's no tax deduction). For information about **Mortgages**, see page 97. If you're a resident you can sell a principal home and defer paying capital gains tax (see page 115) on the profits, providing you plan to buy another US property with the proceeds within a certain period.

When you agree to buy a property in Florida you should receive a copy of the HUD Guide produced by the US Department of Housing and Urban Development, which covers every financial aspect of the purchase and settlement costs. If you don't receive a copy, you should ask for one, preferably before signing a contract. Free real estate booklets and magazines listing properties for sale are published in all regions, many of which are published in regional editions throughout Florida (and the rest of the US). They are available in local realtors, stores, offices, restaurants, hotels, supermarkets, universities and libraries.

FEES

When calculating the cost of buying a home in Florida, you should allow around 5 per cent of the purchase price for closing or settlement costs if you require a US mortgage (without a mortgage, fees are around 2 per cent). Under US law a buyer can request disclosure of all the costs associated with the purchase of a property, a list of which should be provided before you sign the purchase contract. Note that it's possible to shop around and compare closing rates before choosing a company or individual to complete the closing (which may be conducted by real estate brokers, lawyers, lenders, title insurance companies and escrow companies). Fees may include the following:

- inspection fees (e.g. condition and termite inspections and land survey);
- title search and insurance premiums;
- legal fees;
- notary fee;
- government recording fees for the transfer of ownership and mortgage to be recorded at the county courthouse (i.e. around $6 for the first page of a document plus $4.50 for subsequent pages);
- property taxes (which may be payable in advance);
- apartment (condominium) or community maintenance fees for a community property (see page 144), which may need to be paid in advance;
- one year's homeowner's insurance premium;

If you obtain a mortgage you will also incur various costs totaling around 3 per cent of the mortgage sum (see page 97), which may include the following:

- mortgage application fee;
- credit report fee;

- appraisal fee;
- lender's legal fees;
- lender's title insurance fee;
- loan origination fee;
- loan discount points (see page 99);
- document preparation;
- documentary stamps, e.g. 35¢ per $100 on mortgages and promissory notes and 70¢ per $100 on real estate deeds and other documents associated with real property;
- a local intangible tax of 20¢ per $100 of the loan amount, e.g. $200 on a $100,000 mortgage.

When you buy a new property most mortgage fees are paid by the builder and your contribution usually amounts to no more than around 1 per cent of the purchase price. When a mortgage isn't required, many builders offer a cash discount of around 2 per cent, which is the amount saved on closing costs.

Before you engage a buyer's agent or any agent, make sure you know exactly who will pay his fees. Who pays the various fees is usually negotiable, with the exception of mortgage fees which are paid by the borrower (usually assisted by the builder when buying a new home), although some may be waived. Usually the seller's and buyer's agents' commission are split between the buyer and seller, but this isn't always the case. Sometimes an agreement stipulates that a buyer's broker will be paid his commission by the seller's broker or by the buyer. You must have sufficient cash to pay the deposit, closing fees, mortgage costs, insurance and furnishings, plus ideally enough to run a home for at least six months without any income from it (if applicable). Also bear in mind that non-resident buyers must usually make escrow payments comprising an advance of three to six months' mortgage payments (principal and interest), property taxes and insurance premiums (see page 97).

Running Costs: In addition to the fees associated with buying a property, you must also take into account the running costs of a home. These usually include local property and other taxes; community fees for a property in a community development (see page 144); homeowner's insurance; deposits and standing charges for utilities (electricity, water, gas, telephone); building maintenance; lawn, garden and pool maintenance; pest control; 'renting' taxes; and management fees. Annual running costs usually average around 2 to 3 per cent of the cost of a property or around $300 a month for the average home. If you rent a home (see **Rental Income** on page 176) the monthly costs for a three-bedroom home with pool will be around $600 or approximately double those incurred by an owner-occupier.

NEW HOMES

New homes are popular in Florida, particularly among foreign, non-resident buyers. Although new properties may lack the charm and character of older buildings, they offer attractive financial and other advantages. These may include lower closing fees and property taxes; better quality and a builder's guarantee; no costs or problems associated with remodeling or refurbishment; and a wide range of standard fixtures and fittings. If required, a new property can usually be rented immediately. It's also often cheaper to buy new rather than remodel (refurbish) an older property as the price is fixed, unlike the cost of remodeling which can soar way beyond original estimates.

On the other hand, new homes may be smaller than older properties and are generally built on smaller lots. When you're planning to buy a new single-family home, you can usually buy the land and house separately, although it's usual to choose an inclusive land and house deal. Most builders have a number of developments, each of which is divided into lots, and offer what is called 'custom building'. This means that you choose the site and size of your lot (e.g. one third to half an acre) and select a style from a wide range of standard designs (builders offer up to 100 designs and floor plans).

The most important consideration when choosing a new home is the reputation of the builder. Inspect other homes a builder has built and check with the owners what problems they have had and whether they're satisfied. Building standards in Florida are generally high and new building codes were introduced after the widespread devastation (estimated to have cost over $20 billion) caused by hurricane Andrew in 1992. Most new single-family homes in Florida are purchased off-plan and builders don't usually start work until a lot has been selected and a contract signed (the main exception is apartment and townhouse developments). A good agent or builder will keep you informed about the construction of your home and may send you regular photographs showing the progress of building work. Most homes are completed within 90 to 120 days of signing a contract.

Standard Features: Standard fixtures and fittings in new homes are usually more comprehensive and of better quality than those found in older homes. Builders often offer limited and standard feature options. Standard features in single-family homes include a fitted kitchen with a range and possibly also a dishwasher, refrigerator, pantry and breakfast nook; deluxe bathroom suites with mirrored cabinets; master bedrooms with walk-in closets (usually with mirrored doors and ventilated shelving); air-conditioning and heating (climate controlled); screened patios and terraces; and a single or double garage. Homes may also contain quality fixtures and fittings such as recessed kitchen lighting, humidifiers, electric door chimes, window blinds, exhaust fans in bathrooms, ventilated closet shelving, and smoke alarms.

Floors in the foyer, kitchen and bathrooms are usually non-wax vinyl in less expensive homes, although you can pay extra to have tiles (fitted as standard in luxury homes). All other rooms are carpeted. New homes usually include a range of energy-efficient, low maintenance features in the latest materials and are pre-wired for TV (e.g. living or family room and master bedroom) and telephone connections (e.g. kitchen and master bedroom), although if you want more than two points you may have to pay extra. Homes are also usually pre-wired for ceiling fans (with switches), garage door openers, front and rear exterior electrical outlets, a cold water line for an ice-maker, and washer/dryer connections. Ensure that utility 'hookups' (connections) are included in the price.

Luxury Features: More expensive homes often offer better value for money with a larger lot, larger living and total built area, superior fixtures and fittings, and many luxury features included as standard. These may include a tiled foyer, kitchen and bathrooms; a tiled roof (tile roofs cost around $5,000 more than shingle roofs, don't absorb as much heat and last much longer); better quality interior and exterior doors; volume ceilings; window blinds; large walk-in closets; extra electrical outlets; plant shelves; security metal-clad external doors (including patio doors) with deadlocks; emergency lighting; fire extinguisher; garage door opener; pull-down stairs in garage to access an attic (which are usually small); large garden plant tubs; separate shower with glass enclosure; cultured marble vanity tops and marble window sills; mirrored closet doors and medicine cabinets; screened lanai (patio); an automatic lawn sprinkler system; better quality carpeting; European-style or decorator/designer (favorite words of builders) kitchen cabinets; luxury light fixtures (some builders provide an allowance to buy lighting fixtures of your choice); an upgraded appliance package (e.g. washer, dryer, refrigerator, dishwasher and microwave); a fireplace; an alarm system; and a larger garage.

Large luxury homes come with three or four-car garages, a large backyard (garden) with room for RV and boat parking, a swimming pool, gourmet-style kitchens and high (vaulted/cathedral/volume) ceilings as standard. Some builders offer incentives such as free swimming pools or even free cars to buyers of luxury homes when sales are slow. The standard fixtures and fittings vary depending on the building (and price) and some homes may include extra features (options) as standard. **Note that it's often possible to negotiate for a number of options to be included in the basic price at no extra cost. When buying a new home it certainly pays to haggle!** This is particularly true if a builder if offering a new home that's already built. Most builders can show you examples of all their designs, but bear in mind that model or show homes often include many optional features, so check exactly what is included in the basic price.

Options: Options are many and varied and may include a refrigerator; microwave oven; washer and dryer; intercom and music system; fireplaces; security system; automatic garage door opener; full landscaping and automatic sprinkler system; swimming pool; jacuzzi or spa; and ceiling fans (which are cheaper to operate than air-conditioning); to name but a few. Note that some options may be cheaper to have installed independently rather than by the builder, e.g. a swimming pool or sprinkler system. However, many builders won't allow buyers to install a pool simultaneously with a home unless it's purchased through them. A sprinkler system may be included in a landscaping package, in which case it won't be possible to have it installed separately (unless you also have the landscaping done separately). If you wish to furnish a property solely for renting, all builders offer furniture packages which are usually good value for money. Some builders offer 'turnkey' properties (furnished with all appliances), although these are usually confined to apartments and townhouses.

Furniture Packages: Many builders offer furniture packages (or a 'turn key' service) which includes all furniture, electrical apparatus, cutlery, crockery, linen and miscellaneous items for an inclusive price. Typical furniture packs contain absolutely everything necessary from a color TV, washing machine and refrigerator down to lamps, ashtrays and teaspoons, and are particularly designed for buyers who are planning to rent their homes. Although packages generally offer better value than buying items individually, you should obtain separate quotations from suppliers. Wholesale furniture stores usually offer a good deal when you buy a complete home package, rather than buying individual items or doing a room at a time. When comparing value for money, make sure that you're comparing the same quality! Note that homes must be furnished to a high standard if you will be renting. Many buyers opt for a standard furniture pack, although if you will be renting you should ensure that furniture and furnishings (particularly carpets) will stand up to hard wear.

Most builders offer economy and luxury furniture packs and most items can be customized or upgraded to suit your tastes and pocket. Upgrades and options may include pool furniture and umbrellas, an electrical package, and extra pictures and other decorative items. A typical furniture package costs from $7,000 for an economy package for a two bedroom, two bathroom property, around $10,000 for a three bedroom, two bathroom home, up to $15,000 for a luxury package for a four bedroom, two bathroom home with a family room. There's generally a difference of some $2,000 between economy and luxury furniture packages. Note that sales tax of 6 or 7 per cent (depending on the county) must be added to quoted prices. Furnishings must be financed separately and can't be included in the mortgage. See also **Furniture & Furnishings** on page 69.

Customization: If you're buying a new apartment or single-family home off-plan, you can usually choose your bathroom suite, plumbing fixtures, kitchen, fireplace, wallpaper and paint, wall and floor tiles, and carpets, which may be included in the basic price. You can also choose the interior and exterior decoration and may also be able to alter the interior room layout of the property, although this will increase the price. The exterior can be finished in practically any color you choose (e.g. yellow, blue, orange, green, salmon, pink and white) and homes usually have a contrasting colored roof. Note that two similar houses are rarely, if ever, built side by side, and even then one would need to have a different facade, thus ensuring individuality.

Single-family homes are often part of a community development (see page 144) offering a wide range of community facilities such as indoor and outdoor swimming pools, tennis courts and landscaped gardens. Some communities have their own golf or country club providing a wide range of facilities including golf, swimming pools, tennis and racquetball courts, health spa, gymnasium, sauna, jacuzzi, plus a restaurant and bar.

Pre-Closing Inspections: Your representative (e.g. a broker) will carry out an inspection or 'walk thru' (also called 'snagging') on your behalf prior to closing, which is a legal requirement. It's necessary to ensure the house is completed in every detail, the color schemes are as ordered and all options are installed. You should make a list (known as the 'punch list') of anything with which you aren't satisfied, which should be rectified before the closing. Your representative will arrange for services (water, electricity, gas, electricity) to be connected and switched on and deposits paid; arrange for a furniture package to be delivered and installed; and check that everything is in working order. There's a further building inspection after six months when any minor faults that have arisen are recorded and rectified.

Warranties: New homes (including single-family homes, townhouses and apartments) must, by law, have a 10 or 15-year Home Buyer's Warranty (HBW) or Home Owner's Warranty (HOW). With these warranties workmanship and materials are guaranteed for the first year and some systems, e.g. electrical, plumbing and ventilation, are guaranteed for two years against certain defects. The HBW also provides a guarantee against structural defects in the building for 10 or 15 (optional) years and an HOW for 10 years. Warranties are transferable when a property is sold during the warranty period. New homes are supposedly inspected at various stages of their construction, although inspections aren't always carried out thoroughly and building codes are easily circumvented by dishonest builders.

When buying a used home, it's also possible to buy a home warranty or a home protection insurance plan from a number of insurers covering major systems such as heating and plumbing. **When you have a limited warranty, such as the first two years of the HBW or HOW warranties, you should ensure that a claim is made during the relevant period, e.g. a claim for poor workmanship must be made in the first year.** If necessary (e.g. to support a claim), you can have a professional inspection carried out before the warranty expires.

Information: A number of free booklets and magazines such as *New Homes* magazine (published by New Homes America) are available in Florida, many of which are published in regional editions (in Florida and throughout the US) covering all the most popular areas (see also page 143). It also helps to study property magazines such as *International Property Magazine* and *World of Property*, and to visit overseas property exhibitions such as those organized by Overseas Property Match (see addresses in **Appendix A**) and Homebuyer Events Limited.

Warning: Prospective buyers are often captivated by the modern designs, spacious styles, quality finish, and the excellent value for money provided by Florida homes. However, it's easy to be seduced by the attractions of an American home, without giving the transaction sufficient thought. Take your time and don't allow yourself to be rushed. Remember, the developer is only a phone call away, even if you're half way round the world! See also **Avoiding Problems** on page 124.

RESALE HOMES

Resale or secondhand properties are often better value than new homes, although you must carefully check their quality and condition. There are always some excellent bargains around, particularly repossessions which are often exceptional value and well under replacement cost. Note, however, that you may need to be a cash buyer to take advantage of a quick sale. It's often possible to get a larger lot with a resale home than with a new home. Resale apartments with two bedrooms and one or two bathrooms are available from around $30,000 and a one bedroom one bathroom apartment from $20,000. Resale four bedroom, single-family properties can be bought for $80,000, three bedrooms from $50,000 and two bedrooms from as little as $30,000. Note, however, that these prices are for older homes that may need some work. The deposit on a resale house should be large enough to indicate that you mean business, e.g. 10 per cent of the agreed price, with an offer limited to 7 to 10 days, after which your offer automatically expires if it isn't accepted and your deposit is returned. Inexpensive apartments and townhouses are sometimes sold fully furnished, although the quality of furnishings varies considerably and may not be to your taste ('luxury' apartments and villas are rarely sold furnished).

Owners often advertise properties for sale in local newspapers (Sunday editions are best) or simply by putting a for sale sign in their yard. Homes are also advertised on cable TV. Note that although it may be cheaper buying direct from an owner, particularly when he's forced to sell, you should *always* employ a lawyer to carry out the necessary checks (see page 156) and draw up a contract. If you're unsure of the value of a property, you should obtain an appraisal (independent valuation) from a professional appraiser. It's often possible to take over (assume) a mortgage from the previous owner and some owners offer financing.

Advantages: The advantages of a resale home, in addition to better value for money, may include an established community or development with a range of services and facilities available in the local neighborhood; more individual design and style; the eradication of 'teething troubles'; furniture and other extras included in the price; a mature garden and trees; a larger lot; no (or fewer) rental restrictions; and the possibility of assuming a mortgage, owner financing or a lease purchase. With a resale property you can see exactly what you will get for your money (unlike when buying off-plan), most problems will have been resolved, and the previous owners may have made improvements or added extras such as a swimming pool, which may not be fully reflected in the asking price.

Disadvantages: The disadvantages of buying a resale home may include a poor state of repair and need for refurbishment; few of the benefits of a modern home unless modernized/remodeled; in need of redecorating and new carpets; poorer build quality (e.g. not built to withstand hurricanes) and inferior design to a new home; no warranty (e.g. on a home that's over 10 or 15 years' old); termite or other infestations; lack of mains sewerage and water in older properties; and the possibility of high assessments (fees) for repairs in community properties. Before buying a resale property in a community development (see **Community Properties** on page 144), it's advisable to ask the neighbors about any problems, community fees, planned developments and anything else that may affect your enjoyment of the property. Most residents will usually be happy to tell you, unless of course they're trying to sell you their own property!

Inspections: You should always consider having an inspection (see page 154) on a resale property, particularly an older single-family home, which may have been built with inferior materials. Common problems include rusting water pipes, lead-based paint (used on older homes prior to 1978, which can cause lead poisoning), poor wiring, humidity and rising damp, uneven flooring, collapsing facades, subsidence, and cracked internal and external walls, which can even be evident in fairly recent homes. Note that when a property is older than 10 or 15 years you must ensure that it's structurally sound, as it will no longer be covered by a warranty. Warranties are transferable if a property is sold during the warranty period. Although Florida is noted for its high building standards, you should never assume that a building is sound (many cases of shoddy workmanship came to light after hurricane Andrew in 1992). It's advisable to hire an architect, building expert or engineer to carry out an inspection and check that building standards have been met (preferably employing someone outside the county building inspector's office, which may have done the original inspection). The cost of an inspection is a small price to pay for the peace of mind it affords.

Agents & Brokers: You can employ a buyer's broker to find a property in a particular area and price bracket. Note that most real estate agents who advertise in the foreign press usually work exclusively for one or two builders or developers and sell new properties only. Few overseas agents handle resale properties and those that do don't handle the cheaper properties as there's too little commission to be made from them. The US Department of Housing and Urban Development (HUD) sells homes deeded to HUD/FHA by mortgage companies which have foreclosed on FHA-insured mortgage loans. HUD homes are advertised in local papers and sold to the highest bidder. You can also save money by buying a foreclosure (repossession) sold by a bank. For information obtain a copy of *The Foreclosure Magazine* (tel. 1-800-895-1432, ext. 506) or the *Florida Foreclosures Report* (tel. 407/995-7550).

Publications: A wealth of property catalogs, magazines and newspapers are published in Florida, many containing both new and resale properties. Many are free nationwide publications produced for a number of Florida regions, including all of the major metropolitan areas (e.g. Jacksonville, Orlando, Miami and Tampa).   These include *Harmon Homes* (tel. 1-900-773-7356), published every two weeks, and the monthly *Real Estate Photo Guide* (tel. 1-800-982-2677).   A comprehensive resale homes catalog ($1) is *Buy Owner* (1719 West Kennedy Blvd, Tampa, FL 33606, tel. 1-800-408-1999), a real estate magazine in which owners advertise their homes and no agents' fees or commission is involved.   Some brokers such as Coldwell Banker (Coldwell Banker Residential Real Estate, 3322 Bee Ridge Road, Sarasota, Florida 34239) publish their own *Real Estate Buyer's Guide*.   Coldwell Banker also provide a telephone information service which allows you to hear descriptions of properties for sale via an interactive telephone system.

COMMUNITY PROPERTIES

In the US, properties with common elements (whether a building, amenities or land) shared with other properties are owned through a system of co-ownership or community ownership.   Community properties (also called group housing) include apartments (condominiums and cooperatives), townhouses (also called attached houses or townhomes), mobile home parks (see page 148), and single-family (detached) homes on a private estate with communal areas and facilities.   Under co-ownership rules, owners of community properties not only own their homes (e.g. an apartment or townhouse), but also a share of the common elements of a building or development that don't comprise an integral part of any unit and are shared by all owners, e.g. foyers, hallways, elevators, patios, gardens, roads, and leisure and sports facilities.

The most common community properties in Florida are condominiums, usually shortened to 'condo', which are also referred to as units (cooperatives are rare in Florida).   There are over one million condos in Florida (50 per cent of the total in the US), mostly located in high density developments in cities and beach areas where land is expensive and in short supply.   A condo can be an apartment in a low or high-rise apartment block, townhouse or penthouse, and there are also condominium hotels where condos are usually bought as an investment and rented on a daily basis to visitors. In Florida there's a whole division of state government dedicated to the regulation and enforcement of condominium and cooperative laws.

Although they aren't strictly community developments in the way that condos and co-ops are, single-family homes are increasingly built on community developments and given fancy names such as lifestyle oriented communities, design or planned communities, and retirement communities.   Many are very exclusive and home ownership often includes membership of an owners' country or golf club. Community developments made up of single-family homes are particularly popular with retirees. In general, the only properties that don't belong to a community are detached houses on an individual lot in a public street or a house on a lot of rural land.

Advantages: The advantages of owning a community property may include improved security (possibly including neighbors looking after your property when you're away); lower property taxes than single-family homes; a range of communal sports and leisure facilities; community living with lots of social contacts and the companionship of close neighbors; no garden, lawn or pool maintenance; fewer responsibilities of home ownership; ease of maintenance; and they are often situated in locations where owning a single-family home would be prohibitively expensive, e.g. a beach-front or city center.

Disadvantages: The disadvantages of community properties may include excessively high association and recreational fees (owners may have no control over increases); restrictive rules and regulations; a restricting living and social environment and possible lack of privacy; noisy neighbors (particularly if neighboring condos are rented to holiday-makers); lack of control over community fees; limited living and storage space; and limited or no covered or secure parking; and acrimonious association meetings, where management and factions often try to push through unpopular proposals (sometimes using proxy votes).

Sports & Leisure Facilities: What all community properties have in common is that they share private grounds and provide a variety of communal leisure and sports facilities. These may include swimming pools, parks, playgrounds, volleyball, basketball, bocci ball, shuffleboard courts, horseshoe pits, ball parks and fields, golf courses (with pro shop, driving ranges and practice putting greens), fitness/walking/jogging/biking trails, children's playgrounds, health clubs or fitness centers (with jacuzzis, saunas and heated spas), racquetball and tennis courts, equestrian facilities, polo club, private beaches, fishing, boat rentals/charters, full service marinas, and RV/boat storage. Other facilities may include private gardens, parks and lakes with picnic and barbecue areas; a clubhouse (with banquet and meeting rooms, activity/hobby clubs, arts and craft rooms, billiards/pool, card rooms, video games room, large screen TV, restaurant and bar); and a variety of stores. Many communities have a neighborhood watch scheme and are completely fenced and gated with security lighting and patrols.

Some developers create a community of 'villages' with a 'town center' with shops, banks, restaurants, youth centers and schools, to provide a sense of neighborhood and a village atmosphere. In many community developments there's a good spirit of community among residents. Note, however, that new developments initially have few facilities, which may be provided only after a high percentage of homes have been sold. If you're planning to buy in a community development, check the services both within the community and the local neighborhood, as not all community developments offer a wide range of services. Before buying in a community development it's advisable to ask current owners about the community. For example, do they like living there, what are the fees and restrictions, how noisy are other residents, are the recreational facilities easy to access, would they buy there again (why or why not), and, most importantly, is the community well managed. You may also wish to check out your prospective neighbors.

Condominiums: When you buy a condo, you buy a piece of real property and receive a deed as if you were buying a house. You pay your own mortgage to a bank and your own real estate taxes. You also pay monthly maintenance fees for the common elements of a building including caretaking, upkeep of the garden and surrounds, lift and swimming pool maintenance, and garbage collection. All condo complexes have a 'homeowners' association', a non-profit organization comprising all owners, that administers the development and assesses mandatory fees for common area maintenance and improvements. The regulations governing buying a condo are much more flexible than those for buying a co-op apartment (see below) and you require no approval from shareholders, can pay as little as 10 per cent as a deposit, and generally have the same rights as the owner of a single-family home.

Due to their smaller size, condos are often much cheaper than single-family houses and resale homes can be purchased from as little as $20,000 for one bedroom and from around $30,000 for two bedrooms. On the other hand, the price of a three bedroom luxury condo in a prime, beach-front location can easily be over $300,000. Location is of primary importance in determining the price of a condo and a unit in a high-rise, beach-front location costs three or four times that of a unit in an inland setting. In cities and beach-front locations condos are considered luxury housing and developments are invariably high-rise with panoramic views, while inland they are often located in attractive low rise (e.g. two or three-story) buildings. Townhouses, which may also be classed as condos, are priced from around $55,000 for a two bedroom, two bathroom property and from $65,000 for three bedrooms and two bathrooms. Note that apartments and townhouses don't usually have individual private garages, but a car port or parking space only, which may be in an underground car park when a condo is located in a tower block. Condos are often sold 'turn-key furnished', which literally means all you need do is turn the key and they are ready to live in (but don't forget your toothbrush!).

Check the price paid for similar apartments or townhouses in the same development in recent months (note, however, that the price you pay may have more to do with the seller's circumstances than the price fetched by other condos in a development). Find out how many condos are for sale in a particular development; if there are many on offer you should investigate why as there could be management or structural problems. If you're still keen to buy you can use any negative aspects to drive a hard bargain.

Cooperatives: A cooperative building is owned by a non-profit apartment corporation and tenants don't actually own their apartments in the same way as they would a condominium. Each owner of a cooperative apartment owns a number of 'shares' in the corporation, depending on the size of his apartment. Owners pay expenses for the building's mortgage, real estate tax, employee salaries and expenses for the upkeep of the building, depending on the number of shares they own. A managing agent and staff are hired to run and secure the safety of the building and its apartments, and a board of directors is elected by the tenants to supervise and control the management of the corporation. The tenant-owners of the co-op interview and decide on each potential owner of a co-op apartment and can veto a sale. Note also that should you wish to sell, you could be forced to sell your shares back to the cooperative for less than the market value. Apart from the difference in how a property is owned, there's little difference between a condo and a co-op under Florida law, and many of the statutory provisions are the same. Condo ownership is far more prevalent in Florida than co-ops.

Community Fees: Condos are administered by an elected 'board of administration' which prepares an annual operating budget including all operating, maintenance, service and personnel costs. This forms the basis for the fees paid by owners, plus a share of the costs associated with a recreational lease, e.g. a country club, golf course or marina. Fees are calculated according to each owner's share of a development or apartment building, with shares apportioned according to the actual size (e.g. in square meters) of properties. For example, 20 properties of equal size in an apartment block would each pay 5 per cent of the community fees. The percentage to be paid is detailed in the property deed. Shares not only determine the share of fees to be paid, but also voting rights at general meetings. Fees are set forth in the condominium association documents and vary considerably depending on the location, quality and the facilities provided, with the average being around $200 a month, although the sky's the limit for luxury developments. However, high fees aren't necessarily a negative point (assuming you can afford them), providing you get value for money and the community is well managed and maintained. The value of a community property depends to a large extent on how well the development is maintained and managed.

Community fees go towards road cleaning; green zone maintenance; cleaning, decoration and maintenance of buildings and lifts; caretaking; communal lighting in buildings and grounds; guard house and security patrols; water supply (e.g. swimming pools, gardens, lawns); swimming pool maintenance; building insurance; exterior pest control; parking lots; administration fees; development taxes; maintenance of radio and TV aerials; cable TV; sports and leisure facilities, including social membership of a clubhouse; and garbage collection. There may also be a fund which provides for exterior painting, roof, road and pool refurbishment. If central heating and hot water are provided communally, the cost is divided according to the share of the utility allocated to each property. Owners must pay for their own interior pest control and insurance.

Always check the level of general and special charges before buying a community property. Fees are usually billed two or three times a year and adjusted at the end of the year when the actual expenditure is known and the annual accounts have been approved by the association. If you're buying a resale apartment, you should ask to see a copy of the receipts for fees paid in previous years, as sellers may be 'economical with the truth' when stating fees. Note that a new owner can be held liable for unpaid association fees and therefore it's important to verify that all fees have been paid by the previous owner before buying. An association has a lien on each unit for unpaid fees and assessments, and can foreclose (as with a mortgage lender) and obtain a deficiency order against the owner.

Maintenance & Repairs: If necessary, owners can be assessed an additional amount to make up any shortfall of funds for maintenance or repairs. You should check the condition of the common areas (including all amenities) in an older development and whether any major maintenance or capital expense is planned for which you could be assessed. Beware of bargain condos in buildings requiring a lot of maintenance work or refurbishment. Note, however, that under Florida law disclosure of impending expenditure must be made to prospective buyers of condos before they sign a contract. Many condo associations set aside a reserve account for capital expenditure, which can be ascertained by examining the annual budget. Note that association meetings can become rather heated when finances are discussed, particularly when assessments are being made to finance capital expenditure.

Community Property Rules & Regulations: Sellers of condos must give prospective buyers a copy of the 'declaration of condominium'; a copy of the 'articles of incorporation' of the association; a copy of the bylaws and the current rules and regulations of the condominium association; and a copy of the 'frequently asked questions and answers' (DBR form 33-032) containing information such as recreational fees, leasing restrictions, any pending lawsuits, and a copy of the latest association budget and financial statements. These are prepared for sellers by condo associations for a small fee and must be given to buyers at least three working days before they sign a contract. Note that the buyer of a condo has the right to cancel a contract (called a 'cooling-off' period) in writing within 15 days of signing it. If you don't understand any of the above documents you should have them explained to you.

Restrictions: Association rules allow owners to run their community in accordance with the wishes of the majority, while at the same time protecting the rights of the minority. The bylaws of a condominium association are the governing rules of the condo and are detailed in the covenants, conditions and restrictions (CC&Rs) of the association (see also the documents listed above). They usually include such things as noise levels; the keeping of pets (dogs are often prohibited); the occupation by children under a certain age; renting and guests (e.g. visits by young children may be restricted in retirement communities); rental restrictions; exterior decoration and plants (e.g. the placement of shrubs); garbage disposal; the use of swimming pools and other recreational facilities; parking; and the hanging of laundry. Permanent residents should avoid buying a condo in a complex with a high percentage of rental units, i.e. units that aren't owner-occupied. You should be particularly aware of any limitations placed on homes in retirement communities. Check the regulations and discuss any restrictions with residents. Note that smoking is prohibited in the common areas of condos and co-ops including hallways, lobbies, rest rooms, stairwells, entryways and conference rooms.

Holiday Apartments: If you're buying a holiday apartment that will be vacant for long periods (particularly in winter), don't buy in a block where heating and/or hot water charges are shared, although this isn't standard practice in Florida. You should also check whether there are any rules regarding short or long term rentals or leaving a property unoccupied for any length of time. Note that when buying in a large development, communal facilities may be inundated during peak periods, e.g. a large swimming pool won't look so big when 100 people are using it and getting a game of tennis or using a fitness room may be difficult.

Information: For further information about condominiums or cooperatives or for an answer to specific questions about existing or planned developments, you can call the following offices of the Division of Florida Land Sales, Condominiums, and Mobile Homes of the Department of Business Regulation; Fort Lauderdale (1-800-226-4472), Tallahassee (1-800-226-9101) or Tampa (1-800-226-6028). These offices will also provide a copy of the Condominium Act (chapter 718 of Florida Statutes) on request.

MOBILE HOMES

Mobile homes, or manufactured homes as they are called by the industry, come in an almost unlimited variety of styles, shapes and sizes. Modern mobile homes are quite luxurious and are built to a high standard, with luxury mobile homes almost indistinguishable from permanent homes. However, they aren't as structurally sound as site-built homes and are vulnerable to fires and high winds (mobile homes were decimated during hurricane Andrew in 1992). Note that despite the name, the modern mobile home isn't very mobile, particularly as many have added rooms and carports permanently attached to the ground, and they aren't to be confused with trailers (caravans).

There are some 5,500 mobile home parks and over 850,000 mobile homes in Florida, which has more than any other US state. However, most are holiday homes and only a small percentage are owned by residents. The price of a new mobile home ranges from around $10,000 for a single-section model to $100,000 for a top of the range multi-section model, with average prices around $20,000 for a single-section and $35,000 for a multi-section. Mobile homes generally cost around half to two-thirds of the price of a similar size site-built home. Resale homes are often sold furnished. Note that sales tax is payable on both new and resale mobile homes. When comparing prices, check the standard features of each home and exactly what the price includes. Mortgages are available, although if you buy a mobile home without a lot you pay a higher rate of interest and must usually repay it over a shorter period, e.g. a maximum of 15 years. Note that it's important to take the same precautions when buying a mobile home as when buying a traditional home and to always have a sales contract checked by a lawyer before signing it.

Most mobile homes are permanently sited in mobile home parks where owners are required to rent or buy a lot. Parks are usually situated in attractive locations, for example on a waterfront or golf course, and most offer a range of facilities such as swimming pools, a clubhouse, tennis courts and possibly even a golf course. Rents vary considerably depending on the facilities provided and are typically around $200 a month for a two bedroom, two bathroom home, which usually includes water, sewerage, garbage pickup and property tax (although owners may need to pay tax separately). Other fees include a license tax costing between $20 and $80 a year depending on the length of a mobile home (however, a mobile home may be classified as real property, in which case real property taxes are payable in lieu of the license tax). Note that homeowner's insurance is higher on mobile homes than on conventional homes with an equivalent value, due to the higher risk of fire and storm damage.

Before choosing a mobile home park, you should talk with other owners and ask them about a park's fees, facilities and management. Read a rental contract carefully, so that you know exactly what's included and excluded from the monthly fee. Note that many parks have raised their rents considerably in recent years, while at the same time cutting back on amenities. Check any fee rises in the last five years. It isn't advisable to rent a lot if you're on a low fixed income, as rent rises could blow your budget and reduce the resale value of a home. You can also buy lots in some mobile home parks, costing from around $8,000 to $40,000. In some parks all owners own their lots and have an interest in the communal areas and facilities (similar to a condominium), or parks are cooperatives where owners own an interest in the entire park with a right to use their lot (see **Community Properties** on page 144).

There are a number of free magazines for mobile home buyers in Florida including the *The Mobile Home Advertiser* (4275 34th Street So. # 318, St. Petersburg, Florida 33711, tel. 1-800-295-8899). Prospective owners can also contact the Federation of Mobile Home Owners of Florida, PO Box 5350, Largo, Florida 34649 (tel. 813/530-7539).

TIMESHARE & PART-OWNERSHIP SCHEMES

If you're looking for a holiday home abroad, you may wish to investigate a scheme that provides sole occupancy of a property for a number of weeks each year. In Florida these include timesharing, a leasehold interest, co-ownership and a holiday property bond. **Don't rush into any of these schemes without fully researching the market and before you're absolutely clear what you want and what you can realistically expect to receive for your money.**

Timesharing (also called various other names including 'holiday ownership', 'vacation ownership', 'co-ownership' or 'holidays for life') is easily the most popular form of part-ownership. Timesharing was invented in the US, where it doesn't have the dreadful reputation that it has earned in some European countries, although it's still a hard sell. A timeshare purchase contract in Florida can be either 'interval ownership' or 'right to use'. Interval ownership gives you the same rights as any other property purchase with the right to sell, rent, give away or bequeath the property. Title insurance is, however, necessary. A 'right to use' contract can be a club, lease or licence, and your rights are different in each case. For example, a leasehold interest is usually for 20 to 40 years, after which the rights revert to the freehold owner. This isn't such a good investment as interval ownership, particularly as your rights could be worthless if the owner goes bankrupt.

The best timeshare developments are beautifully presented and on a par with luxury hotels offering a wide range of facilities including bars, restaurants, entertainment, shops, swimming pools, tennis courts, health clubs, and other leisure and sports facilities. If you don't wish to take a holiday in the same place each year, choose a timeshare development that's a member of an international organization such as Resort Condominium International (RCI) or Interval International (II), which allow you (usually for a fee) to exchange your timeshare with one in another area or country. The highest rated RCI timeshares are classified as Gold Crown Resorts and allow you to exchange with any timeshare anywhere in the world (RCI has over 2,000 resorts in some 70 countries).

Timeshare touts are rife in central and southern Florida throughout the year, where they compete vigorously to induce tourists to attend a 'presentation' (sales pitch) by offering free or reduced tickets to attractions and possibly also a free breakfast if you agree to inspect a timeshare property. If you're tempted to attend a sales pitch (usually lasting at least two hours), you should be aware that you may be subjected to some of the most persuasive, high-pressure sales methods employed anywhere on earth and many people are simply unable to resist (the sales staff are experts). If you do attend, don't take any cash, credit cards or check books with you so you won't be pressured into paying a deposit without thinking it over. However, the good news is that there's a 10-day cooling off period after signing a contract for a timeshare in Florida, during which you can cancel without penalty and have your deposit repaid in full (a refund must be paid within two days of notice of cancelation). **Not surprisingly, many people cancel within the 10-day period after having had time to think it over and away from the high-pressure sales staff.**

It isn't difficult to understand why there are so many timeshare companies and why salespersons often employ such intimidating, hard-sell methods. A week's timeshare in an apartment worth around $60,000 to $75,000 can be sold for up to $10,000, making a total income of some $500,000 for the timeshare company if they sell 50 weeks (at least six times the market value of the property!), plus management and other fees. **Most property experts believe that there's little or no advantage in a timeshare over a normal holiday rental and that it's simply an expensive way to pay for your holidays in advance.** It doesn't make any sense to tie up your money for what amounts to a long term reservation on an annual holiday. Often you aren't even buying anything and have no freehold title in perpetuity, but are simply leasing an apartment and paying your rent for years in advance. Often timeshares are difficult or impossible to sell at any price and 'pledges' from timeshare companies to sell them for you or buy them back (a buy-back 'guarantee') at the market price are usually just a sales ploy, as companies aren't usually interested once they have made a sale.

Top-quality timeshares usually cost around $10,000 for one week in a one or two-bedroom apartment in a top-rated resort at a peak period, to which must be added annual management fees, e.g. $200 to $300 or more for each week, and other miscellaneous charges. Timeshares can also be bought on the instalment plan, e.g. $150 per month for five years (total $9,000). Don't be taken in by discounts and 'once-in-a-lifetime' special offers or a special reduction 'because the salesman has a relative in your home country'. These are all sale's ploys which confirm that you can drive a hard bargain if you really want to buy. Most financial advisers believe that you're better off putting your money into a long term investment, where you retain your capital and may even earn sufficient interest to pay for a few weeks' holiday each year. If you wish to buy a timeshare, it's best to buy a resale privately from an existing owner or a timeshare resale broker, which sell for a fraction of the original cost. When buying privately you can usually drive a hard bargain and may even get a timeshare 'free' simply by assuming the current owner's maintenance contract. **Note that there's no real resale market for timeshares and if you need to sell you're highly unlikely to get your money back.**

Co-Ownership: Co-Ownership includes schemes such as a consortium of buyers owning shares in a property-owning company and co-ownership between family, friends or even strangers (some builders and developers offer this option). A common deal is a 'four-owner' scheme (which is usually the maximum recommended number of co-owners), where you buy a quarter of a property and can occupy it for up to three months a year. Owners don't need to have equal shares and can all be made direct title holders. Some developers offer a turn-key deal where a home is fully furnished and equipped and a car is provided for the owners' use. Co-ownership can be a good choice for a family seeking a holiday home for a few weeks or months a year and has the added advantage that (because of the lower cost) a mortgage may not be necessary. Note that it's cheaper to buy a property privately with friends than through a developer, when you may pay well above the market price for a share of a property (check the market value of a property to establish whether the share is good value). **Co-ownership is much (much) better value than a timeshare and needn't cost much more.** Note, however, that a water-tight contract must be drawn up by an experienced lawyer to protect your interests.

The **Holiday Property Bond** is a good alternative to timesharing for those with a minimum of £2,000 to invest. Holiday Property Bond (operated by Villa Owners Club Ltd., HPB House, Newmarket, Suffolk CB8 7BR, UK, tel. 01638-660066) own over 600 properties in some 10 countries, including Florida. Each £1 invested is equal to one point and each week's stay in each property is assigned a points rating depending on its size, location and the time of year. There are no extra fees apart from a 'user' charge when occupying a property to cover cleaning and utility costs. Furthermore, there's a buy-back guarantee after two years, when an investment can be sold at the current market value.

REAL ESTATE AGENTS & BROKERS

Most people in Florida buy and sell their homes through real estate agents, brokers or realtors, who must be licensed by the Florida Real Estate Commission (FREC). In Florida, you should do business only with a licensed agent or broker, preferably one who's a member of a professional organization. Monies (such as deposits) must be paid only into an escrow (trust) account held by a licensed broker. Note that the terms 'agent', 'broker' and 'realtor' are used variously (in this section and throughout this book) to refer to real estate sales professionals, licensed to practice in the state of Florida.

Under Florida law anyone who advertises, buys or sells real estate must be licensed, although this doesn't prevent a few crooks from trying to make a fast buck. Note, however, that an 'agent' who's on a salary and employed by a single builder or developer needn't be licensed. Many overseas buyers use agents and brokers based in their home countries. These 'agents' aren't usually licensed in Florida and aren't permitted to take clients to Florida unless they're working with a licensed Florida-based agent (if they do and you have a problem, you will have no redress under Florida law). A real estate broker is a professional who's licensed by the state of Florida. A real estate salesperson is also licensed by the state under the title of either real estate salesperson or real estate broker-salesperson (someone who has passed the broker's examination, but chooses to work for another licensed broker). Always ask to see a broker's license as licensed brokers are covered by a state-run 'errors and omissions' insurance scheme to compensate buyers (up to a maximum of $50,000) who lose money as a result of a broker's actions. All licensed agents must conform to a code of practice established by the Florida Real Estate Commission (FREC), 400 W. Robinson Street, PO Box 1900, Orlando, FL 32802 (tel. 407/423-6071). If you have a genuine grievance against an agent, simply threatening to report him to the FREC should help get it resolved.

Realtors: An agent or broker with the title 'realtor' (a registered term) is a member of a local real estate board that has an affiliation with the National Association of Realtors (NAR), the largest and most respected national organization for brokers, or the Florida Association of Realtors (7025 Augusta National Drive, PO Box 725025, Orlando, FL 32822-5017, tel. 407/438-1400). Realtors subscribe to the NAR's code of ethics and must have completed a course of study. Note, however, that because an agent or broker doesn't belong to a professional organization it doesn't mean that he's any less qualified or competent to perform real estate services for you. However, although real estate agents can be licensed to sell real estate, they aren't bound by a code of ethics. If you have a problem with an agent or broker who's a member of NAR or another professional organization you have a better chance of satisfactory redress. If a broker contravenes the code or acts in an unprofessional manner he risks losing his license and having to reimburse a buyer for any losses incurred because of his actions. You can file complaints against a realtor in the same way as you can against a lawyer or other professional. A 'realtist' is a member of the National Association of Real Estate Brokers, which also sets professional standards and has a code of ethics for members.

Buyer's Brokers: Many experts recommend that buyers always employ an agent or broker as a buyer's broker (some individual brokers and companies conduct business exclusively as buyer's brokers), which ensures that there isn't a potential conflict of interest. Otherwise a broker could also be acting as the seller's broker, although this would be illegal without disclosure. A buyer's broker will negotiate the price, terms and conditions of a purchase, and will analyze market data to insure a low offer price (taking into account the weaknesses and strengths of a property). A broker who conducts business exclusively as a buyer's broker doesn't take listings from sellers or other agents. There are a variety of fee arrangements depending on the particular broker. A common arrangement, and the best for a buyer, is for the broker to charge the buyer nothing and to negotiate with the seller or his broker to split the seller's commission. Some buyer's brokers charge their clients a fee as a retainer. Note that buying a new home through a broker is usually better than buying direct from a builder or developer as it provides important extra safeguards and costs you nothing. Buyer's brokers advertise in the local Yellow Pages, in the 'Homes for Sale' classified ads in newspapers and magazines, and in the publications listed in **Appendix A**.

Agency Contracts: Since 1995 there have been three types of real estate contracts in Florida:

- **Single Agency:** An agent is employed solely by either the buyer (buyer's agent) or seller (seller's agent).

- **Dual Agency:** An agent works for both the buyer and seller.

- **Transactional Agency:** An agent is directly employed by neither the buyer or seller, but is an intermediary employed to ensure that all necessary documents are provided to complete the transaction.

Under Florida law a broker must disclose in writing whether he is acting as a single or dual agency or as a transactional broker. A broker acting for a buyer or seller must, by law, disclose all relevant information to his client, while a transactional broker, although having a duty of honesty and fair dealing, does not. As a dual agent a broker must give full disclosure to both parties, although few brokers offer this option. Therefore if you're buying you should engage a buyer's broker who's acting for you only and owes a duty to obtain the best price and terms solely for you, the buyer. Similarly, if you're selling you should employ a seller's agent who has only your best interests in mind.

Choosing a Broker: There are many ways to find a broker including asking lenders, lawyers and other professionals, and calling the local real estate board and obtaining the names of the local 'highest achievers' or the local 'realtor of the year'. You may also wish to contact existing foreign owners and ask them for their recommendations. Note that if you have a special property in mind such as a business or farm, it's advisable to choose an agency or broker specializing in that sort of property. It will come as no surprise to most people to learn that according to the Consumer Federation of America (CFA), many homebuyers using real estate agents are unrepresented and overcharged.

Be particularly wary of agents who try to sell you something outside your price range or properties which don't match your specifications. If an agent tries to dictate to you or argue about an offer, go elsewhere. An agent must, by law, forward all offers to a seller, no matter how low, and if he refuses you can complain to the Florida Real Estate Commission (FREC). Always be cautious about what you say to an agent who's working for the seller, as by law he must report everything you say if you make an enquiry or offer. Naturally you must never tell an agent your highest price or how high you're willing to bid on a particular property.

Commission: Agents usually receive a 5 to 7 per cent commission (average 6 per cent) on sales, although this may be negotiable, particularly when market conditions favor the seller's position. When both buying and selling brokers are involved, they will split the commission. Note that it's illegal for a broker to offer to pay you a part of his commission as an inducement to buy. You must never pay an agent in advance, as commission is paid only on the successful completion of a purchase at the closing (see page 164).

Listings: Most agents use a multiple listing service (MLS), which is a broker information network that publicizes homes for sale, where the selling agent splits the commission with the agent who finds a buyer. Most homes are multiple listings and therefore most agents offer the same properties for sale. It's possible for prospective buyers to obtain a list of all homes fitting a particular description, (e.g. three bedrooms, two bathrooms, double garage and pool), for a certain price (e.g. between $100,000 and $125,000) in a particular area or town. Lists may be updated daily. However, some properties have a so-called 'exclusive' listing, which means that a property is listed with one agent only and prospective buyers must deal with this agent. Note that agents are naturally biased towards their own listings because they don't need to split the commission with another agent. If you view a property with one agent, you aren't permitted to buy it through another agent without paying the commission of the first agent.

Buying Direct From The Owner: Around 25 per cent of homes sold in the US are sold direct by owners without using the services of an agent or broker. This saves owners $thousands in agent's fees, part or all of which they may pass on to the buyer. It's particularly recommended when you're selling an attractive home at a *realistic* price. **However, when buying direct from the owner, you should always use the**

services of a lawyer, an appraiser (if necessary) and have a home inspection on a resale home, before going through with a deal.

HOME INSPECTIONS & SURVEYS

When you have found a property that you like, you should make a close inspection of its condition. Obviously this will depend on its age and whether it has been restored or renovated, called remodeling (see page 165) in the US, or is a new property. A common problem with a remodeled home is that you don't usually know how well work has been carried out, particularly if the previous owner did it himself. If work has been done by a professional builder, you should ask to see the bills and check whether there's a warranty. Note that a seller has a duty under Florida law to inform you of any defects which aren't readily apparent and which materially affect the value of a property (which should be in writing). Note, however, that a seller may be able to deny any knowledge of a problem after the sale and it could be costly or impossible to prove otherwise.

Some simple checks you can do yourself include testing the electrical system, plumbing, mains water, hot water boiler, central heating and air-conditioning. Don't assume that these are functional, but check them for yourself. If a property doesn't have electricity, mains gas, mains water, or a telephone link, check the nearest connection point and the cost of extending the service to the property. If a home has a well and septic tank, you should have them tested. An older building may show visible signs of damage and decay, such as bulging or cracked walls, rising damp, missing roof slates and rotten woodwork. Some areas are prone to flooding, severe storms (e.g. hurricanes) and subsidence. It's advisable to check an older property after a heavy rainfall, when any leaks should come to light.

The whole of Florida is infested with wood-boring insects such as subterranean termites, dry wood termites and powder post beetles, which can do thousands of dollars worth of damage. You should always have a termite inspection on a resale property in Florida and the soil on a new house site must be treated against insect and vermin infestations. You may also be advised to have a radon test if a property is in an area susceptible to high levels of radon (a naturally occurring radioactive gas which can cause cancer). If you find or suspect problems, you should have a full home inspection carried out, which is always advisable for a resale property. Many older properties were built with inferior materials and common problems include rusting lead water pipes; asbestos; poor wiring; defective plumbing and drains; lead-based paint (which is poisonous and now banned); rising damp; dry and wet rot; uneven flooring; collapsing facades; subsidence; woodworm and termites; bulging walls; and cracked internal and external walls. Serious problems are often found in properties built in the boom years of the 1980s and can even be found in properties less than five years old. Generally if you would have a home inspection carried out if you were buying the same property in your home country, then you should have one done in Florida.

Some experts even recommend a home inspection on a new property with a warranty, as some builders occasionally use short cuts and inferior materials which can lead to problems later. Alternatively you could hire a contractor, architect, engineer or other expert to check a building during construction to ensure that the building code has been met. You shouldn't assume that everything is okay as shoddy workmanship and violations of the building code are fairly common in Florida. The good news is that with a new home you do at least have a warranty (see page 138).

Home inspections aren't usually performed prior to signing a contract in Florida, and therefore if you decide to have an inspection done you *must* make the purchase contract contingent on a satisfactory report. If serious faults are revealed the inspection contingency clause (see page 162) allows you to obtain compensation for any work necessary or to cancel the contract and have your deposit returned. The contract should state who will pay for the inspection and any necessary repairs, although the inspector should *always* be working solely for (and under the instructions of) the buyer.

Always discuss with an inspector exactly what will be included in the inspection, and most importantly, what will be excluded (you may need to pay extra to include certain checks and tests). A general inspection should include the structural condition of all buildings (particularly foundations, roofs, walls and woodwork); plumbing, electrical, heating and air-conditioning systems; and anything else you want inspected such as a swimming pool and its equipment (e.g. filter system or heating). A home inspection can be limited to a few items or even a single system only, such as the electrical wiring or plumbing in an old house. The average home inspection costs $250 to $500, which is small price to pay when tens of thousands of dollars are at risk.

Always use a certified and licensed professional inspector who's a member of the American Society of Home Inspectors (tel. 202/842-3096) or another professional organization. Whoever you employ, you should ensure that he's experienced in the idiosyncracies of local properties and that he has professional indemnity insurance (which means you can confidently sue him if he does a bad job!). Most companies provide a comprehensive one-year warranty. You should receive a written report on the structural condition of a house, including anything that could become a problem in the future. Some experts recommend that you accompany the inspector, who may produce a video film of his findings in addition to a written report.

Surveys: Before buying a single-family home on its own lot you should walk the boundaries and look for fences, driveways, roads, and the overhanging eaves of buildings that might be encroaching upon the property. If you're uncertain about a property's boundaries or that of a neighboring property, you should have a survey done. A survey usually applies to unplatted land and provides that the lot on which a property is built is substantially as stated in terms of its size and location. It's also intended to reveal any encroachments by neighboring buildings or the shifting of boundary markers.

GARAGES & PARKING

A garage or private parking space may not be provided when you buy an apartment or townhouse, although there's usually a general parking lot for both residents and visitors. Single-family homes always have a car port or garage for one or more cars. Smaller or older homes may have a single car port or garage only, while larger homes often have garaging for up to four cars. Note that because of the absence of basements in Florida homes, the garage usually doubles as a storage area and workshop, and may also house the laundry room. Garages are usually an integral part of a house, with direct access to first (ground) floor rooms (detached garages are rare). New homes and apartment buildings usually have adequate parking for both residents and visitors (over 75 per cent of new homes have a two-car or larger garage).

When buying a property (whether it's an apartment, townhouse or a single-family home) the cost almost always includes the garage or garage space (if applicable), which isn't sold separately as in some countries. If you wish to live in a city center, it may be difficult to find an apartment or townhouse with a garage or parking space, although high-rise apartment blocks usually have underground parking lots where spaces are allocated to owners. A private lock-up garage is useful, particularly in areas with a high incidence of car theft, e.g. most cities. Free on-street parking may be difficult or impossible to find in cities and in any case isn't advisable for anything but a wreck.

CONVEYANCING

Conveyancing is the legal term for processing the paperwork associated with transferring the deeds of ownership of a property (a conveyance is a deed or legal document which conveys a house from the seller to the buyer, thereby transferring ownership). In Florida conveyancing usually comes under the heading of title services, which are provided by lawyers or more often by title insurance companies. The title company examines the public records to ensure that the seller owns the property, after which they issue a commitment that insures the property against a third party making a claim to it apart from the exceptions stated in the title policy.

Unlike in most other countries, the vast majority of home sales in Florida are completed without the direct involvement of a lawyer (with the exception of lawyers acting on behalf of title companies). However, the proving of the title, which usually takes 30 to 60 days, can be performed by a lawyer who's regulated by the Florida Bar Association and licensed to do conveyancing for property transactions. A lawyer may also be a title agent for the purpose of issuing land title insurance. If you engage a lawyer, it's advisable to hire one who's a title insurance agent, in which case he can examine the abstract and do a title examination himself (see page 156). Fees charged by title companies or lawyers include title certification, document preparation, closing and notary fees (a notary may be required to witness signatures on some closing documents). Before hiring a company, compare the fees charged by a number of companies. A lawyer or title insurance company should check the following:

- That a property belongs to the seller or that he has legal authority from the owner to sell it;

- That there are no pre-emption rights or restrictive covenants over a property (such as rights of way) and that there are no plans to construct anything which would adversely affect the value, enjoyment or use of the property such as roads, railway lines, airports, shops, factories or any other development. Note that a lawyer may check only planned developments directly affecting the property itself and not those that might affect its value, such as a new railway line or freeway in the vicinity. Obviously a new freeway or railway that disturbs the peace of your home will be something of a disaster, although on the other hand, a new freeway junction or railway station within a few miles may enhance its value considerably. The local planning department can tell you whether there are any plans for major development or public works in an area. Your lawyer should check the land use and zoning ordnance maps for the surrounding area and what (if anything) can be built there, for example whether an apartment building, supermarket, gas station or factory can be built alongside a single-family house. You can find out who issues building permits from the building department at the local city hall or county administration building.

- Whether the land has been registered at the local land registry and a new property has the necessary building permits and planning permission (and that they are genuine), and that a building was built in accordance with such plans. All building work must comply with the Florida building code and be approved by a county inspector. If alterations or improvements have been made to a property, any necessary planning permission should have been granted.

- That there are no encumbrances or liens, e.g. mortgages or loans, against the property or any outstanding debts such as property taxes, community charges, electricity, gas, water/sewerage, telephone or any other debts. **Note that certain unpaid debts on a property are usually inherited by the buyer. For example, if there's an outstanding loan or taxes on a property, the lender or local authority has first claim on the property and has the right to foreclose on a property and sell it to recover the debt.**

- Ensuring that a proper title is obtained and arranging the necessary registration of ownership. A lender will insist on title insurance to protect his interests. It's also advisable (but not a legal requirement in Florida) for a buyer to have owner's title insurance to protect against a future claim on the title by a third party. A title insurance policy issued to the lender *doesn't* protect the buyer. Compare rates charged by various title insurance companies and check any limitations on cover when comparing fees. If a home has changed hands within the last few years it may be unnecessary to do a full title search and you may be able to get the company which issued the existing policy to issue a new policy at a lower 're-issue' rate. A survey (see page 154) may be necessary to verify a property's boundaries as detailed in the title, although it may be possible to get an updated document from the surveyor who carried out the previous survey.

   A title insurance company may issue a summary of their findings a few weeks prior to closing called a 'Commitment to Insure' dossier, listing any defects or liens against a title. This is usually sent to a lender to verify the state of the title until a title insurance policy is issued after closing. The buyer should also receive a copy of the summary so that he can check whether there's anything affecting the title with which he didn't agree when he signed the purchase contract.

The cost of conveyancing for a home in Florida depends on whether you employ a local or overseas lawyer or both. If you employ a foreign-based lawyer, i.e. a lawyer who isn't based in Florida, you can expect to pay heavily for his services, e.g. around £100 an hour in Britain. **Note that while engaging a lawyer based in your home country when buying a home in Florida may provide added peace of mind, you won't usually receive any extra services and will simply pay more.** Most experts believe that when buying property in Florida you should employ the services of an experienced, local lawyer (if you don't speak fluent English, you may be able to engage a lawyer who speaks a language that you speak fluently).

PURCHASE CONTRACTS

A contract to buy real estate in Florida is usually a standard 'Contract for Purchase and Sale of Real Estate' produced by the Florida Association of Realtors and Florida Bar Association. You should be wary if a seller doesn't use the standard contract, which can be tailored to your individual requirements, in which case it's vital to have it checked by a lawyer. Note that if you're entering into an agreement to buy a new home off-plan, a different contract is used to that required to purchase an existing or resale home. The contract sets forth the legal description of the property, the purchase price and the terms of payment. It also includes the time limit within which it must be accepted by the seller and the terms of financing. The contract also provides that the seller proves he owns title to the property and sets forth a closing date (see **Closing** on page 164). It also includes any restrictions on the use of the house and any special clauses affecting the purchase. **Note that verbal agreements aren't enforceable under US law.**

In Florida, a freehold title is usually called a 'fee simple'. When a married couple purchase a property together they own it as joint tenants ('joint tenancy by the entireties') and upon the death of either partner, ownership automatically transfers to the other partner (called the 'right of survivorship') without the need for probate, although there may be tax consequences. You should investigate the consequences of US income, gift and inheritance tax before buying a home in Florida, whether under joint ownership or any other method. Note that if joint ownership is held other than as a husband and wife it becomes a 'tenancy in common' and can have complicated legal ramifications.

Lawyers: It's advisable to have a contract checked by an experienced real estate lawyer, which will cost you around $200 and is worth every penny, if only for the peace of mind it provides. If a lawyer is acting for you as the title agent this should be part of his brief (see page 156). Shop around and compare fees charged by a number of lawyers. Most contracts are fine providing nothing goes wrong, when you're likely to find the odds stacked against you (particularly if you're buying a new home). Most builders hire clever lawyers to write contracts that limit your rights and their liability, and some contracts are so biased that they're actually illegal! **Note that in order to avoid possible conflicts of interest, you should never hire a lawyer who's acting for any other parties in a property transaction.**

Deposits: Usually a buyer pays an initial 'good faith' or binder deposit, e.g. $1,000 to $5,000, in the form of 'earnest' money, to show that he means business. When buying a new home it's usual to pay a holding deposit of $1,000 to $2,000 to reserve a lot, after which you have 15 days to change your mind before signing the purchase contract. Most agents and builders, not surprisingly, advise prospective buyers to take the binder deposit with them when on an inspection trip. They know only too well that if you're tempted to go away and think about it you may not buy. A deposit paid on an option or reservation contract on a yet to be built property is returnable if you don't proceed. A second deposit of 5 per cent of the purchase price is paid on signing the contract for a new home, with the balance paid in stages or at the closing. When payment is made in stages, the first payment is usually for the lot (land). You should bear in mind that deposits are lost far more frequently in the new home than the resale market. When buying a resale home the deposit is negotiable, although 10 per cent is normal.

The deposit and all other funds must be placed with a neutral third party, called an 'escrow agent', who's usually selected by the buyer's broker, but is subject to approval by all parties. He's responsible for compiling and checking the documents and ensuring that the transaction can 'close' within the escrow period specified in the purchase contract. Once the deal closes, the escrow agent records the deed and disburses the funds to the appropriate parties. When buying a new home, a deposit must *never* be paid into a builder's general operating fund. If you don't complete a purchase you will lose your deposit or can even be forced to go through with a purchase. On the other hand, you can sue the seller if he refuses to go through with a sale. **You should always ensure that you know the terms regarding the forfeiture or reimbursement of a deposit.**

Making an Offer: You should never make a sloppy offer in the expectation that it will be rejected, as if it's accepted many important details may be unresolved or in an ambiguous state. Always make an offer with the expectation that it will be accepted, as when it is you can be legally bound by the terms and details of your offer. All offers should be made in writing and must be signed by all prospective buyers, e.g. a husband

and wife. If the owner rejects it, he may make a counter-offer by changing some of the terms in the contract. Any changes made to a printed contract form must be initialed by all parties and changes instigated by a buyer *must* obviously be made before the form is sent to the seller. This can go on for several rounds until the parties agree or one of them rejects an offer. In some cases it's better to deal directly with a seller and hammer out a deal face to face. Note that if you really want a particular property you must be prepared to haggle. All amendments and clauses to the contract must be agreed before it's signed. Once signed the contract is binding upon all parties and the seller is prohibited from selling the property to a third party while the contract is in force.

Inheritance & Capital Gains Tax: Before registering the title deed for a Florida property, you should carefully consider the tax and inheritance consequences of the person(s) in whose name the deed will be registered. Property can be registered in one name; both names of a couple; joint buyers' names; the name or names of children, giving a surviving parent sole use during his or her lifetime; or in the name of a US or foreign company. **Whatever you decide, it should be done at the time of purchase, as it can be difficult or expensive to change later and may even be impossible.** Consult a lawyer who's experienced in US inheritance law (and gift, estate and capital gains taxes) before signing a contract. See also **Capital Gains Tax** on page 115, **Estate & Gift Tax** on page 117 and **Wills** on page 119.

Company Ownership: If you're a non-resident, owning a Florida property through a foreign company may have significant tax advantages. For example, a sale can be effected simply by transferring the company shares, thus avoiding documentary stamps and recording fees, US Gift and Estate Taxes, US capital gains tax and the 10 per cent withholding (see page 115). However, gift or inheritance tax may apply in the owner's country of residence. Note that a mortgage and title insurance may be more difficult to obtain for a property owned by an offshore company. If a property owned by a foreign company is rented and you choose to pay taxes on a 'net basis' (see page 112), then rental income is subject to US Federal Corporate Income Tax (although it's levied at a low rate and is deductible against federal tax). A foreign company may also be liable to taxation in another country. Buying and owning a Florida property through a foreign company requires expert advice and administration and is generally advisable only for very expensive properties and for individuals whose situation permits them to take maximum advantage of the tax benefits. It involves extra costs, both in setting up the company and in administration and running costs, although the tax advantages can be significant.

Basic Contract Details

The following basic details are contained in all real estate sales contracts:

- **Names of Parties:** A contract contains the names of all the parties to the contract, i.e. the buyers and the sellers. The full names of all the sellers in whose name the title is held and all the buyers (e.g. a husband and wife) must be listed and each person named must sign the contract.

- **Property Description:** The identity of the property, which is its legal description not its address (which may also be included). Properties in subdivided areas (such as municipalities) are described by their lot and block number; the name of the subdivision; and the plat book and page number where there's a graphic description of the property (a plat is a printed survey of an area that has been subdivided by a developer). A property may also be described by metes and bounds, which are surveyor's directions used to mark the boundaries of a property.

- **Purchase Price**: The total purchase price must be listed with a breakdown of where the money will come from, for example the deposit, mortgages (including assumed mortgages), owner financing, and the value of personal property or other real property that's part of the agreement. Assumed mortgages or owner financing must be supported by official documentation.

- **Extras & Options:** Everything that's included in a home purchase must be listed in the contract. This may include both standard items and any extras you have paid for and applies equally to new and resale properties. Personal property which is to be included in a sale may include appliances, furniture, furnishings, pool equipment, garden ornaments, and even shrubs and trees. If you're in doubt whether an item is an integral part of the property or personal property, it's advisable to list it as personal property. Fixtures which are part of the property should also be listed if there's any doubt whether the seller may remove them. When you're buying a new property all standard features and options (and their specific quality or brand names) should be listed in a contract or added as an addendum, whether they are provided 'free' or at an additional cost.

- **Closing Date:** The closing or settlement (see page 164) date must be specified, which is the date when the final documents will be signed, contracts exchanged and the balance of the purchase price paid. The date must allow sufficient time for both parties to perform anything required under the contract and for the buyer to obtain a mortgage (if necessary).

Standard Contract Clauses

Contracts usually include the following standard clauses, some of which may not be applicable. Standard clauses describe the obligations of both the seller and buyer with respect to such things as proof of title; surveying and termite inspection; expenses, fees and taxes; home inspection, maintenance and repair; risk of loss; requirements for escrow; and the closing procedure and place. If a clause involves the services of a third party, it should be stated in the contract who's to pay the fee. The actual content of each clause (and who pays any fees involved) is negotiable between the parties.

- **Acceptance:** The time period, e.g. 14 days, during which the seller must accept or reject an offer.

- **Access:** A contract may include an ingress and egress clause; ingress means that you have access to the property from a public road and egress to the public road from the property. This could be a problem in rural areas when access to a property is via someone else's land.

- **Addendums & Riders:** Some clauses are included in riders or addendums in order to keep the contract as short as possible. However, they must be referred to in the contract and be attached to it. Riders may refer to the withholding of 10 per cent of the price by the buyer in lieu of capital gains tax (see page 115) when the seller is a non-resident of Florida; condominium association rules; a list of items or options included in a sale; and permission to rebuild a property located in a coastal or other sensitive area after its destruction (e.g. by a hurricane).

- **Assignability:** Usually a buyer can assign his rights to a property to a third party, unless otherwise stated in the contract. For example, if you were unable to go through with a purchase after paying a hefty deposit, you could assign your rights to another buyer who would reimburse your deposit.

- **Broker's Commission:** If a broker is involved there should be a clause recognizing his right to a commission, which is signed by the broker's agent and the party who's to pay the broker's commission.

- **Closing Documents:** A list of the documents required for closing, who's to provide them and, most importantly, who's to pay for their preparation. Usually the seller pays for documents that he signs (such as the deed and bill of sale) and the buyer for those he signs, e.g. loan documents.

- **Closing Venue:** The office, e.g. a broker's or lawyer's office, where the closing is to take place.

- **Conveyance:** The contract should state that the seller 'convey the property by statutory warranty deed', which means that the seller owns the property and has the right to sell it. A buyer must *never* accept a quit claim deed instead of a warranty deed, as this merely transfers the seller's interest in the property, which could be zero.

- **Deadline:** A contract may include a 'time is of the essence' clause, which simply means that the failure to meet a deadline stated in the contract is a default of the contract.

- **Deposits:** The escrow agent should verify in the contract the receipt of any monies deposited with him.

- **Easements, Limitations & Restrictions:** A contract should contain a clause stating that there are no easements (third party rights to use or access a property), limitations or other restrictions that would prohibit the use of the property for whatever purposes you have in mind. These may include zoning, building or subdivision restrictions, payment of taxes, assumed or new mortgages, or defects. The contract should require the seller to correct any breaches prior to closing. A survey (see page 154) may be necessary to determine whether a property is free of easements, limitations and restrictions.

- **Inspections & Repairs:** The seller must certify in writing that a property is in good condition and that all equipment is in proper working order. Special facilities or equipment (e.g. a swimming pool) should be specifically mentioned. It's advisable to hire a home inspection company to establish the condition of a property before closing (see page 164).

- **Legal Fees:** There's usually a clause in the contract stating that in the event of a lawsuit over the contract, the winner of the lawsuit can recover his lawyer's fees and legal costs from the loser.

- **Liens:** A property must be free and clear of any liens (debts) at closing and the seller should provide a testimony to this effect.

- **Loss:** The contract should state that the seller bears the risk of loss should the property be damaged or destroyed before closing. You should check the state of the property immediately prior to closing to make sure it hasn't fallen down or been damaged (see **Closing** on page 164).

- **Mortgages:** When the buyer is taking out a mortgage to finance a purchase or assuming the seller's mortgage, the purchase must always be contingent (see below) on obtaining this financing.

- **Occupancy:** Usually a buyer will have sole occupancy of a property after closing. If another agreement is made, for example the seller or a tenant will be permitted to remain after the closing or the buyer is permitted to move in before the closing (which isn't advisable as the contract could be canceled for any number of reasons), this must be included in the contract.

- **Other Agreements:** Contracts usually contain a clause stating that this agreement and no other is the legal agreement between the parties. This nullifies any subsequent claims regarding a previous verbal or written agreement.

- **Payment & Closing:** The contract provides that monies due to the seller (or buyer) be paid in cash or by certified check (e.g. cashier's) at the closing.

- **Payment of Fees & Taxes:** The contract states who pays the transfer taxes and recording fees, which is usually shown on the first page of the contract. The seller usually pays for documentary stamps on the deed and other documents required to transfer clear title, while other documentary stamps for recording and the state intangible tax on a mortgage are normally paid by the buyer.

- **Prorations:** The annual expenses on a property such as property taxes, interest on assumed mortgages, and special assessments are usually divided between the buyer and seller on the day a sale takes place, termed prorating the expenses, or prorations. The daily (or 'per diem') rate is calculated and multiplied by the number of days assigned to each party. The amount due to the buyer, as it's the buyer's responsibility to pay them, is credited to him and deducted from his closing costs.

- **Signatures:** Each party must sign and date the contract. A spouse must sign even when a contract is in the name of the other partner only.

- **Special Assessment Liens:** Any special assessment liens on a property at the time of closing should be paid by the seller, and this should be stated in the contract.

- **Termite Inspection:** You should always have a termite inspection on a resale property in Florida, where it isn't unusual to find termite damage. A termite inspection is often required by lenders. If any damage is discovered, the contract should state that the seller must pay an amount equal to a percentage (e.g. 2 to 5 per cent) of the purchase price to repair the damage. **If this clause is rejected by the seller it should set the alarm bells ringing!**

- **Title:** The seller must prove that he has clear and good title to the property, free from third party claims. He provides his 'Abstract of Title' as proof of ownership, which is a document outlining all deeds and other legal events affecting the property. This may be checked by a lawyer or a 'title company' who will issue 'title insurance' providing it's 'clear', i.e. valid and free of any encumbrances. If you apply for a mortgage your lender will require title insurance to protect his loan, although this *doesn't* protect the buyer. It's always advisable (but not a legal requirement in Florida) for a buyer to have owner's title insurance to protect himself against a claim on the title by a third party. Who pays for the owner's title insurance is usually negotiable.

Contingency Contract Clauses

A contract usually contains a number of conditions, called contingencies or riders, which must be met before it becomes valid and binding. Contingency clauses state that if certain conditions or events aren't met the contract can be suspended or canceled by one or both parties without penalty. Clauses may include deadlines in the contract if the failure to meet them permits cancelation without penalty (otherwise deadlines aren't considered to be contingencies and may result in the loss of a deposit or legal redress). Contingency clauses are designed to permit either party to enter into a contract without being sure that he can do everything necessary to complete the sale (such as obtain a mortgage) or when certain facts won't be known until later, e.g. after a home inspection. Both parties can agree to contract to do anything that's legal and contracts can be contingent on any number of events. The most common contingency clauses include the following:

- **Appraisal:** A lender will make an appraisal (valuation) of a property before agreeing to a loan. The contract must be contingent on the appraisal not being below the agreed purchase price. In certain cases a lender may insist on two appraisals to prevent fraud. An appraisal usually costs between $250 and $300 and is paid by the prospective buyer.

- **Approval by Third Parties:** If either party requires the approval from a third party (perhaps tied to financial assistance), the sale should be contingent on obtaining this approval. For example, a cooperative association may be able to veto a sale or exercise a first right of refusal and a buyer may want to obtain approval from a family member before going ahead.

- **Financing:** This clause is applicable when the buyer needs to obtain a mortgage or to assume a mortgage from the seller. The buyer must usually apply within 7 to 10 days and must be turned down by the lender for the contract to be canceled, i.e. he can't reject a mortgage offer if it meets the criteria stated in the contract. The terms of the financing must be stated, e.g. the amount, term, type of mortgage, maximum interest rate, discount points and monthly payments. The mortgage application must usually be approved within a limited period, e.g. six weeks. This clause must always be present if you require a mortgage, otherwise if you don't get a planned loan you could lose your deposit and be sued for damages or even be forced to go through with a purchase. It isn't advisable to give up your right to obtain a mortgage if there's any possibility that you will need one, because if you change your mind and fail to obtain a mortgage you will lose your deposit.

- **Home Inspection:** When buying a resale home, it's *always* advisable to make a contract contingent on a satisfactory home inspection (see page 154), called a survey in some countries. The inspection can apply to a few items or even a single system only, such as the wiring or plumbing in an old house. The contract should state who should pay for the inspection and any necessary repairs.

- **Sale of Buyer's House:** If you need to sell a home in order to complete a purchase, this *must* be included as a contingency clause in the contract. A seller may be wary of agreeing to this unless the buyer makes some concessions (or the seller is desperate).

- **Survey:** In Florida a survey (see page 154) simply indemnifies a property by reference to a map and its legal description and doesn't refer to an inspection of the buildings located on the land (see **Home Inspections & Surveys** on page 154). It costs around $200 and is usually paid by the buyer.

- **Other Contingencies:** There are numerous other possible contingencies such as a seller needing to remove a tenant before closing, re-zoning for an extension, approval of repairs made by the seller, and proof of certain rights. When buying a community property (see page 144), you may wish to include a clause relating to restrictions and covenants such as those concerning renting, the keeping of pets or visitors. This protects you if you discover a restrictive covenant after signing the contract that would have deterred you from buying.

CLOSING

The final act of a property purchase is the closing or settlement, the date of which is stated in the contract. The closing involves the signing of the deed of sale, transferring legal ownership of a property, and the payment of the balance of the purchase price plus any other payments due, e.g. closing costs, taxes and insurance. The balance of the price after the deposit and any mortgages are subtracted must be paid by the buyer in cash or with a certified or cashier's check. The parties are given a closing statement, e.g. the HUD-1 form approved by the US Department of Housing and Urban Development, which sets out all the costs and fees (see page 137) for which they are responsible.

Before the deed of sale is signed, the closing agent checks that all the conditions contained in the preliminary contract have been fulfilled. The agent collects any fees or taxes due, witnesses the signing of the deed and arranges for its registration (in the name of the new owner) at the local property register. **He doesn't, however, verify or guarantee the accuracy of statements made in a contract or protect you against fraud.** The closing agent may issue other documents including an IRS form 1099 to the sellers (to declare their sale) - or a *Sale or Exchange of Principal Residence* (form 2119). The buyers and sellers are required to sign a state tax return (DR-219) confirming that the documentary stamps have been paid on the sale. If applicable, the seller will need to sign a certificate stating that he isn't a non-resident alien for the purpose of US income tax, otherwise 10 per cent of the sale price must be withheld by the closing agent against a possible capital gains tax liability (see page 115) under the Foreign Investment in Real Property Tax Act (FIRPTA).

Final Check: Property is sold subject to the condition that it's accepted in the state it's in at the time of closing, therefore you should be aware of anything that occurs between signing the contract and closing. Before signing the deed of sale, it's *imperative* to check that the property hasn't fallen down or been damaged in any way, e.g. by a storm or the previous owners. If you have employed a broker he should accompany you on this visit (failing that, take your lawyer). You should also do a final inventory immediately prior to closing (the previous owner should have already vacated the property) to ensure that the seller hasn't absconded with anything that was included in the price.

You should have an inventory of the fixtures and fittings and anything that was included in the contract or paid for separately, e.g. carpets, light fittings, curtains or kitchen appliances, and check that they are present and in good working order. This is particularly important if furniture and furnishings (and major appliances) were included in the price. You should also ensure that expensive items (such as kitchen apparatus) haven't been substituted by inferior (possibly secondhand) items.

If you find anything is missing, damaged or isn't in working order you should make a note and insist on immediate restitution or an appropriate reduction in the amount to be paid. In such cases it's normal for the closing agent to withhold an appropriate amount in escrow from the seller's proceeds to pay for repairs (etc.) or replacements. **You should refuse to go through with the closing if you aren't completely satisfied as it will be difficult or impossible to obtain satisfaction later.** If it isn't possible to complete the closing, you should contact a real estate lawyer about your rights and the return of a deposit and any other funds already paid.

Overseas Buyers: It's usual for both parties to be present when the deed of sale is read, signed and witnessed, although it's possible to give a US representative power of attorney (proxy). This is quite common for foreign buyers and can be arranged by your broker, builder or lawyer. It's usually necessary for an overseas buyer to sign certain documents in the presence of a notary who will witness his signature. There are US authorized notaries in most countries (contact your nearest US consulate or embassy for information). There are also US lawyers in many countries, although (if possible) you should choose one who's licensed to practice in Florida and has experience of Florida property law. If you need to send documents to Florida from overseas, you should always use a courier company such as Federal Express or DHL. On the other hand if you have any questions you should fax them to Florida rather than waste money on expensive telephone calls.

Registration: After the deed of sale has been signed by the closing agent he will give you a certified copy. A notarized copy is lodged at the county property registry office and the new owner's name is entered on the registry deed. **Note that only when the deed is registered do you become the legal owner of the property.** Following registration, the original deeds are retained by the lender until a mortgage is paid off or are returned to the owner.

REMODELING

Remodeling (or rehabilitation) is the name used in the US for modernization, renovation and restoration of a property. Although there are few really old properties in Florida requiring total restoration, many older properties require some sort of renovation or modernization. It's generally recognized in Florida that a new home will require remodeling after 25 to 30 years. It's possible to save money when buying a home that needs some work, particularly if you're a keen do-it-yourself fan. The most common renovations include timber treatment, new windows and doors, landscaping, a new roof or repairs, a modern kitchen, adding a new or additional bathroom, re-wiring, central heating and air-conditioning, new carpets, and painting and decorating. Buildings with seriously defective foundations or walls are best avoided, as it's usually cheaper to demolish them and erect a totally new building! If a property doesn't have electricity, mains gas or water, or a telephone link, check the nearest connection points and the cost of extending the service to the property, which can be expensive.

Before buying a home needing remodeling, it's advisable to employ a home inspector to provide a detailed estimate of the cost of repairs. Use the market price of a similar home in good condition as a guide and total all the costs involved in the remodeling to get an accurate assessment of what you should pay. Note that spending an extravagant amount on remodeling may not be reflected in a home's market value and it may be impossible to recoup the expenditure when you sell. Before making a capital improvement it's advisable to consider how a property will be viewed on the resale market and how long you intend to own it. You should only make improvements if the cost will be recouped in your family's enjoyment or on resale. Remodeling costs can usually be offset against income tax payable on rental income (see **Taxation of Rental Income** on page 112) and against capital gains tax when selling a property.

One of the first decisions you need to make regarding restoration or modernization is whether to do all or some of the work yourself or have it done by local contractors. You shouldn't tackle jobs yourself unless you're sure that you're doing them correctly.

When renovations and 'improvements' have been botched, there's often little that can be done except to start again from scratch. It's important not to over-modernize an old period property, so that too much of its natural charm and attraction is lost (it may also be illegal to change the character or outward appearance of an old home). If the modernization of an old property involves making external alterations such as building an extension you will need planning permission and a building permit from the local town hall (which may also be necessary to install larger windows or new doorways). **You should never start any building work before you have official permission in writing.** Note that if you want to remodel a community property such as a condo, you will need to check the covenants, conditions and restrictions (CC&Rs) of the condominium association. All home improvements must comply with the Florida building code.

The home repair and improvement business in Florida is fraught with scams (cons) and shoddy workmanship and is second only to auto repairs in the number of complaints it generates. There are both federal and state laws governing the work of contractors and contracts for home repairs, although they are little consolation if you get into a dispute, which could drag on for years and end in disappointment. However, a law introduced in 1993 established a compensation fund to meet claims of up to $25,000 when a dispute can't be resolved through the courts. Before hiring anyone you should obtain recommendations from local people you can trust, e.g. a real estate broker, lawyer or a neighbor. You can also contact the local Chamber of Commerce for a list of contractors and check with the local Better Business Bureau or Office of Consumer Affairs whether any complaints have been recorded against a particular contractor. Ask a contractor for the names of satisfied customers (but check that they aren't relations) and question them about the work done. **Although they are difficult to find, a good contractor is worth his weight in gold!**

You should obtain written quotations from *at least* two contractors before hiring anyone. Note that for estimates to be accurate, you must describe in detail the work required, e.g. for electrical work this would include the number of lights, points and switches, and the quality of materials to be used. If you have only a vague idea of what you want, you will receive a vague and unreliable estimate. Make sure that an estimate includes everything you want done. You may have to pay for a detailed estimate, although the cost should be reimbursed by a contractor if he's awarded the contract. If you change the specifications after work has started, you should renegotiate the price, otherwise you may get a shock when you receive the final bill. Look out for any terms in an estimate that allow the price to be increased for inflation or a general rise in prices, and check whether a quotation is definitive or provisional, i.e. dependent on further exploratory work. It's advisable to have a contract checked by a lawyer.

Other things you should check include whether a contractor is state licensed (imperative, where applicable); provides a performance bond guaranteeing satisfaction; has third party insurance (to protect your home and contents) and worker's compensation insurance; belongs to a trade association; or offers a warranty. Many businesses are required to be licensed and bonded. **Beware of employing a company that employs sub-contractors (e.g. to build a swimming pool), as if the company goes broke before paying the sub-contractor, you must pay again!** You shouldn't pay for a job in advance (apart from a small deposit) and should agree a stage payment schedule for a large job. If you have work done on a home while you're absent from Florida, you should appoint a 'clerk of works' (e.g. an architect or builder) to oversee it, otherwise it could drag on for months or even be left half-finished.

It's possible to obtain a mortgage which includes the cost of remodeling. For example, the Federal Housing Administration (FHA) offers a special program (203k) whereby owners can secure a single loan to finance both the purchase and remodeling of a property. Home improvement loans are also available from banks and savings and loan associations, and contractors may also offer loans, although they may not apply to non-residents.

MOVING HOUSE

If you're moving to Florida from abroad, it usually takes from four to eight weeks to have your personal effects shipped, depending on the distance and route. It's advisable to obtain at least three written quotations before committing yourself. Moving companies or movers (in the US movers are never called removals or removal men, who are undertakers!) usually send a representative to provide a detailed estimate. Most companies charge by the cubic foot and will pack your belongings and provide packing cases and special containers, although this is naturally more expensive than packing them yourself. Ask a company how they pack fragile and valuable items, and whether the cost of packing cases, materials and insurance (see below) are included in the quotation. If you're packing yourself, most shipping companies will provide packing crates and boxes. If you're moving within the continental US it's advisable to use a member of the American Movers Conference, 2200 Mill Road, Alexandria, VA 22314, who publish a number of free leaflets.

For international moves, it's best to use a shipping company that's a member of the International Federation of Furniture Removers (FIDI), the Overseas Moving Network Inc. (OMNI) or the Association of International Removers Ltd. Members usually subscribe to a payment guarantee or bond scheme, so that if a member company fails to fulfill its obligations to a customer the contract will be completed at the agreed cost by another company or your money will be refunded. Make a complete list of everything to be shipped and give a copy to the shipping company. Don't include anything illegal (e.g. guns, bombs, drugs, pornographic materials, etc.) with your belongings as customs checks can be rigorous and penalties severe. It's also pointless shipping obsolete items such as 220V electrical apparatus (Florida has a 110V system), TVs (see page 72) and wardrobes (most American homes have walk-in closets). Give your shipping company a telephone number and an address in the US, where you can be contacted. **Fully insure your belongings with a well established insurance company during shipment or while they are in storage (warehouses have been known to burn down!). Around 50 per cent of all moves result in some damage to possessions!** It may not be wise to use a moving company's insurance policy as this may limit their liability to a paltry sum. It's advisable to make a photographic or video record of any valuables for insurance purposes. If your stay in Florida will be for a limited period, it may be wise to leave your most valued possessions at home (e.g. with relatives or friends), particularly if their insured value wouldn't provide adequate compensation for their loss or damage. Unless you're trying to save money, it's advisable to use a major shipping company with a good reputation and to always use a specialist company for international moves. If there are any breakages or damaged items, these must be noted and listed before you sign the delivery bill. If you need to make a claim, be sure to read the small print. Claims must usually be made within a limited period, sometimes within a few days, and be sent by registered mail.

For house moves within the US you can rent a van or truck by the hour, half-day, or day, and many people moving personal effects only rent a 'U-Haul' trailer ('Make Moving an Adventure'). Many transport companies sell packing boxes in various sizes and rent or sell house moving equipment (trolleys, straps, boxes, etc.), for those who feel up to doing their own move. See also the **Checklist** on page 195 and **Customs** on page 191.

MOVING IN

One of the most important tasks to perform after moving into a new home (rented or purchased) is to make an inventory of the fixtures, fittings and, if applicable, the furniture and furnishings. If you have bought a property, you should check that the previous owners haven't absconded with any fixtures and fittings which were included in the contract or anything which you specifically paid for, e.g. carpets, light fittings, curtains, cabinets, kitchen appliances, garden ornaments, plants, doors or walls. It's common to do a final check or inventory, called a 'walk-thru', when buying a new property, which is usually done a few weeks before closing. If you discover defects or missing items after the closing you may have a case for fraud if the property was misrepresented by the seller or agent. Make a note of everything that was said and take legal advice from a real estate lawyer. You can also make a complaint to an agent's professional association (if applicable) and the Florida Real Estate Commission (FREC).

One of the most important tasks on moving into a rented home is to complete an inventory of the contents and a report of its condition. This includes the condition of fixtures and fittings, the state of furniture and furnishings, the cleanliness and state of the decoration, and anything damaged, missing or in need of repair. An inventory may be provided by your landlord or agent and may include every single item in a furnished property (down to the number of teaspoons). The inventory check should be carried out in your presence, both when taking over and when terminating a rental agreement. If it isn't provided by your landlord, you should make your own inventory and ask a witness and your landlord to sign it. Note the reading on your utility meters (e.g. electricity, gas, water) and check that you aren't overcharged on your first bill. The meters should be read by utility companies before you move in, which you may have to organize yourself.

It's advisable to get written instructions from the previous owner about the operation of appliances and heating and air-conditioning systems; maintenance of grounds, yard and lawns; care of special surfaces such as wooden floors; and the names of reliable local handymen who know a property and its quirks. Check with your local town hall regarding local regulations about such things as recycling, parking, and the upkeep of your yard, drive and front lawns (if you don't cut the grass your local authority may do it for you and send you a bill). Many communities have local regulations requiring owners to maintain buildings in good condition and paint them regularly. The storage of vehicles, trailers and boats, and the erection of fences and sheds is usually strictly controlled.

HOME SECURITY

When moving into a new or resale home, it's often advisable to replace the locks (or lock barrels) as soon as possible and fit high security (double cylinder or dead bolt) locks, as you have no idea how many keys are in circulation for the existing locks (builders often give keys to a number of sub-contractors). In any case it's advisable to change the external locks or lock barrels (called re-keying and costing $15 to $20) regularly, e.g. annually, particularly if you rent a home. You may wish to have an alarm system fitted, which is usually the best way to deter thieves and could also reduce your homeowner's insurance premium (see page 59). It costs around $500 for a system including all external doors and windows, internal infra-red security beams, numerically coded keypad entry (which can be frequently changed and is useful for clients if you rent) and 24-hour monitoring. Many towns operate 'crime watch' or 'neighborhood watch' areas, where residents keep a look out for suspicious characters and report them to the local police.

Note that many door locks in the US don't lock automatically and you need a key to lock as well as open them. Patios are usually protected by security pins, which must be secured at night and when a home is unoccupied, as must all windows. Most outside doors, particularly apartment doors in major cities, are fitted with spy-holes and chains so that you can check the identity of a visitor before opening (or completely opening) the door. Inside doors often have locks that are operated by pressing and/or twisting a button on the center of the door knob or by pushing or twisting the knob itself (these locks should be replaced if found on outside doors, as they are insecure). However, no matter how secure your door and window locks, a thief can usually obtain entry if he's sufficiently determined, often by simply smashing a window (although you can fit unbreakable glass or external steel security blinds). You can deter thieves by ensuring that your house is always well lit, particularly when no one is at home, when it's wise to leave a TV or radio on (a timer switch can be used to randomly switch on and off radios, TVs and lights). If you have a single-family home, you should install external 'motion detector' lights.

Most security companies provide home security systems connected to a central monitoring station. When a sensor, e.g. smoke or forced entry, detects an emergency or a panic button is pushed, a signal is sent automatically to a 24-hour monitoring station. **Remember, prevention is better than cure as people who are burgled rarely recover their property.** See also **Crime** on page 75.

If you lock yourself out of your home (or car) there's usually a local locksmith on emergency call day and night to help you. However, if you live in a small community it's advisable to call the local police, who may help you free of charge. A locksmith's services are expensive and it may be cheaper to break a window to gain entry to your home (but difficult if you live on the 39th floor!). If you vacate an apartment or townhouse for an extended period, it may be obligatory to notify your community association or insurance company, and to leave a key with the building superintendent or caretaker in case of emergencies.

UTILITIES

Electricity, gas and water companies in the US are called 'utility' companies (see also **Telephone** on page 25), and are owned by private companies, local municipalities or the federal government (there are also cooperatives in some rural areas). Because utility companies are monopolies, state governments have established public utility or public service commissions (PUCs or PSCs) to set rates and regulate their operation in accordance with state law. In many cities and regions you may be billed for both electricity and gas (and water) by the same utility company or by your municipality. However, electricity, gas and water bills are always itemized separately.

You should apply in person to utility companies to have your electricity, gas or water service switched on, sometimes called an 'initiate application' (take with you proof of ownership or lease and a photo ID, such as a passport or driver's license). You may be required to pay a security deposit, depending on your credit history. When payable, a deposit may vary depending on the size of the property, but is typically $100 for electricity and around $60 for gas and water. Deposits are usually held in an interest-earning escrow account. A deposit may be returned after you have been billed for a number of consecutive billing cycles or have paid your bills promptly for a year or two. When moving into a property there's a 'start-up' (connection) fee to switch on the service (e.g. $10 to $25) and read the meter, which is included in your first bill. You must contact your electricity, gas and water companies (usually at least 48 hours in advance) to get a final meter reading and bill when vacating a property.

Electricity and gas meters are read and customers billed monthly in most areas, although billing is bi-monthly or even quarterly in some areas (the number of billing days is shown on the bill). Bills include a service or customer charge, e.g. $3 to $5 per month. If a meter reader is unable to read your meter, you will receive an estimated bill, usually denoted by 'EST', 'Avg' or 'A'. A utility company may send out a revised bill based on a meter reading provided by the householder. State regulations require at least one actual reading a year. You're usually given 14 to 28 days in which to pay a bill before it becomes overdue. If you miss paying a bill (or your payment arrives after the due date) it will be added to your next bill and you may be charged a late payment penalty. If you don't pay a utility bill, you will eventually receive a 'notice of discontinuation of service', when you should pay the bill within the period stated, e.g. 15 days, even if you dispute the amount. Utility companies are required by law to give adequate notice and a hearing before they can terminate your service, and there are strict laws regulating all utilities.

Your utility company may offer a 'levelized billing' or 'budget' plan, where your annual energy costs are spread evenly throughout the year. You can also have a copy of your bills sent to a relative, friend or organization, which is intended to assist those who are ill, elderly or absent from their homes for long periods. Overseas owners can have their utility bills sent to them abroad or paid by direct drafting (direct debit) from a Florida bank account, which is the best method (if available). Otherwise you should prepay a sum in advance, e.g. an amount equal to a quarter's charges, and make further payments when necessary after receiving your bills. Some utility companies have what is termed a 'lifeline rate' or a 'baseline allowance', which is a special low rate designed to cover the service necessary to meet the energy requirements of the average household. Energy used above the lifeline rate is billed at a higher rate. State and local taxes are levied on utility bills. Note that if you're a 'returning or seasonal customer' and spend three months or more a year away from Florida, you can have your utility services temporarily suspended when you're away, thus saving the monthly customer service charge. There's a connection fee, e.g. $10, although the service charge for three months exceeds this. You must usually give at least two weeks' notice to have your utilities reconnected.

Most utility companies publish a number of useful booklets explaining how to conserve energy, e.g. through improved insulation, and thus reduce your bills. However, this has little impact on most Americans, who are the most profligate consumers of energy in the world and habitually light, heat and cool their homes to extremes, even when they are empty. Most utility companies will perform a free home energy conservation survey of your home and private companies will conduct a more in-depth investigation for around $200. Always check the identity of anyone claiming to be a utility employee (or any kind of 'serviceman') by asking to see a photo ID card.

Electricity

The electricity supply in Florida (and most of the US) is 110/120 volts AC, with a frequency of 60 hertz (cycles). Over 75 per cent of electricity in Florida is supplied by private electricity companies such as the Florida Power & Light Company in Miami, Jacksonville Electric, the Gulf Power Company, the Florida Power Corporation and the Tampa Electric Company. The remainder is provided by numerous municipal systems, rural electricity cooperatives and federal systems.

Every household, whether an apartment or a single-family home, has its own electric meter. This is usually located either in the basement of an apartment block or outside a house, where it can be read when the occupants aren't at home. In some areas electricity is charged at peak and slack period (off-peak) rates at different times of the day, and during different seasons of the year (usually summer and winter). Electricity in Florida is among the cheapest in the US, with 1,000KWh usually costing between $70 and $80 or from 7¢ to 10¢ per kilowatt-hour (KWH or KWHR). The typical Florida electricity bill for an average household is around $100 a month (it's higher in summer if air-conditioning is used extensively). The standing customer charge varies considerably and is typically $6 to $9 a month. You can reduce your electricity bills by running high-consumption appliances during off peak times and using timers to regulate the use of water heaters and air-conditioning systems.

It's possible to operate electrical equipment rated at 240 volts AC in Florida with a converter or a step-up transformer to convert it to 110 volts AC, although generally it isn't worth bringing electrical appliances to Florida that aren't rated at 110 volts AC. Some electrical appliances (e.g. electric razors and hair dryers) are dual-voltage, and are fitted with a 110/240 volt switch. Check for the switch, which may be inside the casing, and make sure it's switched to 110 volts *before* connecting it to the power supply. Most people buy new electrical appliances in Florida, which are of good quality and reasonably priced. Shop around before buying electrical appliances, as prices vary considerably and check comparison tests in consumer magazines.

An additional problem with some electrical equipment that isn't manufactured for the North American market is that the frequency rating is designed to run at 50 Hertz and not the US's 60 Hertz. Electrical equipment *without* a motor is generally unaffected by the increase in frequency to 60 Hz (except TVs). Some equipment with a synchronous motor may run okay with a 20 percent increase in speed; however, automatic washing machines, ranges (cookers), electric clocks, record players and reel-to-reel tape recorders are unusable in the US unless designed for 60 cycle operation. To find out, look at the label on the back of the equipment; if it says 50/60 Hertz, it should be okay. If it says 50 Hz, you might try it anyway, but first ensure that the

voltage is correct as outlined above. If the equipment runs too slowly, seek advice from the manufacturer or the retailer. For example, you may be able to obtain a special pulley for a reel-to-reel tape deck or record turntable to compensate for the increase in speed.

The standard American plug has two flat pins (live and neutral) plus an optional third pin (neutral). It's possible to buy adapters for many foreign plugs, both in the US and abroad, although it's more economical to change plugs. All appliances sold in the US are fitted with a molded two-pin plug, which will run off any outlet in the country. Some electrical appliances are earthed, which means they have a three-core wire and are fitted with a three-pin plug. If you need to fit a plug, the color coding is usually white (neutral), black (live) and green (earth). **Always make sure that a plug is correctly and securely wired, as bad wiring can prove fatal. Never fit a two-pin plug to a three-core flex.** Note that you should unplug electrical appliances during electrical (thunder) storms and fit a power strip surge protector, which although it won't protect against lightning, makes it easy to disconnect the system.

In American homes there are generally no switches on wall sockets, so electrical appliances should be fitted with their own on/off switches. Light switches usually operate in the opposite way to some other countries, where the UP position is ON and the DOWN position is OFF; some switches operate from left to right. The ON position may be indicated by a red spot on the switch. Standard and other lamps often have two or three-way settings which provide two or three levels of brightness (e.g. bright, medium and dim). Often lamp switches (or knobs) must be turned in a clockwise direction or pushed and pulled. Electric light bulbs have a standard size screw fitting for all lamps and sockets, which may differ from those in other countries. Bulbs for older appliances or foreign appliances may not be available in the US, so take a few spares with you.

Most American apartments and all houses have their own fuse boxes. If a fuse blows, **first turn off the mains switch**. This may be on the consumer unit or on a separate switch box nearby. Fuses in modern homes and homes with modern wiring are usually of the circuit breaker type, which when a circuit is overloaded trips to the OFF position. Switch off the main switch and open the circuit breaker box. After locating and remedying the cause of the failure (if possible), just switch the circuit breaker to the ON position. Close the circuit breaker box and switch on the main switch. Note that in Florida only a qualified electrician is permitted to install electrical wiring and fittings, particularly in connection with fuse boxes. Most electricity companies will service your major electrical appliances, e.g. heating or air-conditioning system, and some provide service contracts.

Gas

Natural gas, which is piped from the Gulf Coast area of Texas and Louisiana, is available in most metropolitan areas in Florida and to a lesser extent in rural areas. There are around ten private natural gas companies in Florida, the largest of which is the Peoples Gas System of Tampa, which serves some 250,000 customers. Most modern houses in Florida are all electric and don't have a mains gas supply (it's generally considered a bonus if a home has a gas supply). Outside cities and in remote areas, gas is usually available in bottles. The same company may supply you with both gas and electricity, when you will receive one bill for both, with gas and electricity costs itemized separately.

Gas is much less expensive than electricity for heating, hot water and cooking. It usually costs around 70¢ to 80¢ a therm (100 cubic feet), although the price fluctuates depending on the time of the year. Bills include a customer charge averaging around $7 (the cost of billing and meter reading), the energy charge and a pass-through gas charge. Gas is primarily used for cooking and hot water heating in Florida, with the typical monthly bill being between $25 and $50. You can install an electrically-operated gas detector that activates an alarm when a gas leak is detected. Gas leaks are extremely rare and explosions caused by leaks even rarer (although spectacular and therefore widely reported).

Water

Florida has some 4,750 public water systems and around 180 large water community systems serving some 80 per cent of the population. The state is divided into five water management districts which were created to preserve and conserve the state's waters. Despite the state's many lakes, only some 10 per cent of Florida's water comes from surface water sources, most being provided by underground aquifers and drawn to the surface by wells. With the exception of northern Florida, most of the state has a water shortage and experiences occasional droughts and routine restrictions, particularly coastal areas where some 80 per cent of the population lives. An added problem is Florida's millions of visitors who use around 175 gallons of water a day, compared with the US average of some 110 gallons (less than one gallon of which is used for cooking and drinking).

Rates: All homes in Florida have water meters. Water rates range from around $10 (Orlando, Tampa) to over $25 (Sarasota) for 10,000 gallons, although water and sewerage charges are usually lower within cities. Your water bill may double in summer when the garden and lawn need frequent watering. There's often a higher charge for water in rural areas than in metropolitan (city) areas. Water companies charge an additional monthly fee, e.g. $20 to $30, for waste-water (sewerage) costs. Note that you can have a second 'irrigation' water meter installed for external use (e.g. watering the garden, filling the pool and washing the car), in which case no sewerage fee is added. **You must ensure that a plumbing system is in good condition and not leaking or wasting water, which can result in high water bills.**

Restrictions: There are water shortage restrictions throughout the state and information is published regularly. The following lawn and landscape irrigation restrictions are in force in the southwest Florida water management district (from Levy to Charlotte counties). Even-numbered addresses (or names beginning with the initials A-M) may water on Tuesday and/or Saturday, and odd-numbered addresses (or names beginning with the initials N-Z) may water on Wednesdays and/or Sundays. No watering is permitted between 10am and 4pm on any day or at any time on Mondays, Thursdays or Fridays. New lawns and landscaping are exempt from watering restrictions for the first 30 days after installation, although irrigation is still prohibited between 10am and 4pm. **Note that restrictions vary depending on the town and region and the above is just an example.**

However, restrictions aren't strictly enforced and there's little individual effort to conserve water in Florida, where single-family homes don't even have water storage tanks to catch rainwater (water conservation in Florida consists of washing the car every other day, rather than every day). In Florida vehicles may be washed on any day at any time, although automatic shut-off nozzles should be used on hoses, and the washing of windows, mobile homes, boats and boat motors isn't restricted. The filling and maintenance of pools isn't restricted, providing water use is kept to a minimum. However, the hosing down of porches, sidewalks, driveways and other impervious surfaces (except for health and safety reasons) is prohibited.

Quality: Most water is of reasonable or good quality, although there are some areas where ground water is contaminated, e.g. by chemicals, waste and salt water, particularly in central and southeastern Florida. You can check the quality of water in your home by having your water analyzed by your local office of the Department of Environmental Regulation. Note that houses within a few miles of each other may have a different water supply, one of which is far superior to the other. Most Americans drink water straight from their house supply, although some people find the taste of the water or the purifying (e.g. chlorination) chemicals unpleasant and prefer to drink bottled spring or mineral water (or American beer, which tastes like water). In many areas people fit kitchen cold-water faucets (taps) with charcoal or other filters, to cleanse water for drinking or cooking. You shouldn't drink water from rivers, wells, and streams, unless you know it's okay, as it may be polluted (although in rural areas homes may have well water, which is usually excellent).

Faucets: American faucets can be complicated for the uninitiated and may be fitted with a variety of strange controls, e.g. one common design is operated by a handle that works on a universal joint arrangement, where an up-and-down movement controls the

flow and a left-to-right movement the temperature (left is usually hot). In the US the left faucet is almost always the hot faucet. Note that when there are separate hot and cold faucets in a shower, sometimes both faucets turn in the same direction and sometimes in opposite directions; check them out before scalding or freezing yourself. Where a shower and bath are combined, a lever or knob is commonly used to convert the flow from bath to shower and vice versa. Most American baths and washbasins have a single mixer spout. Sometimes faucets must be pulled or pushed rather than turned and a lever may also control the plug. Before moving into a new home, you should enquire where the main stop-valve or stopcock is, so that you can turn off the water supply in an emergency. If the water stops flowing for any reason you should ensure that all faucets are closed to prevent flooding from an open faucet when the supply starts again.

HEATING & AIR-CONDITIONING

Americans don't believe in doing anything by halves and heated and air-conditioned buildings are either boiling or freezing (or the exact opposite of outdoor temperatures). In Florida most Americans live in air-conditioned homes, ride in air-conditioned cars to air-conditioned offices and stores, and never spend more than a few seconds in the heat (lest they melt). Summer is very hot and humid throughout most of Florida and air-conditioning is considered to be essential by most people (providing they can afford to install and run it). In most regions of Florida, heating is necessary in winter and most new homes have a combined, thermostatically-controlled, heating and air-conditioning system (some luxury homes even have *outdoor* air-conditioning, e.g. pool-side). Homes can also be fitted with ceiling fans, which are useful to keep the air circulating and reduce temperatures, and are cheaper to operate than air-conditioning.

Note that central heating dries the air and may cause your family to develop coughs and other ailments. Those who find the dry air unpleasant can increase the indoor relative humidity by adding moisture to the air with a humidifier, vaporizer, steam generator or even a water container made of porous ceramic. Humidifiers that don't generate steam should be disinfected occasionally. You can also buy a dehumidifier to recirculate room air and reduce the relative humidity.

The advantage of air-conditioning is that it extracts the excess moisture in the air and reduces humidity. Most people set the thermostat at a comfortable temperature and simply leave it. Many people leave their air-conditioning on a low setting when a property is empty, which helps prevent mildew and mold forming, although whether it's necessary (and the times) depends on the location. It's possible to fit a 'humidity meter' to the A/C system which switches on the A/C when the humidity reaches a certain level (and off again when it drops), irrespective of the temperature.

Installing a heat pump (a reverse cycle, air-conditioning system that uses the heat energy in the outside air to warm your home) in place of a conventional heating and air-conditioning system can save considerably on energy costs. Although you will save on heating bills in Florida, you're likely to spend any savings on air-conditioning, particularly if you're a permanent resident. Solar power systems are rarely installed in Florida due to the high start-up costs (solar power is most commonly used to heat swimming pools). Most power companies publish useful booklets detailing how you can save money on cooling and heating costs, and will perform a free energy survey of your home.

In older apartment buildings and single-family homes there's usually no central air-conditioning system and window air-conditioning units may be installed. These can be purchased in most appliance or department stores and fitted directly into windows. You can install them yourself or most suppliers will install them for a fee. If you do it yourself, make sure that the size and power of the unit is correct. Most window air-conditioning units have a choice of fan speeds and the fan can usually be switched on separately from the cooling system. The cooling system can be adjusted for temperature and units often have a vent that can be opened to allow air into the room when they aren't in use. When using air-conditioning, all windows and outside doors should be closed. You may find that some air-conditioners are noisy and that you need to switch them off at night to get to sleep. Air-conditioners can be rented on a monthly basis during the hottest months of the year.

GARBAGE COLLECTION & DISPOSAL

Americans are the ultimate consumers and produce considerably more household garbage per head than any other nation (people in developing countries could live quite comfortably on what Americans throw away!). Kitchens in modern homes are usually fitted with garbage-disposal units, which will dispose of anything up to and including chicken bones. Some apartments have trash compactors, which are rubbish bins incorporating a unit which crushes and compresses garbage to make it easier to dispose of. American homes have their own individual trash cans (dustbins) and apartment blocks have large communal trash bins.

Garbage pickup (collection) is usually organized by local communities or city authorities and may be contracted to a private company (in some areas you may need to arrange your own collection). There are usually two collections a week. The cost is either included in local property taxes (particularly in rural areas) or you're billed monthly or bi-monthly, e.g. around $15 a month, perhaps with your water and sewerage bill. You may be billed separately for the months prior to a charge appearing on your tax bill. All rubbish must be put into plastic trash bags and tied, and cans may need to be placed in a certain position, e.g. by the roadside, at a particular time (if you put your garbage out too early you can be fined).

Although recycling in the US remains well below that of many other countries, it has become a topical issue in recent years and many states have introduced mandatory recycling laws (although more thought could be given to creating less waste in the first place!). Generally all paper (e.g. newspapers, magazines), aluminum cans and glass *must* be recycled, and many communities also recycle corrugated cardboard, plastic bottles, steel cans, bulk metals, motor oil, lead acid batteries and vegetative (compost) materials such as leaves, grass and garden debris.

Waste for recycling is usually stored in special containers (e.g. barrels) provided by communities and is collected on specific days of the month by the local authorities. Waste pickup information and schedules are published and delivered to all households. Household rubbish and bulk trash such as furniture is picked up on certain days. Hazardous waste may need to be taken to special collection facilities. In some communities, residents maintain their own recycling centers, where some waste (such as garden waste) is taken to sites (staffed by community volunteers) by residents. This saves communities hundreds of thousands of dollars in landfill tipping fees, in addition to the revenue earned by selling recyclable materials.

RENTAL INCOME

Many people planning to buy a holiday home in Florida are interested in owning a home that will provide them with an income to cover the running costs and help with mortgage payments. If you wish to rent a property, you must check before buying that it's permitted in the area or development (see **Rental Restrictions** below). Non-residents are permitted to occupy their Florida homes for a maximum of six months a year and many choose to rent their homes when they're absent. **Note that in most areas of Florida you're highly unlikely to meet mortgage payments and running costs from rental income.** Buyers who overstretch their financial resources often find themselves on the rental treadmill, constantly struggling to find sufficient rentals to cover their running costs and mortgage payments. In the early 1990s many overseas buyers lost their homes after they defaulted on their mortgage payments when rental income failed to meet expectations. Note that buying property in Florida (and in most other countries) isn't a good investment compared with the return on income that can be achieved by investing elsewhere. **Most experts recommend that you don't purchase a home in Florida if you need to rely on rental income to pay for it.**

Location: To maximize rental income, a property should be located as close as possible to the main attractions and/or a beach, be suitably furnished and professionally managed. A swimming pool is obligatory, as properties with pools are much easier to rent than those without (unless a property is situated on a beach). It's usually necessary to have a private pool with a single-family home, but a shared pool is sufficient with an apartment or townhouse. The best rental prospects are with a three bedroom, two bathroom home, with a single or double garage and a heated pool. For maximum rental income a property should be located within 20 minutes (preferably 10 to 15) of Disney World.

Note, however, that while it's the best location for rentals, the Disney World area definitely isn't the best place to live permanently due to the incessant crowds and traffic gridlock caused by visitors. Other popular areas include the Gulf Coast from around Naples in the south to Crystal River in the north, and the Atlantic coast between Miami and Daytona Beach. Key West is also a popular holiday destination. A property in a coastal location should be no further than 15 minutes' drive from a beach. Rental demand falls off dramatically outside the most popular areas, although coastal areas within day-trip distance of Disney World also offer reasonable rental potential.

Rents: Rental rates vary considerably depending on the area and the time of year. Rates for a property 10 to 20 minutes from Disney World range from around $600 per week for a two bedroom, two bathroom home with a community pool, to around $1,000 a week for a four bedroom, two bathroom home with a private heated pool. A 'standard' three bedroom, two bathroom home with private pool rents for between $700 and $900 a week, depending on the area. US source rental income drops dramatically outside the US peak rental season from Christmas to Easter. The season for European visitors is dominated by school holiday periods including Christmas and the New Year, Easter, summer (e.g. July and August) and the October mid-term break. The off peak months for European visitors are generally November/December and January to March (excluding school holiday periods).

Occupancy: Don't always believe a developer's rental and occupancy rates, which are sometimes highly exaggerated. Note that it's illegal under Florida law to offer guaranteed rental income (not that this stops some agents from doing it abroad, where they are out of reach of Florida law). You should always err on the conservative side when estimating rental income and bear in mind that in some cases your home may need to be available to rent for 40 weeks a year (80 per cent occupancy) to cover all your costs. However, an occupancy level of around 50 to 60 per cent is usually break-even point, although it's possible to get 75 per cent in a popular area.

A management company may offer a guaranteed number of weeks rental occupancy (e.g. 30), which isn't the same as a guaranteed income. To qualify for a guaranteed rental scheme a property must have a private heated swimming pool (the water can get cold in winter), which can improve bookings considerably in winter. However, a guaranteed rental deal may apply only if a property is available 52 weeks a year and the weeks when a property is used by the owner (or by owner-booked clients or friends) may be deducted from the guaranteed number of weeks' rental.

Furnishings & Keys: If you rent a property, don't fill it with expensive furnishings or valuable personal belongings. While theft is rare, items will certainly get damaged or broken over a period of time. When buying a new property that you plan to rent you should choose hard-wearing, dark colored carpets which won't show the stains, and should bear durability in mind when choosing the furniture and furnishings. It's common practice to install a credit card telephone (see page 25) which allows free local calls, but all other calls must be charged to a credit card (installation may be taken care of by a management company). You will also need several sets of spare keys, which will inevitably get lost at some time. If you employ a management company, their address should be on the key fob and not the address of the house. If you rent a home yourself, you can use a 'keyfinder' service, whereby lost keys can be returned to the keyfinder company by anyone finding them. You should ensure that you always get 'lost' keys returned, otherwise you may have to change the locks (it's advisable to change the external locks annually in any case if you rent a home). You don't need to provide clients with keys to all the external doors, only the front door (the others can be left in your home). If you arrange your own rentals, you can mail keys to clients in your home country, otherwise they can be collected from a management company's offices in Florida. It's also possible to install a security key-pad entry system (see **Home Security** on page 168).

Rental Restrictions: Short term (i.e. less than 28 or 30 days, but possibly less than six months) rental restrictions are becoming commonplace in Florida and have increased dramatically in the last few years in areas popular with foreign buyers. There are restrictions in a number of counties, cities and communities and if you wish to earn income from short term rentals it's *vital* to check that they are authorised in the area, development or community where you're planning to buy a home. You also need to check whether there are plans to introduce restrictions, which can be applied retrospectively. The reason for the restrictions is partly because many full-time residents don't wish to live in a community or development where short term rentals are permitted, although the main reason is pressure from the hotel lobby who don't want the competition.

Some counties such as Orange County have county-wide restrictions, other than in developments or zones where unrestricted rentals have previously been permitted. In some counties such as Osceola County, rentals are permitted only in developments that have been specifically zoned for short term rentals. In some areas, short term rentals are prohibited or a property may be restricted to just one rental a year only, irrespective of its duration. Many condo and cooperative owners' associations also restrict or ban short term rentals, even in areas where short term rentals are generally permitted. If there are restrictions in an area or development you should be notified before buying, but must also make your own investigations (also regarding possible future restrictions). **It's important to ask whether a sub-division (area) is zoned for short term rentals and whether there are any community or association restrictions, e.g. imposed by a condo association, and obtain documentary evidence.**

Note that Orange and Seminole counties in Florida don't permit short term rentals of less than 30 days. However, you can have rentals of less than 30 days as it isn't possible for owners to compel tenants to stay for the entire duration of their 30-day rental agreement, but the number of rental agreements in a calendar year can't be more than 12. In some counties homes built before the introduction of short term rental restrictions can still be rented for short periods (e.g. one week) if they were rented prior to the new regulations coming into force (called 'grand-fathering'), although short term rentals may be allowed to continue for a limited period only, e.g. five or ten years. Properties built before the late 1970s don't generally have any rental restrictions, but may not have the benefits of modern homes, and many condo apartment blocks also don't have any short term rental restrictions.

Licenses & Regulations: A Florida home used for rentals must be licensed annually by the state and county. A property used for short term rentals must be registered as such with the State of Florida (i.e. the Florida State Division of Hotels and Restaurants) and an annual state hotel (and occupational license in some counties) licence obtained. The license and sales tax number (see below) must be clearly displayed in your home. Safety equipment such as approved fire extinguishers, smoke detectors (if they aren't already installed), and two locks on front and patio doors is also necessary. Fire and safety rules are constantly being revised and extended and the cost of compliance has escalated in recent years to around $1,000. There's an inspection to ensure that owners comply with fire and security regulations. Note that if you rent a home without a license you face stiff penalties, e.g. a fine of up to $1,000 per day, imprisonment and possibly confiscation of your property. Check with the local county hall exactly what's required as the procedure varies depending on the county. Note, however, that fire and safety regulations are sometimes wrongly interpreted by counties and cities, and you should obtain the latest rules from the relevant state office.

Sales tax must be levied on short term property rentals of less than six months' duration and owners must register before starting business (see **Sales Tax** on page 117). Some counties also levy additional taxes on short term rentals such as tourist development, tourist impact and convention development taxes (see page 117). All taxes are based on gross receipts and must be levied on rents by the managing agent or owner. Rental income earned by non-resident aliens is also subject to US income tax, although all expenses can be deducted if you elect to be taxed on a 'net basis' (see **Taxation of Rental Income** on page 112).

Management Companies: If you're renting a second home, the most important decision is whether to rent it yourself or use an agent (or agents). If you don't have much spare time then you're better off using an agent, who will take care of everything and save you the time and expense of advertising and finding clients. However, an agent charges commission of around 15 per cent of gross rental income, plus various other fees for management services. You will need a local management company or employee to arrange for cleaning, maintenance, repairs and the payment of bills (although it's best to pay all regular bills by direct drafting). If you want your property to appear in an agent's catalog, you must contact him the summer before you wish to rent it.

Take care when selecting a rental agent, as a number have gone bust in recent years owing customers thousands of dollars. Make sure that your income is kept in an escrow account and paid regularly. Some foreign tour operators such as Florida Homes Direct in Britain (tel. UK 0181-715 9646) undertake to pay owners *before* guests arrive for their holiday. It's absolutely essential to employ an efficient, reliable and honest company, preferably a long-established company owned by (or with strong ties to) a local builder or developer. Note that anyone can set up a short term rental agency in Florida, which doesn't require a license (although long term agencies need a license). Always ask a management company to substantiate rental income claims and occupancy rates by showing you examples of actual income received from other properties. Ask for the names of satisfied customers and check with them.

Other things to ask a management company include who they rent to; where they advertise; whether they have contracts with holiday and travel companies; whether you're expected to contribute towards marketing costs; and whether you're free to rent the property yourself and use it when you wish. The larger companies market homes via newspapers, magazines, overseas agents and color brochures, and have representatives in many countries. Management contracts usually run for a year (renewable) and can be terminated by either party by giving around 90 days' notice.

Letting agents usually charge set fees for their services (see **Management Fees** below), which may include cleaning, gardening and laundry; paying utility bills and taxes; organizing maintenance and repairs and replacing damaged equipment; and dealing with tenants' problems on the spot. Companies have someone available at all hours to meet and greet clients, hand over the keys, check that everything is in order and be available in case of emergencies. If required, management companies will provide a welcome pack of groceries and they usually have extra equipment for hire such as roll-away beds, cribs (baby's cot), high chairs, gas grills and barbecues.

Companies also make periodic checks when a property is empty to ensure that it's secure and that everything is in order.

Owners pay the management company a 'float', which is usually equal to around four months' management fees (e.g. $500 or around $300 for a condo) to pay for bills, expenses and repairs. There may also be a separate contingency fund for redecoration, replacements and repairs. All funds must be held in an escrow (trust) account, which is a legal requirement. Management companies provide a monthly statement showing all income and expenses. Check all charges listed in your monthly statement and question anything you think is too high or incorrect.

Management Fees: The typical monthly management fee is around $100 which includes a 'meet and greet' service (meeting clients at the airport and accompanying them to your home); key delivery and collection; providing a welcome grocery pack; collection and handling of post; arranging routine and emergency repairs; routine maintenance of house and garden, including lawn cutting and pool cleaning; arranging cleaning between rentals; advising guests on the use of equipment; and providing guest information and advice (possibly 24-hours a day for emergencies). All bills are extra and there's usually an additional fee for check writing (paying bills on your behalf) and completing tax returns (sales and income tax on rental income). Typical monthly management fees are shown below:

Service	Fee ($)
general management	100
bill paying service	40
sales/tourist tax returns	10
grocery welcome pack*	30 (from)
cleaning & laundry 3 bed*	50 per visit
garden/grass cutting (standard lot)	75
pool maintenance (chemicals, etc.)	85
pest control (full service)	25
cable TV	25
garbage collection	25
utilities	100
telephone	20
TOTAL*	**$765**

* The total includes two charges for grocery welcome packs and four charges for cleaning & laundry.

To the above costs must be added mortgage payments (if applicable), insurance and taxes. **Note that if a person renting your home is assaulted there, you could be sued for negligence, and therefore it's important to have liability insurance that covers this eventuality (see page 63).** Note that a home which is rented must have a 'short term rental dwelling' policy. Maintenance fees are payable for the common elements of a community property and if communal facilities are provided you must also pay an 'amenities' fee. Note that electricity bills can easily amount to $150 to 200 a month in summer when you're running air-conditioning 24-hours a day (many owners leave their air-conditioning on a low setting even when a home is unoccupied, as the high humidity can cause mildew and mold in a warm house).

Renting Yourself: Some owners prefer to rent a property to family, friends, colleagues and acquaintances, which allows them more control (and *hopefully* the property will be better looked after). In fact, the best way to get a high volume of rentals is usually to do it yourself, although many owners use a local rental company in addition to doing their own marketing in their home country. If you wish to rent a property yourself, there's a wide range of newspapers and magazines in which you can advertise in most countries (e.g. *Dalton's Weekly* and the broadsheet Sunday newspapers in Britain). You will need to experiment to find the best publications and days of the week to advertise. There are also companies which produce catalogs of properties rented directly by owners in Florida, e.g. *Private Villas* in Britain. You can also advertise among friends and colleagues, in company and club magazines (which may even be free), on TV bulletin boards (e.g. ITV's Oracle 'Florida Villas Direct' in Britain), and on notice boards in companies, stores and public places. The more you advertise, the more income you're likely to earn. It will pay you to have a telephone answering machine and a fax machine.

To get an idea of the rent you should charge simply ring a few rental companies and ask them what the rent would be for a property such as yours at the time of year you plan to rent. They are likely to quote the highest possible rent you can charge. You should also check the advertisements in newspapers and magazines. Set a realistic rent as there's a lot of competition. Add a returnable deposit (e.g. $150) as security against loss (e.g. of keys) or breakages. If you plan to rent a home yourself you will need to decide how to handle enquiries about flights and car rentals. It's easier to let clients do it themselves, but you should be able to offer advice and put them in touch with airlines, travel agents (see **Appendix F**) and car rental companies (see page 40). Some owners leave a car and/or boat at their home for the use of their clients.

It's advisable to produce a colored brochure containing external/internal pictures (or a single color brochure with colored photographs glued to it, although this doesn't look so professional), important details, the exact location, local attractions, details of how to get there (with a small map), and the name, address and telephone number of your local management company. It's necessary to make a home look as attractive as possible without distorting the facts or misrepresentation. You should also provide an information pack for clients explaining how things work (such as air-conditioning); what not to do; where to shop; recommended restaurants; local emergency numbers and health services such as doctors, hospitals and dentists; and assistance such as a general repairman, plumber, electrician and pool maintenance. It's also beneficial to have a visitor's book where your clients can write their comments and recommendations.

If you want to impress your guests you may wish to arrange for fresh flowers, fruit, a good bottle of wine and a grocery pack to greet them on their arrival. It's little touches like this that ensure repeat business and recommendations. Many people return to the same property each year and you should do an annual mailshot to previous clients and send them a few brochures. **Word-of-mouth advertising is the cheapest and always the best.** Note that even when you rent a property yourself, you will still need a local management company to arrange for cleaning, maintenance, repairs and the payment of bills. A management company shouldn't charge extra fees when an owner finds his own tenants. **Note that when buying a home in Florida for rental, you must plan well in advance so that you're ready to rent it as soon as possible after the closing.**

Long Term Rentals: Long term rentals are generally for at least six months or a year and are often unfurnished. However, it's possible to rent a furnished home for three to six months, particularly during the winter when many retired Canadians and Americans from northern states spend the winter in Florida (known locally as 'snowbirds'). Rates aren't as high as for short term rentals, e.g. weekly, although you can expect to receive from $1,500 to $2,500 a month in the high season and $750 and $1,000 a month in the low season for a three bedroom, two bathroom home for a minimum three-month rental. There's also a market for long term rentals of six months or longer to Americans or foreign residents (many foreigners buying businesses in Florida rent a home for a few years before buying). With long term rentals, tenants usually take pay most of the running costs including utilities, pool and lawn maintenance, cable TV and telephone.

See also **Taxation of Rental Income** on page 112 and **Sales Tax** on page 117.

SELLING A HOME

Although this book is primarily concerned with buying a home in Florida, you (or your descendants) will probably want to sell your Florida home at some time in the future. Before offering your Florida home for sale, it's advisable to investigate the state of the property market. For example, unless you're forced to sell, it definitely isn't advisable to sell during a property slump when prices are depressed. It may be wiser to rent your home long term and wait until the market has recovered. It's also unwise to sell in the early years after purchase when you will almost certainly make a loss. Having decided to sell, your first decision will be whether to sell it yourself (or try) or use the services of a real estate agent. In Florida the majority of homes are sold through real estate agents, although many owners also sell their own homes. Note that in cities and popular areas of Florida the average home sells in around 100 to 120 days, although the majority of homes take over a year to sell. If you need to sell your existing home before buying a new home, this must be included as a contingency clause (see page 162) in the purchase contract for a new home.

Price: It's important to bear in mind that (like everything) property has a market price and the best way of ensuring a quick sale (or any sale) is to ask a realistic price. If your home's fairly standard for the neighborhood you can find out its value by comparing the prices of other homes on the market or those which have recently been sold. Note that you need to compare similar homes with more or less the same lot size and built area; number of bedrooms and bathrooms; garage size; build quality and fixtures and fittings; the heated and air-conditioned area (referred to as the heated/cooled square footage); and extras such as a pool. If you use an agent he will recommend a price and most agents will provide a free appraisal of your home's value in the hope that you will sell it through them. However, don't believe everything an agent tells you, as he may over-price it simply to encourage you. You can also hire a real estate appraiser to determine the market value of your home. Note that you should be prepared to drop the price slightly (e.g. 5 or 10 per cent) and should price it accordingly, but shouldn't grossly over-price a home as it will deter buyers.

Presentation: The secret to selling a home quickly lies in its presentation (always assuming that it's competitively priced). First impressions (both exteriors and interiors) are vital when marketing your home and it's important to make every effort to present it in its best light and make it as attractive as possible to potential buyers. It may pay to invest in new interior decoration, new carpets, exterior paint and landscaping. Note that when decorating a home for resale, it's important to be conservative and not to do anything radical (such as install a red or black bathroom suite); white is a good neutral color for walls, woodwork and porcelain. It may also pay you to do some remodeling such as installing a new kitchen or bathroom, as these are of vital importance (particularly kitchens) when selling a home. Note, however, that although remodeling may be necessary to sell an old home, you shouldn't overdo it as it's easy to spend more than you could ever hope to recoup on the sale price. If you're using an agent, you can ask him what you should do (or need to do) to help sell your home (some large real estate chains publish free seller's guides and magazines).

If your home is in poor repair this must be reflected in the asking price and if major work is needed which you can't afford, you should obtain a quotation (or two) and offer to knock this off the asking price. Note that you have a duty under Florida state law to inform a prospective buyer of any defects which aren't readily apparent and which materially affect the value of a property. There are special disclosure requirements for condos and other community properties (see page 144).

Selling A Home Yourself: While certainly not for everyone, selling your own home is a viable option for many people and is particularly recommended when you're selling an attractive home at a *realistic* price in a favorable market. It may allow you to offer it at a more appealing price, which could be an important factor if you're seeking a quick sale. How you market your home will depend on the type of home, the price, and the country or area from where you expect your buyer to come. For example, if your property isn't of a type and style and in an area desirable to local inhabitants, it's usually a waste of time advertising it in the local press.

Advertising is the key to selling your home. The first step is to get a professional looking 'for sale' sign made (showing your telephone number) and erect it in your garden. Do some market research into the best newspapers and magazines for advertising your property, and place an advertisement in those that look most promising. The best day for Florida newspapers is Sunday. There are also resale homes magazines such as *Buy Owner* (1719 West Kennedy Blvd, Tampa, FL 33606, tel. 1-800-408-1999), where owners can advertise their homes for sale directly to potential buyers and no agents' fees or commission is involved.

You could also have a leaflet printed (with pictures) extolling the virtues of your property, which you could then drop into local letter boxes or have distributed with a local newspaper (many people buy a new home in the immediate vicinity of their present home). You may also need a 'fact sheet' printed if your home's vital statistics aren't included in the leaflet and could offer a finder's fee (e.g. $1,000) to anyone who finds you a buyer. Don't omit to market your home around local companies, schools and organizations, particularly if they have many itinerant employees. Finally, it may help to provide information about local financing sources for potential buyers. With a bit of effort and practice you may even make a better job of marketing your home than a broker!

Unless you're in a hurry to sell, set yourself a realistic time limit for success, after which you can try a broker. If you have an unusual property such as a period building, you could try selling it at auction, which may increase the price (although you must pay the auctioneer's commission). When selling a home yourself, you will need to obtain legal advice regarding contracts and to engage an escrow agent to hold the deposit and close the sale (if not done by your lawyer). Obtain quotations from a number of professionals in your area. A useful book for property sellers is *How to Sell Your Home in the '90s* by Hafferty and Carolyn Janik (Penguin).

Home Marketing Services: A new scheme to surface in recent years are marketing service companies such as Homeowners Concept and Help-u-Sell, who charge owners a flat fee (usually plus optional services) in exchange for assistance in selling your home. Services usually include a 'for sale' sign, a standard sales contract, a book of marketing tips, advertising suggestions, advertisements in locally distributed real estate magazines and possibly other advertising. Check the circulation and number of copies of publications printed and where they are distributed. Note that marketing service companies don't show or actually sell your home, which is up to you, and although it's cheaper than using a broker you won't have the benefit of a listing service. Using a marketing company is a halfway house between doing everything yourself and using an agent, and generally offers little or nothing that you can't do for yourself.

Using An Agent: Most owners prefer to use the services of an agent or broker, either in Florida or in their home country, when selling a holiday home. If you bought the property through an agent, it's often advisable to use the same agent when selling, as he will already be familiar with it and will have the details on file. You should take particular care when selecting an agent as they vary considerably in their professionalism, expertise and experience (the best way to investigate an agent is by posing as a buyer). Many experts recommend that owners engage a seller's broker, who works exclusively for the seller and ensures that there's no potential conflict of interest (otherwise a broker could also be acting for the buyer, although this would be illegal without disclosure). Note that many agents cover a relatively small area, e.g. a city or county, so you should take care to choose one who regularly sells properties in your area and price range. If you own a property in an area popular with foreign buyers, it may be worthwhile using an overseas agent or advertising in foreign newspapers and magazines, such as the English-language property publications listed in **Appendix A**.

Contracts: Before offering a property for sale, an agent must have a signed authorization from the owner or his legal representative. There are two main types of contract in Florida: a listing contract, using a multiple listing service (MLS), and an exclusive contract. With a listing contract your broker circulates details of your home to all brokers subscribing to the MLS and splits the commission with the broker who finds the buyer. MLS brokers (see **Listings** on page 153) usually gain access to MLS properties through a device called a 'lock box', a box attached to your home containing your house key, to which all MLS brokers have a master key. This allows agents to show your home when nobody is at home. You can decide whether you want to have a lock box installed, but it's generally advisable and guarantees maximum exposure.

An exclusive contract gives a single agent the exclusive right to sell a property, although you should reserve the right to find a private buyer. **Note that if you sign a contract without the right to find your own buyer, you must still pay the agent's commission even if you sell your home yourself.** Most people find that it's best to sign a listing contract, and if possible, reserve the right to sell your own property, although a broker may insist on receiving half his commission. Note that if an agent finds a buyer willing to pay cash for the full asking price without any contingencies (which is highly unlikely unless a home is an absolute bargain), you must pay the agreed commission even if you decide not to sell. You may also be required to pay an agent's commission if you decide not to sell and take your house off the market during the contract period, although the contract should restrict the agent's fee to out-of-pocket expenses only.

Contracts are always for a limited period only (e.g. six months) and state the agent's commission, what it includes, and most importantly, who must pay it. The agent usually provides a 'for sale' board, photographs, information leaflets and may include some advertising other than in his office window (although advertising may be charged separately). **Generally you shouldn't pay any fees unless you require extra services,**

and you should never pay commission before a sale is completed. Check the contract and make sure you understand what you're signing. See also **Agency Contracts** on page 152.

Commission: Agents usually receive a 5 to 7 per cent commission (average 6 per cent) on sales, although it can be as high as 10 per cent and may be negotiable, particularly when market conditions favor the seller's position. You may be able to negotiate a lower rate (e.g. 4 to 5 per cent), depending on the area and the appeal of your home, but if you do you may be required to actively assist in the sale, e.g. by paying for advertising. An agent usually receives a lower commission when he has an exclusive rather than a listing contract. When a number of brokers are involved in a sale, they split the commission. Shop around for the best deal as there's fierce competition among agents in most areas. The agent's commission is usually allowed for in the sale price of a property.

As when buying a home abroad, you must be very, very careful who you deal with when selling a home. Make sure that you're paid with a certified (e.g. cashier's) check before signing over your property to a buyer, as once the deed of sale has been signed the property belongs to the buyer, whether or not you have been paid. Sales should always be conducted by a lawyer. Note that when selling a second home in Florida you must pay capital gains tax (see page 115) on any profit and 10 per cent of the sale price must be retained by the closing agent when the seller is a non-resident, against a possible capital gains tax liability. If you're a US resident you must file an information schedule *Sale or Exchange of Principal Residence* (form 2119) with your income tax return (form 1040). A non-resident seller must file a tax return (form 1040NR) at the end of the tax year to report a capital gain or loss on a property sale.

When selling a holiday home in Florida, you may wish to include the furnishings (plus major appliances) in the sale, particularly when selling a relatively inexpensive property with modest furnishings. You should add an appropriate amount to the price to cover the value of the furnishings, or alternatively you could use them as an inducement to a prospective buyer at a later stage, although this isn't usual in Florida. See also **Purchase Contracts** on page 157, **Real Estate Agents** on page 151 and **Capital Gains Tax** on page 115.

5.

ARRIVAL & SETTLING IN

On arrival in Florida your first task will be to negotiate immigration and customs. Fortunately this presents few problems for most people. Note, however, that with the exception of certain visitors (see **Visa Waivers** on page 19), all persons wishing to enter the US require a visa (see page 17). In addition to information about immigration and customs, this chapter also contains checklists of tasks to be completed before or soon after arrival in Florida and when moving house, plus suggestions for finding local help and information.

ARRIVAL/DEPARTURE RECORD

Before you arrive in Florida you will be given an INS *Arrival/Departure Record* card (I-94/I-94W) to complete by the airline. If you're a visa-free visitor (see **Visa Waivers** on page 19), you will be given an I-94W card *Nonimmigrant Visa Waiver Arrival/Departure Form*. The I-94/I-94W card is divided into two parts, an 'Arrival Record' (items 1 through 11) and a 'Departure Record' (items 14 through 17). You must complete it in pen in block capitals and in English. If you make a mistake you may be asked to complete a new card. If you don't have an 'address while in the United States' (item 10), it's often wise to enter the name of an hotel in an area or city where you're heading or write 'touring', rather than leave it blank. Complete both the 'Arrival' and 'Departure' parts before arrival.

You're authorized to remain in the US until the date stamped on your I-94 card (departure record), entered by the immigration officer when you arrive. The I-94 card departure record will be stapled into your passport and must be carried at all times. **Note that it's this date and not the expiration date of your visa (if applicable), that determines how long you may remain in the US.** When you leave the US, the card will be removed from your passport by an airline official. If you fail to surrender your I-94 card (departure record) when you leave, a future entry may be delayed. All I-94 cards are recorded in a computer, which makes it easy for immigration officials to check whether you returned your card or overstayed your last visit. If you overstay your visit (i.e. the date stamped on your I-94 card), it's a violation of the immigration law. If you lose your I-94 card, you should replace it at the nearest US Immigration and Naturalization Service (INS) office, a list of which can be obtained from the INS, Central Office Information Operations Unit, #5044, 425 I St., NW, Washington, DC 20536 (tel. 202/633-1900).

Occasionally an INS officer will stamp your I-94 card with a date that permits a shorter stay than the date on a non-immigration visa. Although this is technically incorrect, it's best not to argue with an INS admitting officer. If this happens to you, apply for an extension up to 60 days and not less than 15 days before the date on your I-94 card becomes due. Many non-immigrant visas are of the multiple-entry type, which allows you to enter and leave the US as often as you wish during the visa validation period, e.g. 10 years for a B-1/B-2 visa. However, the period that you will be allowed to remain will also depend on the expiration date of your passport. For example, if you have a non-immigrant visa valid for three years and your passport is valid for three months only, you will be admitted for just three months, as stamped on your I-94 card. If you have a valid multiple-entry, non-immigrant visa and obtain a new passport, retain your old passport and take it with you when traveling to the US, as the visa will remain valid. You must *never* remove a visa from your old passport, as this will invalidate it.

IMMIGRATION

When you arrive in the US, the first thing you must do is go through US Public Health Immigration & Naturalization. This is divided into two sections, 'US Citizens' and 'All Other Passports'; make sure you join the correct line. Once you enter the US, you're under the jurisdiction of the INS who have dictatorial powers over you, and have been variously described as aggressive, brusque, bullying, stern and intimidating (on a good day). You should always remain polite and answer any questions in a direct and courteous manner, however personal or irrelevant you may think they are. It never pays to antagonize immigration officials, for example by questioning the relevance of certain questions.

American immigration officials are trained to suspect that *everyone* who doesn't have the right to live and work in the US is a potential illegal immigrant (most Americans believe that, given the choice, any sane person couldn't possibly wish to live anywhere other than in the US). Nationals of some countries may be singled out for 'special treatment', e.g. persons from a country that's hostile towards the US or which has a reputation for illegal immigrants. It's an unfortunate fact of life that many immigration officials (like most people) are prejudiced against certain groups. If you're white, English-speaking, smartly dressed, sober and polite, you will have a much easier time than a black bohemian who doesn't speak English.

Immigration officers have the task of deciding whether you're permitted to enter the US and have the necessary documentation, including a visa if necessary. Note that even with a visa, you don't have a *right* to enter the US as only the immigration officer can make that decision. The length of time you will be permitted to remain in the US also depends on the immigration officer, irrespective of how long your visa is valid. If the officer believes that you may participate in activities, e.g. employment, prohibited by the terms of your visa, he can refuse to admit you. Present the following to the immigration officer, as applicable:

* your passport (plus an old passport if it contains an unexpired visa);

* your completed arrival/departure record card (I-94/I-94W);

* your green card, if you're a permanent resident.

Also have any documents or letters on hand that support your reason for visiting the US. After entering the US with an immigrant visa, your passport is stamped to show that you're a permanent resident. You're permitted to travel abroad and re-enter the US by showing this passport stamp until you receive your green card, which you will receive by mail a few months later.

Among those often subject to the closest scrutiny are certain visitors, as people intending to live or work illegally in the US commonly enter the country as tourists. However, most people are admitted to the US with few formalities. If the immigration officer suspects you of not telling the truth he can search you and your baggage. If a search of your person or baggage turns up evidence that contradicts the stated purpose of your visit or your visa status, e.g. work references and a curriculum vitae; letters from American companies or employment agencies offering you employment; letters from friends working illegally in the US; tools of your trade; or anything else which suggests you may look for work illegally, you may be excluded from the US. If you plan to visit the US before applying for a job or an immigrant or non-immigrant visa, you should mail any documents you may require (e.g. to a friend or to yourself c/o a post office), rather than bring them with you. Note, however, that a detailed search of your baggage and person is extremely rare (particularly a strip search).

The degree of questioning you're subject to may depend on many things, not least your nationality; the documentation you provide supporting the reason for your visit or why you must return abroad (see below); the amount of money you have; whether you have friends or relatives in the US who can support you; whether you have a return ticket to your 'home' country; and your age and appearance. Immigration officials may ask you about the following:

Duration: If you're asked how long you intend to remain in the US, take care how you answer. For example, if you're a visa-free visitor (maximum stay three months) or have a B-2 visitor's visa (maximum stay six months), you should be specific about the amount of time you intend to stay, and be prepared to support it with a timetable and sufficient funds (or access to funds) to maintain yourself during this period. If you intend to stay for the maximum period permitted, you should be able to provide a full schedule, otherwise the immigration officer may suspect that you intend to overstay your visit.

Accommodations: An official may ask you where you intend to stay in the US. If you will be staying with relatives or friends, it will help if you can provide a letter of invitation and provide their address and telephone number. If the officer has any doubts, he may telephone your hosts (irrespective of the time of day or night) to check your story. Relatives are better than friends, as in the eyes of immigration they are more likely to provide you with financial help (if necessary). If you have no friends or relatives with whom to stay and no hotel reservations, the immigration officer may be suspicious, particularly if you don't have adequate funds.

Money: You may be asked how much money you have with you, which should be an appropriate amount for the purpose and length of your trip. This may include cash and travelers' checks (a pile of low denomination checks look more impressive than a few high value checks). You should have a minimum of $100 to $200 for each week you intend to stay if you're staying with friends or relatives, and much more if you're touring and staying in hotels. You should also mention any credit or charge cards you have with you. You may be asked to show your money and credit cards. The immigration officer may also ask you what you will do if you run out of money, so you should have an answer ready.

Tickets: If you're a visitor, you should always have a return or onward non-transferable ticket that's non-refundable except in the country of issuance or your country of residence. The date of your return flight (e.g. if you arrive by air) should agree with the information you provide about the length of your intended stay in the US.

Home Situation: If the immigration officer suspects you may be planning to work illegally, he may ask you about your circumstances in your country of residence, e.g. whether you have a job to return to and where you live. If you're a student, a letter from a future employer or a college stating that you're on holiday or plan to return to study during the next term will be useful. If you're unemployed or self-employed you may have more trouble convincing immigration that you don't intend to work in the US. If you own a home in your home country or have been renting one for some years, it will obviously be more convincing than if you have no permanent address.

Be extremely careful how you answer seemingly innocent questions from the immigration authorities, as you could find yourself being refused entry if you give incriminating answers (immigration officials *never* ask innocent questions). Whatever the question, don't imply that you may remain in the US longer than the period permitted, or for a purpose other than that for which you have been granted permission. If you're singled out for closer examination, your passport and other documents may be placed in a red folder and you will be asked to go to a separate waiting room for an interview. Try to remain calm and patient as if you become nervous and anxious an official may become even more suspicious.

If you enter the US from certain countries, you may be required to have immunization certificates. Check the requirements in advance at an American embassy or consulate before traveling. An immigration officer can decide to send you for a routine (and random) health check, before allowing you to enter the US. Clearing immigration during a busy period can take a number of hours, so it's advisable to be prepared and take a thick book or a few newspapers and magazines. Among the most notorious entry points for delays is Florida's Miami airport. Immigration lines are shorter at smaller airports, although you may have little choice of entry point, depending on where you start your journey.

CUSTOMS

If you travel to the US by air you will be given a *Customs Declaration* form (6059B) to complete by the airline. You must complete it in English in block capitals in blue or black ink (if you make a mistake you may be asked to fill in a new card). Hand your completed form to the customs officer at your port or frontier of entry. The head of a family may make a joint declaration for all members residing in the same household and traveling together to the US. There are no restrictions on the amount of money you may take into the US, although if you have over $10,000 in currency or 'monetary instruments', you're required to state this on your customs declaration form (large sums of cash are often carried by criminals, particularly drug traffickers).

Some American ports and international airports operate a system of red and green 'channels', as are common in Europe. Red means you have something to declare and green means that you have nothing to declare, i.e. no more than the duty free customs allowances, no goods to sell, and no prohibited or restricted goods. **If you're certain you have nothing to declare, go through the 'green channel', otherwise go through the red channel.** US customs checks are usually much stricter than in Europe and many other countries, and even when you go through the green channel you will usually be stopped, your customs declaration form inspected and you may be asked to open your bags. At ports without red and green channels, your baggage may be given a thorough inspection. Note that there are stiff penalties for smuggling.

A list of all items you're bringing in is useful, although the customs officer may still want to examine your bags. If you're required to pay duty or Internal Revenue Service (IRS) tax, it must be paid at the time goods are brought into the country. If you're unable to pay on the spot, customs will keep your goods until you pay the sum due. This must be paid within a certain period, noted on the back of your receipt. Postage or freight charges must be paid if you want your goods sent on to you.

Note that if you're discovered trying to smuggle goods into the US, customs may confiscate them, and if you hide them in a vehicle, boat or plane, they can confiscate that also! If you attempt to import prohibited items, you may also be liable to criminal charges or deportation.

Importation of Personal Effects: When you enter the US to take up residence, either temporarily or permanently, you can usually import your personal belongings duty and tax free. Any duty or tax payable depends on where you arrived from, where you purchased the goods, how long you have owned them, and whether duty and tax has already been paid in another country. Personal effects owned and used for at least one year prior to importation are usually exempt from import duty. The duties levied on non-exempt items vary according to the classification of goods and their original value. If you're coming to live in the US and are sending your personal effects unaccompanied, you must provide US customs with a detailed list of everything brought into the country and its value. The detail officially required is often absurd and you're even expected to list such things as the titles of books, although in practice less detail is acceptable. A person emigrating to the US may bring professional equipment such as books and tools of a trade, occupation or employment. American embassies and consulates provide a free information package and a sample inventory list.

You're required to complete customs form 3299 *Declaration for Free Entry of Unaccompanied Articles*, for presentation to the examining customs officer when your belongings are cleared through customs. It's unnecessary to employ a broker or agent to clear your belongings through customs, as you can do this yourself after you arrive in the US or you can authorize someone to represent you. Your belongings must be cleared through customs within five working days after their arrival in the US, otherwise they will be sent to a warehouse for storage at your risk and expense until customs clearance can be made. Your belongings may be imported up to six months prior to your arrival in the US, but no more than one year after your arrival (after transferring your residence). They must not be sold, lent, rented or otherwise disposed of in the US within one year of their importation or of your arrival (whichever is later) without obtaining customs authorization.

Visitors: If you're a visitor, you can bring your personal belongings to the US free of duty and tax without declaring them to customs providing:

- they are brought in with you and are for your personal use only;

- they are kept in the US for no longer than six months in a 12-month period;

- you don't sell, lend, rent or otherwise dispose of them in the US;

- they're exported either when you leave the US or before they have been in the US for more than six months, whichever occurs first.

General information about US customs regulations is contained in a leaflet entitled *United States Customs Hints For Visitors* obtainable from US customs offices or from the US Customs Service, Office of Public Information, 1301 Constitution Avenue, NW, PO Box 7407, Washington, DC 20229 (tel. 202/566-8195). The US Customs Service also provides detailed information regarding the importation of special items including cars, boats, and animals. If you have any questions regarding the importation of anything into the US, you can also contact the customs representative at your local US embassy or consulate abroad.

REGISTRATION

Registration applies to permanent alien residents only. The US doesn't require the registration of foreign nationals resident in the US (e.g. at a local police station), although a change of address must be registered with the INS within 10 days and you must report your address annually irrespective of whether it has changed. All permanently-resident foreigners over the age of 14 are finger-printed before they are issued with a green card and those who attain the age of 14 while in the US should be finger-printed within 30 days of their 14th birthday. Non-immigrants intending to remain in the US longer than one year who are citizens of countries that require US citizens to be finger-printed are also finger-printed.

FINDING HELP

One of the most important tasks facing new arrivals in Florida, is how and where to obtain help with essential everyday tasks such as buying a car, obtaining medical help and insurance requirements. How successful you are at finding local help will depend on your employer (if applicable), the town or area where you live (those who live in small communities are usually better served than those who inhabit cities), your nationality, English proficiency and sex (women are usually better catered for than men through numerous women's clubs).

Fortunately obtaining information in the US isn't a problem as there's a wealth of information available on every conceivable subject. However, finding up-to-date information, sorting the truth from the half truths, comparing the options available, and making the correct decision is more difficult, particularly as most information isn't intended for foreigners and their particular needs. You may find that your friends, colleagues and acquaintances can help, as they're often able to proffer advice based on their own experiences and mistakes. **But take care!** Although they mean well, you're likely to receive as much false and conflicting information as accurate (not always wrong, but possibly invalid for your particular region, community or situation). Americans are renowned for their friendliness and you should have no trouble getting to know your neighbors and colleagues, who will usually be pleased to help you make yourself at home.

All communities have a wide range of clubs and organizations, the most important of which for new arrivals is the newcomers club. Most American communities and towns pride themselves on the warm welcome they extend to new residents and someone may contact you within a few weeks of your arrival in a new community. Some communities have a senior center where help is provided for senior citizens, usually on a casual walk-in basis (they are also an excellent place to meet people). In most communities there are local volunteer services designed to meet a range of local needs. Services may be listed in telephone directories under a variety of names including helpline, crisis center, hotline, people's switchboard, community switchboard or 'we care'. Volunteer services can usually also direct you to a range of free or inexpensive local services.

Libraries are a mine of local information. Besides keeping reference works, telephone directories, local guidebooks, maps, magazines and local newspapers, they distribute leaflets and brochures for local clubs and organizations of every description. Library staff are helpful in providing information and answering queries, and may even make telephone calls for you. Town halls, police headquarters (the police are usually helpful), visitors bureaus, tourist offices and chambers of commerce, some of which have multi-lingual staff, are also good sources of free maps and local information. Some large companies have a department or staff dedicated to assisting new arrivals or use a relocation company to perform this task. Relocation magazines are published in many areas (contact local chambers of commerce or realtors for information).

There are expatriate and ethnic clubs and organizations in most areas. These may provide members with detailed local information regarding all aspects of living in the US including housing costs, schools, names of doctors and dentists, shopping information and much more. Many clubs produce data sheets, booklets, newsletters and operate lending libraries, and many also organize a variety of social events including day and evening classes ranging from cooking to English-language classes. There are also numerous social clubs in most towns whose members can help you find your way around. Two organizations of particular interest to British readers are the Florida Brits Club and Florida Homes & Travel (see **Appendix F**), both of which provide a wealth of information to anyone owning or planning to buy a home in Florida.

Many businesses (e.g. banks and savings and loan associations) produce books and leaflets containing valuable information for newcomers, and local libraries and bookstores usually have books about the local area. County and local councils and chambers of commerce also publish a wealth of information and maps for both visitors and residents. One way to meet new people and make friends is to enrol in a day or evening class, join a local church or temple, or if you have school-age children, take part in the activities of the local Parent Teacher Association (PTA) or Home and School Association (HSA).

Finally, you should buy a copy of *Living and Working in America* (Survival Books) written by your author David Hampshire (there's an order form at the end of the book), which contains invaluable information about life in the US for both visitors and residents.

CHECKLISTS

The checklists on the following pages list tasks which you need (or may need) to complete before and after arrival in Florida, and when moving your home permanently to Florida.

Before Arrival

The following checklist contains a summary of the tasks that should (if possible) be completed before your family's arrival in the US:

- **Check that your own and your family's passports are valid.**
- If necessary obtain a visa for all your family members (see page 17). Obviously this *must* be done before arrival in the US.
- Arrange health (see page 54) and travel (see page 64) insurance for your family. This is essential if you aren't covered by an international health insurance policy.
- Obtain an international credit or charge card (or two), which will be invaluable in the US.
- Obtain an international driver's permit (if your current licence isn't written in English).
- Open a bank account in the US and transfer funds in US dollars (you can open an account with many American banks while abroad). Have checks printed showing your American address as soon as possible after your arrival.
- It's advisable to obtain some US dollars before arriving in Florida, as this will save you having to line up to change money on arrival.
- If you plan to become a permanent resident you may also need to do the following:
  - Arrange schooling for your children (see page 80).
  - Organize the shipment of your personal and household effects.

- Apply for a social security card from your local US embassy or consulate.
- Obtain as many credit references as possible, for example from banks, mortgage companies, credit card companies, credit agencies, companies with which you have had accounts, and references from professionals such as lawyers and accountants. In fact anything which will help you establish a credit rating in the US.

If you're planning to become a permanent resident don't forget to take all your family's official documents with you. These may include birth certificates, driver's licenses, marriage certificate, divorce papers, death certificate (if a widow or widower), educational diplomas and professional certificates, employment references, curriculum vitaes, school records, student ID cards, medical and dental records, bank account and credit card details, insurance policies (plus records of no claims' allowances) and receipts for any valuables. You may also need copies of official documents and a number of passport-size photographs.

After Arrival

The following checklist contains a summary of the tasks to be completed after arrival in the US (if not done before arrival):

- On arrival at a US airport or port, hand your passport, arrival/departure record card (I-94) and other documents to the immigration official.
- Hand your *Customs Declaration* form (6059B) to the customs officer and if you're importing more than your personal exemption you should provide a list of goods.
- If you haven't already bought a car, you will probably need to rent one (see page 40) until you do, as it's almost impossible to get around in Florida without a car.
- Open a checking account (see page 94) at a local bank and give the details to any companies that you plan to pay by direct debit or standing order (such as utility and property management companies).
- Arrange whatever insurance is necessary such as health, car, homeowner's and third-party liability.
- Contact offices and organizations to obtain local information (see page 193).
- If you plan to become a permanent resident in Florida you will need to do the following within the next few weeks (if not done before your arrival):

  - register as a permanent resident with your local community;
  - apply for a social security card from your local social security office;
  - apply for a state driver's license (see page 35);
  - arrange schooling for your children (see page 80).

Moving House

When moving permanently to Florida there are many things to be considered and a 'million' people to be informed. Even if you plan to spend only a few months a year in Florida, it may still be necessary to inform a number of people and companies in your home country. The checklists below are designed to make the task easier and help prevent an ulcer or a nervous breakdown (providing of course you don't leave everything to the last minute). See also **Moving House** on page 167 and **Moving In** on page 168.

- If you live in rented accommodations you will need to give your landlord notice (check your contract).

- If you own your home, arrange to sell or rent it well in advance of your move.

- Inform the following:

  - Your employer, e.g. give notice or arrange leave of absence.

  - Your local town hall or municipality. You may be entitled to a refund of your local taxes.

  - If it was necessary to register with the police in your home country, you should inform them that you're moving abroad.

  - Your electricity, gas, water and telephone companies. Contact companies well in advance, particularly if you need to have a deposit refunded.

  - Your insurance companies (for example health, car, home contents and private pension); banks, post office (if you have a post office account), stockbroker and other financial institutions; credit card, charge card and hire purchase companies; lawyer and accountant; and local businesses where you have accounts.

  - Your family doctor, dentist and other health practitioners. Health records should be transferred to your new doctor and dentist, if applicable.

  - Your children's schools. Try to give a term's notice and obtain a copy of any relevant school reports or records from your children's current schools.

  - All regular correspondents, subscriptions, social and sports clubs, professional and trade journals, and friends and relatives. Give them your new address and telephone number and arrange to have your mail redirected by the post office or a friend.

  - If you have a driving licence or car you will need to give the local vehicle registration office your new address abroad and in some countries, return your car's registration plates.

- Return any library books or anything borrowed.

- Arrange shipment of your furniture and belongings by booking a shipping company well in advance (see page 167). Major international moving companies usually provide a wealth of information and can advise on a wide range of matters concerning an international relocation. Find out the exact procedure for shipping your belongings to Florida from your local US embassy or consulate.

- Arrange to sell anything you aren't taking with you (e.g. house, car and furniture). If you're selling a home or business, you should obtain expert legal advice as you may be able to save tax by establishing a trust or other legal vehicle. Note that if you own more than one property you may have to pay capital gains tax on any profits from the sale of second and subsequent homes.

- If you have a car that you're exporting to Florida, you will need to complete the relevant paperwork in your home country and re-register it in Florida after its arrival. Contact a local US embassy or consulate for information.

- Arrange inoculations and shipment for any pets that you're taking with you (see page 70).

- You may qualify for a rebate on your tax and social security contributions. If you're leaving a country permanently and have been a member of a company or state pension scheme, you may be entitled to a refund or may be able to continue payments to qualify for a full (or larger) pension when you retire. Contact your company personnel office, local tax office or pension company for information.

- It's advisable to arrange health, dental and optical checkups for your family before leaving your home country (see page 52). Obtain a copy of all health records and a statement from your private health insurance company stating your present level of cover.

- Terminate any outstanding loan, lease or hire purchase contracts and pay all bills (allow plenty of time, as some companies may be slow to respond).

- Check whether you're entitled to a rebate on your road tax, car and other insurance. Obtain a letter from your motor insurance company stating your no-claims' discount.

- Check whether you need an international driving licence or a translation of your current or foreign driving licence(s) for the US. Note that foreigners are required to take a driving test in Florida to buy and register a car.

- Give friends and business associates an address and telephone number where you can be contacted in Florida.

- If you will be living in Florida for an extended period (but not permanently), you may wish to give someone 'power of attorney' over your financial affairs in your home country so that they can act for you in your absence. This can be for a fixed period or open-ended and can be for a specific purpose only. **Note, however, that you should always take expert legal advice before doing this!**

- Allow plenty of time to get to the airport, register your luggage, and clear security and immigration.

- Buy a copy of *Living and Working in America* by David Hampshire (Survival Books).

Have a safe journey!

APPENDICES

APPENDIX A: USEFUL ADDRESSES

The addresses below are intended to help you obtain further information about buying property or a business in Florida.

State Agencies

Agency for Health Care Administration, 325 John Knox Road, Suite 301-Atrium, Tallahassee, FL 32303 (tel. 904/487-2513).

Department of Agriculture & Consumer Service, The Capitol Plaza, Level 10, Tallahassee, FL 32399-0810 (tel. 904/488-3022).

Department of Banking & Finance, The Capitol Plaza, Level 09, Tallahassee, FL 32399-1008 (tel. 904/488-0370).

Department of Business & Professional Regulation, 725 S. Bronough Street, Tallahassee, FL 32399-1000 (tel. 904/487-2252).

Department of Citrus, PO Box 148, Lakeland, FL 33802 (tel. 941/499-2373).

Department of Commerce, 107 W. Gaines Street, Room 535, Tallahassee, FL 32399-2000 (tel. 904/488-3104).

Department of Community Affairs, 2740 Centerview Drive, Tallahassee, FL 32399-2100 (tel. 904/488-8466).

Department of Corrections, 2601 Blair Stone Road, Tallahassee, FL 32399-2500 (tel. 904/489-7480).

Department of Education, The Capitol Plaza, Level 08, Tallahassee, FL 32399-0400 (tel. 904/487-7480).

Department of Elder Affairs, 1317 Winewood Boulevard, Building 1, Room 317, Tallahassee, FL 32399-0700 (tel. 904/922-5297).

Department of Environmental Protection, 2600 Blair Stone Road, Tallahassee, FL 32399-2440 (tel. 904/488-4805).

Department of Health & Rehabilitative Services, 1323 Winewood Boulevard, Building 2, Room 432, Tallahassee, FL 32399-0700 (tel. 904/487-1111).

Department of Highway Safety & Motor Vehicles, 2900 Apalachee Parkway, Room B-443, Tallahassee, FL 32399-0500 (tel. 904/922-9000).

Department of Insurance & Treasurer, 200 E. Gaines Street, Tallahassee, FL 32399-0300 (tel. 904/488-4398).

Department of Juvenile Justice, 2737 Centerview Drive, Tallahassee, FL 32399-3100 (tel. 904/921-5900).

Department of Labor & Employment Security, 2012 Capitol Circle SE, Suite 303, Tallahassee, FL 32399-0201 (tel. 904/488-4398).

Department of Law Enforcement, PO Box 1489, Tallahassee, FL 32302-1489 (tel. 904/488-7880).

Department of Legal Affairs, The Capitol Plaza, Level 01, Tallahassee, FL 32399-1050 (tel. 904/487-1963).

Department of the Lottery, Capitol Complex, Tallahassee, FL 32399-4002 (tel. 904/487-7728).

Department of Management Services, 2737 Centerview Drive, Suite 110, Tallahassee, FL 32399-0950 (tel. 904/488-2786).

Department of Revenue, 501 S. Calhoun Street, Level 02, Tallahassee, FL 32399-0250 (tel. 904/488-6800).

Department of State, The Capitol Plaza, Level 02, Tallahassee, FL 32399-0250 (tel. 904/488-3680).

Department of Transportation, 605 Suwannee Street, Suite 535, Tallahassee, FL 32399-0450 (tel. 904/488-6721).

Department of Veteran Affairs, PO Box 31003, St. Petersburg, FL 33731 (tel. 813/893-2440).

Florida Parole Commission, 1309 Winewood Boulevard, Room 363-B, Tallahassee, FL 32399-2450.

Florida Public Service Commission, 2540 Shumard Oaks Boulevard, Tallahassee, FL 32399 (tel. 904/413-6330).

Florida State Ethics Commission, PO Box 6, Tallahassee, FL 32302 (tel. 904/488-7864).

Game & Fresh Water Fish Commission, 620 S. Meridian, Suite 101, Tallahassee, FL 32399-1600 (tel. 904/488-1960).

Governor's Office, The Capitol Building, Tallahassee, FL 32399-0001 (tel. 904/488-4441).

Office of the Auditor General, 11 W. Madison Street, Room G-11, Tallahassee, FL 32399-1000 (tel. 904/488-5534).

State Board of Administration, PO Drawer 5318, Tallahassee, FL 32314-3518 (tel. 904/488-4406).

Publications

American Holiday & Life, PO Box 604, Hemel Hempstead, Herts. HP1 3SR, UK. Tourist magazine.

Essentially America, Warners Distribution, The Maltings, Manor Lane, Bourne, Lincs. PE10 9PH, UK (tel. 01778-393652). Lifestyle and tourist magazine.

Florida Homes and Travel Newsletter, Freepost, Fleet, Hampshire GU13 0BR, UK (tel. 01252-626273). Monthly newsletter for Florida homeowners and frequent visitors.

Florida Living Magazine, 102 N.E. 10th Avenue, Suite 6, Gainesville, FL 32601-9986 (tel. 352/372-8865).

Florida Trend, PO Box 420072, Palm Coast, FL 32142-9847 (tel. 1-800/829-9203). Business magazine.

Going USA, Outbound Newspapers Ltd., 1 Commercial Road, Eastbourne, East Sussex BN21 3XQ, UK (tel. 0323-412001). Monthly newspaper for those planning to live, work or holiday in the US.

International Property Magazine, 2a Station Road, Gidea Park, Romford, Essex RM2 6DA, UK (tel. 01708-450784).

International Property Tribune, Welbeck House, High Street, Guildford, Surrey GU1 3JF, UK (tel. 01483-455110).

Overseas Property News, E.W. Publicity Ltd., 15 King Street West, Stockport, Cheshire SK3 0DT, UK (tel. 0161-480 0190).

Private Villas (Rentals), 52 High Street, Henley-in-Arden, Solihull, West Midlands B95 5BR, UK (tel. 01564-794011).

Resident Abroad, Subscriptions Department, PO Box 461, Bromley BR2 9WP, UK (tel. 0181-402 8485). Financial magazine for those living abroad.

World of Property, Overseas Property Match, 532 Kingston Road, Raynes Park, London SW20 8DT, UK (tel. 0181-542 9088).

Miscellaneous

Alliance of Real Estate Agents, PO Box 6958, 3256 S. Florida Avenue, Lakeland, FL 33807-6958 (tel. 813/644-4296).

American Association of Retired Persons (AARP), 601 E. Street, NW, Washington, DC 20049 (tel. 202/434-2277).

American Automobile Association (AAA), 1000 AAA Drive, Orlando, FL 32746-5063 (tel. 407/444-7000).

Better Business Bureau of Central Florida, Inc, 1011 North Wymore Road, Suite 204, Winter Park, FL 32789-1777 (tel. 407/621-3300).

Florida Association of Mortgage Brokers, PO Box 6477, Tallahassee, FL 32314-6477 (tel. 904/222-9983).

Florida Association of Realtors, 7025 Augusta National Drive, PO Box 725025, Orlando, FL 32872-5025 (tel. 407/438-1400).

Florida Attractions Association, PO Box 10295, Tallahassee, FL 32302 (tel. 904/222-2885).

Florida Bankers Association, 214 S. Bronough Street, Tallahassee, FL 32301 (tel. 904/224-2265).

Florida Bar Association, 650 Apalachee Parkway, Tallahassee, FL 32399 (tel. 904/561-5600).

Florida Chamber of Commerce, 136 S. Bronough Street, PO Box 11309, Tallahassee, FL 32302 (tel. 904/425-1200).

Florida Division of Tourism, Visitor Enquiries, 126 W. Van Buren Street, Tallahassee, FL 32399-2000 (tel. 904/487-1462).

Florida Home Builders Association, 201 E. Park Avenue, Tallahassee, FL 32301 (tel. 904/224-4316).

Florida Land Title Association, 2003 Apalachee Parkway, Tallahassee, FL 32301 (tel. 904/878-1179).

Florida Real Estate Commission (FREC), 400 W. Robinson Street, PO Box 1900, Orlando, FL 32802 (tel. 407/423-6071).

Mortgage Bankers Association of Florida, 1133 West Morris Boulevard, Suite 201, Winter Park, FL 32789 (tel. 407/647-8839).

National Association of Self-Employed (NASE), PO Box 612067, DFW Airport, TX 75261-2067 (tel. 1-800-232-NASE).

Small Business Administration (SBA), 1320 S. Dixie Highway, Suite 301, Coral Gables, FL 33146 (tel. 305/536-5521) and 7825 Baymeadow Way, Suite 100-B, Jacksonville, FL 32256-7504 (tel. 904/443-1900).

US Customs Service, Office of Public Information, 1301 Constitution Avenue, PO Box 7407, NW, Washington, DC 20229 (tel. 202/566-8195).

APPENDIX B: FURTHER READING

The books listed below are just a small selection of the many books written for those planning to buy a home or work in Florida. Note that some titles may be out of print, but may still be obtainable from book shops and libraries. Books prefixed with an asterisk (*) are recommended by the author.

Buying a Home/Living

Applying for a United States Visa, Richard Fleischer (How To Books)

*The Complete Guide to Life in Florida, Barbara Brumm LaFreniere & Edward N. LaFreniere (Pineapple Press)

*Culture Shock! Successful Living Abroad - A Wife's Guide, Robin Pascoe (Times Books International)

*Culture Shock! USA, Esther Wanning (Kuperard)

The Field Guide to Home Buying in America, Stephen M. Pollan and Mark Levine

*Guide to Home Ownership, The American Bar Association (Times Books)

How to Buy a Home, Ruth Rejnis (Longmeadow Press)

How to Buy a House, Condo or Co-op, Michael C. Thomsett (Consumer Report Books)

Immigrating to the USA, Dan Danilov & Howard David Deutsch

Keys to Buying and Owning a Home, Jack P. Friedman (Barron's)

*Life in America's Small Cities, G. Scott Thomas (Prometheus Books)

Living in Florida, Edward C. Beshara (Robert Hale)

**Living and Working in America, David Hampshire (Survival Books)

Real Estate Buying/Selling Guide for Florida, Richard Badgley (Self-Counsel Press)

Setting Up Home in Florida, Michael Ray (How To Books)

*US Immigration Made Easy, Laurence A. Canter & Martha S. Siegel (Sheridan Chandler)

Your New House, Alan & Denise Fields (Windsor Peak Press)

Tourist Guides

AA Essential Explorer Florida (AA Publishing)

Affordable Florida (Fodor's)

Best Places to Stay in Florida, Christine Davidson (Houghton Mifflin)

*Birnbaum's Official Guide to Walt Disney World, Pamela S. Weiers

Cheap Thrills: Florida, Frank Zoretich (Pineapple Press)

Econoguide: Walt Disney World, Epcot and Universal Studios Florida, Corey Sandler (Contemporary Books)

Entrée to Florida, Peter King (Quiller)

*Florida and Walt Disney World (Collins)

*Florida: Insight Compact Guides (APA Publications)

*Florida: The Rough Guide, Mick Sinclair (Rough Guides)

Florida Road Atlas and Visitor's Guide (Gousha State Atlas)

*Florida Tourbook (AAA)

*Fodor's Walt Disney World and Orlando Area (Fodor's)

Hidden Florida: The Adventurer's Guide, Stacy Ritz & Candace Leslie (Ulysses)
Insider's Guide to Florida, Donald Carroll (Moorland Publishing)
Insight Pocket Guide Florida Keys (Geocenter)
Key to Florida, Reg Butler (Settle)
*Miami and South Florida (Harper Collins)
Nelles Guide to Florida (Nelles Verlag)
On the Road Around Florida, D. Parker (Thomas Cook)
*Orlando and Central Florida (Harper Collins)
Orlando at a Glance (Kuperard)
Places to Go with Children in Miami and Southern Florida, Cheryl L. Juarez &
A.D. Johnson (Chronicle Books)
*Pocket Guide Florida (Berlitz)
*Thomas Cook's Florida (AA Publishing)
Visitor's Guide Florida, Brian Merritt (Moorland Publishing)
Visitor's Guide Orlando and Central Florida, Don Philpott (Moorland Publishing)
*Walt Disney World and Orlando (Berlitz)
Where to Stay in Florida, Phil Philcox (Hunter Publishing)

Florida General

Atlas of Florida (Florida Trend)
The Climate and Weather of Florida, James A. Henry, Kenneth M. Portier & Jan
Coyne (Pineapple Press)
The Economy of Florida (Florida Trend)
*Finding a Job in Florida (Pineapple Press)
*Florida Almanac, Del & Marty Marth (Suwannee River Press)
The Florida Directory (Florida Trend)
Florida Entrepreneur (Pineapple Press)
Florida Facts & Figures (Florida Trend)
Florida Golf Guide: Your Passport to Great Golf, Jimmy Shacky (Open Road)
Florida Guide, Del & Marty Marth (Suwannee River Press)
*Florida Handbook, Allen Morris (Florida Trend)
Florida Law: A Layman's Guide, Gerald B. Keane (Pineapple Press)
Florida: A Pictorial History, Hampton Dunn
*Florida Retiree's Handbook, Elwood Phillips (Pineapple Press)
Florida Statistical Abstract (Florida Trend)
*The Florida Survival Handbook (New Horizons Press)
A History of Florida, Charlton W. Tebeau
Inside Florida State Government (Florida Trend)
*Practical Guide to Florida Retirement, Betty McGarry (Pineapple Press)
Retirement Communities in Florida, Mary Lucier Brooks (Pineapple Press)

APPENDIX C: WEIGHTS & MEASURES

Unlike most of the rest of the world, the US remains stubbornly wedded to Fahrenheit temperatures, inches, miles, gallons and pounds. Although the US decimalized its currency ahead of most European countries, it continues to uses measures derived from the British Imperial system and has abandoned plans to convert to the metric system (*Système Internationale/SI*) for international trade and scientific purposes.

Those who are familiar with the metric system of measurement will find the tables on the following pages useful. The clothes sizes shown include the equivalent European (continental) and United Kingdom (UK) sizes, both of which are different from American sizes. Comparisons shown aren't exact, but are close enough for the accuracy required for most everyday calculations.

Women's clothes:

USA	6	8	10	12	14	16	18	20	22	24
UK	8	10	12	14	16	18	20	22	24	26
Europe	34	36	38	40	42	44	46	48	50	52

Sweaters: **Women's**   **Mens**

USA	32	34	36	38	40	42	44	sm	medium	large		exl
UK	34	36	38	40	42	44	46	34	36	38	40	42	44
Europe	40	42	44	46	48	50	52	44	46	48	50	52	54

Note: sm = small, exl = extra large

Men's Shirts

USA/UK	14	14	15	15	16	16	17	17	18
Europe	36	37	38	39	40	41	42	43	44	46

Men's Underwear

USA	small	medium		large	extra large
UK	34	36	38	40	42	44
Europe	5	6	7	8	9	10

Children's Clothes

USA	2	4	6	8	10	12
UK	16/18	20/22	24/26	28/30	32/34	36/38
Europe	92	104	116	128	140	152

Children's Shoes

USA/UK	2	3	4	4	5	6	7	7	8	9	10
Europe	18	19	20	21	22	23	24	25	26	27	28

USA/UK	11	11	12	13	1	2	2	3	4	5
Europe	29	30	31	32	33	34	35	36	37	38

Men's and Women's Shoes

USA	4	4	5	5	6	6	7	7	8	8	9	9	10	10	11	11
UK	2	3	3	4	4	5	5	6	6	7	7	8	8	9	9	10
Europe	35	35	36	37	37	38	39	39	40	40	41	42	42	43	44	44

Weights:

US (Avoirdupois)	Metric	Metric	US (Avoirdupois)
1 oz	28.35 g	1 g	0.035 oz
1 pound	454 g	1 kg	2.2 lbs
1 US cwt (100 lbs)	45.36 kg	1 tonne	2,205 lbs
1 US ton (2,000 lbs)*	907.2 kg		

* Called a 'short ton; an Imperial ton (2,240 lbs) is called a 'long' ton.

Note: g = gram, kg = kilogram

Length:

USA/UK	Metric	Metric	USA/UK
1 inch	2.54 cm	1 cm	0.39 inch
1 foot	30.48 cm	1 m	3.28 feet
1 yard	91.44 cm	1 km	0.62 mile
1 mile	1.61 km	8 km	5 miles

Note: cm = centimeter, m = meter, km = kilometer

Capacity:

US	Imperial	Metric
1 pint (16 fl.oz)	0.83 pints	0.45 liters
1 quart (two pints)	1.66 pints	0.91 liters
1 gallon	0.83 gallon	3.64 liters

Capacity (cont.):

Imperial	US	Metric
1 pint (20 fl.oz)	1.2 pints	0.57 litre
1 quart	2.4 pints	1.14 liters
1 gallon	1.2 gallons	4.55 liters

Square Measure:

British/US	Metric	Metric	British/US
1 square inch .	6.45 sq. cm	1 sq. cm	0.155 sq. inches
1 square foot	0.092 sq. m.	1 sq. m.	10.764 sq. feet
1 square yard	0.836 sq. m.	1 sq. m.	1.196 sq. yards
1 acre	0.405 hect.	1 hectare	2.471 acres
1 square mile	259 hect.	1 sq. km.	0.386 sq. mile

Temperature:

Fahrenheit	Celsius	
32	0	freezing point of water
41	5	
50	10	
59	15	
68	20	
77	25	
86	30	
95	35	
104	40	

The Boiling point of water is 100 degrees Celsius, 212 degrees Fahrenheit.

Oven temperature:

Gas	Electric	
	F	**C**
-	225-250	110-120
1	275	140
2	300	150
3	325	160
4	350	180
5	375	190
6	400	200
7	425	220
8	450	230
9	475	240

For a quick conversion, the Celsius temperature is approximately half the Fahrenheit temperature.

Temperature Conversion:

Fahrenheit to Celsius: subtract 32, multiply by 5 and divide by 9.
Celsius to Fahrenheit: multiply by 9, divide by 5 and add 32.

Body Temperature:

Normal body temperature (if you're alive and well) is 98.4 degrees Fahrenheit, which equals 37 degrees Celsius.

APPENDIX D: MAP OF FLORIDA

The map below and opposite shows the 67 counties of Florida, listed by region. The county seats (towns) are listed under **Regions** on page 49. A map of Florida depicting the major cities, main attractions and geographical features is shown on page 6.

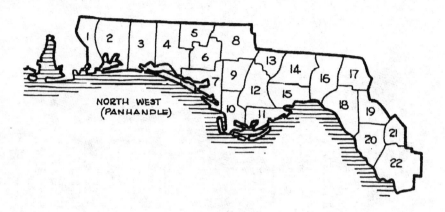

1. Escambia
2. Santa Rosa
3. Okaloosa
4. Walton
5. Holmes
6. Washington
7. Bay
8. Jackson
9. Calhoun
10. Gulf
11. Franklin
12. Liberty
13. Gadsden
14. Leon
15. Wakulla
16. Jefferson
17. Madison
18. Taylor
19. Lafayette
20. Dixie
21. Gilchrist
22. Levy

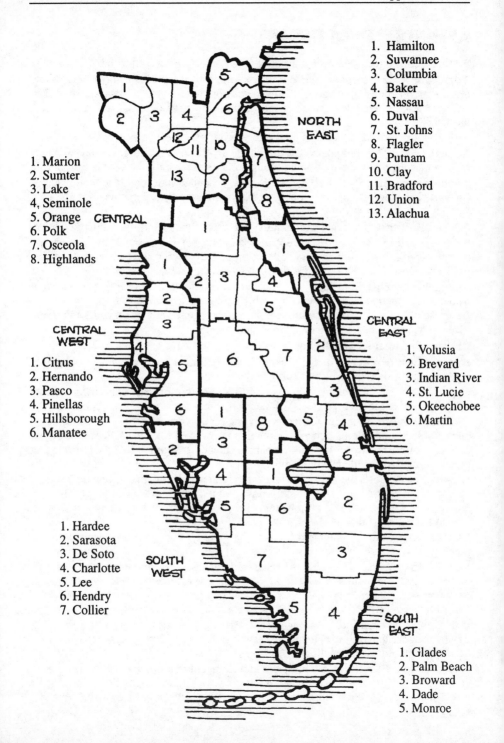

1. Hamilton
2. Suwannee
3. Columbia
4. Baker
5. Nassau
6. Duval
7. St. Johns
8. Flagler
9. Putnam
10. Clay
11. Bradford
12. Union
13. Alachua

NORTH EAST

1. Marion
2. Sumter
3. Lake
4. Seminole
5. Orange CENTRAL
6. Polk
7. Osceola
8. Highlands

CENTRAL WEST

1. Citrus
2. Hernando
3. Pasco
4. Pinellas
5. Hillsborough
6. Manatee

CENTRAL EAST

1. Volusia
2. Brevard
3. Indian River
4. St. Lucie
5. Okeechobee
6. Martin

1. Hardee
2. Sarasota
3. De Soto
4. Charlotte
5. Lee
6. Hendry
7. Collier

SOUTH WEST

SOUTH EAST

1. Glades
2. Palm Beach
3. Broward
4. Dade
5. Monroe

APPENDIX E: GLOSSARY

Acceptance: Agreeing to accept an offer on a property, which constitutes a contract.

Adjustable Rate Mortgage (ARM): A type of mortgage rate loan whose interest rate changes periodically up or down, usually once or twice a year. There are some 150 different ARMs available from lenders nationwide. Also called a 'variable rate mortgage'.

Ad Valorem Tax: A tax based on the value of property, i.e. property or real estate taxes.

Amortization: The gradual process of systematically reducing debt in equal payments (as in a mortgage) comprising both principal and interest, until the debt is paid in full.

Annual Percentage Rate (APR): Everything financed in a mortgage loan package (interest, loan fees, points or other charges), expressed as a percentage of the loan amount.

Appraisal: The professional examination of a property to determine its market value.

Assessed Value: The value placed on a property for tax purposes by the county property appraiser. Unlike in many other countries (and US states), the assessed value in Florida should be equal to the actual market value.

Assumable Mortgage: A loan which the lender is willing to transfer from the current owner of a property to a new owner, possibly with the same interest rate and terms. An Assumable loan may make your home more attractive to buyers when you want to sell.

Balloon Mortgage: A loan with a large final payment.

Broker: See **Real Estate Broker**.

Buyer's Agent/Broker: An agent working solely for the buyer and under obligation to obtain the best price and terms for the him.

Cap: The maximum rate by which an adjustable-rate mortgage can change, either annually or over the lifetime (term) of the mortgage.

Closing: The final procedure in a property transaction when documents are executed and recorded, funds are disbursed and the title transferred from the seller to the buyer. A buyer can give a lawyer (or another person) power of attorney to attend the closing on his behalf. Also called settlement.

Closing Costs: Costs the buyer must pay at the time of closing in addition to the down payment, including broker's commission, points, mortgage insurance premium, homeowner's insurance and prepayments for property taxes. Closing costs average around 5 per cent of the purchase price.

Closing Statement: A statement prepared by a broker detailing the closing costs for both the seller and the buyer.

Common Elements: The parts of a building housing a condominium or cooperative units that aren't individually owned, in which all owners have an indivisible interest. Common elements usually include foyers and hallways, maintenance areas, parking lots, grounds, recreational facilities, and the external structure of a building.

Community Association: An organization which a buyer must usually join when buying in community developments. Note that even single-family home communities can have community associations.

Condominium (Condo): A building or development comprising two or more units (e.g. apartments or townhouses), the interior of which is individually owned. The common elements of the building (see above) are owned in common by all unit owners.

Cooperative: A building or development comprising two or more units (e.g. apartments or townhouses) which is owned by a corporation usually made up of the owner/occupants. No real property is owned by individuals, who own shares in the corporation (allocated to each unit according to its size) entitling them to use a certain dwelling unit or other units of space.

Contingency: A condition placed on an offer to buy or sell a home, e.g. a prospective buyer may make an offer contingent on the sale of his present home.

Conveyance: The act of transferring the title (ownership) of a property and also the document (such as a deed) used to transfer the ownership.

Deed: A written legal document that conveys title to real property.

Deed Restrictions: A clause in a deed that restricts the use of land.

Discount Points: The amount paid to the lender at the time of the origination of a loan to account for the difference between the market interest rate and the lower face rate of the note (see also **Point**).

Down Payment: The amount that needs to be paid in cash to obtain a mortgage, e.g. if you have an 80 per cent mortgage, you must make a 20 per cent down payment.

Earnest Money: Funds submitted with an offer to show good faith to follow through with a purchase. Earnest money is placed by a broker in an escrow (trust) account until closing, when it become part of the down payment or closing costs.

Easement: The interest, privilege or right that a party has in the land of another party, e.g. utility lines.

Encumbrance: Any right or interest in a property that affects its value such as outstanding loans, unpaid taxes, easements and deed restrictions.

Equity: The value an owner has in a property after the deductions of any outstanding liens such as a mortgage, e.g. if a property is valued at $100,000 and the amount outstanding on a mortgage is $50,000, the owner has $50,000 equity.

Equity Loan: A second mortgage where the owner borrows against his equity in a property.

Escrow: A procedure in which documents of cash and property are put in the care of a third party, other than the buyer or seller, pending completion of agreed conditions and terms in sales contracts. An escrow company performs escrow services.

Exclusive Agency Listing: A contract giving one broker the sole right to sell a property for a specified time, while allowing the owner to sell the property without payment of a commission.

Exclusive Right to Sell Listing: A contract giving a broker the exclusive right to sell a property and to collect a commission if the property is sold by anyone, including the owner, within the term of the agreement.

Fee Simple or Fee Absolute: A freehold title or absolute ownership of real property.

FHA Financing/Loan: A loan which is insured against loss by the Federal Housing Administration (FHA), part of the US Department of Housing and Urban Development (HUD). Such financing requires only a 3 to 5 per cent down payment.

Fixed-Rate Mortgage: A mortgage with a fixed interest rate, usually over a period of 15 to 30 years.

Foreclosure: Legal proceedings instigated by a lender to deprive a person of ownership rights when mortgage payments haven't been maintained (called repossession in some countries).

FSBO: An abbreviation for 'For Sale By Owner', when a home is being sold without the assistance of a real estate agent.

Graduated-Payment Mortgage (GPM): A loan requiring lower payments in the early years, with payments increasing in steps until they are sufficient to amortize the loan. Also called a 'flexible payment mortgage (FPM)'.

Growing Equity Mortgage (GEM): A loan in which the payment is increased by a specific amount each year, with the additional payment amount applied to principal retirement. This results in the maturity of the loan being significantly shorter than a comparable level-payment mortgage.

Hazard Insurance: Homeowner's insurance that covers a property against certain risks (hazards) such as fires and storms.

Home Inspection: A home inspection is a thorough examination of the condition of a home before purchase, called a survey and carried out by a surveyor in many countries. It should be completed by a professional home inspection company which provides a detailed written report. You can make a purchase contingent on a satisfactory home inspection.

Homeowners' Association: An organization of owners in a community property such as a condominium or cooperative development, usually for the purpose of managing the common elements of the development and enforcing deed restrictions.

Homeowner's Insurance: An insurance policy that protects a homeowner from 'casualty' (losses or damage to the home or personal property) and from 'liability' (injury to other people or damage to a third party's property). Required by lenders (premiums are usually included in monthly mortgage payments).

HUD: The US Department of Housing and Urban Development (HUD), which sells homes deeded to HUD/FHA by mortgage companies who have foreclosed on FHA-insured mortgage loans. HUD is also responsible for government housing programs.

Impound Account: An account held by a lender for payment of taxes, insurance and other periodic debts against a property. The borrower pays an apportioned amount with each monthly loan payment and the lender pays the bills with the accumulated funds.

Interest Rate: A percentage that when multiplied by the principal determines the amount of money that the principal earns over a period of time (usually one year).

Joint Tenancy: Property ownership by two (e.g. a married couple) or more persons with an undivided interest and the right of survivorship, where if one owner dies the property automatically passes to the joint owner(s).

Jumbo Mortgage: A high value mortgage, usually in excess of $200,000, with a lower than average interest rate.

Lien: A charge against property making it security for a debt such as a mortgage or community fees.

Listing: A property listed for sale, a record of property for sale by a broker, or a written contract between a property owner and an agent authorizing the agent to perform certain services for the owner.

Loan Origination Fee: A fee charged by the lender for evaluating, preparing and submitting a proposed mortgage loan.

Lock-In Period (LIP): The period of a mortgage during which the interest rate is fixed.

Lot: The plot or parcel of land on which a home is built or the land on which a mobile home is located.

Market Value: The current value of a property compared with similar properties, generally accepted to be the highest price a buyer will pay and the lowest price a vendor will accept.

Mortgage: A written instrument that creates a lien against real estate as security for the payment of a loan.

Mortgage Insurance Premium (MIP): A charge paid by the borrower (usually as part of the closing costs) to obtain financing particularly when making a down payment of less than 20 per cent of the purchase price.

Mortgage Pre-Approval: A service offered by lenders whereby they provide pre-approval of a loan (for a maximum sum) thus establishing a buyer's price range, strengthening his buying position and shortening the loan approval period.

Mortgagee: One who holds a lien on property or title to property as security for a debt, i.e. the lender.

Mortgagor: One who pledges property as security for a loan, i.e. the borrower.

Multiple Listing Service (MLS): A broker information network whereby an association of real estate brokers agree to share listings publicizing homes for sale, where the selling agent splits the commission with the agent who finds a buyer. Most homes are multiple listings and therefore different agents offer the same properties.

National Association of Real Estate Brokers (NAREB): An organization of minority real estate salespersons and brokers who are called 'realtists'.

National Association of Realtors (NAR): An Organization of 'realtors' devoted to encouraging professionalism in real estate transactions. NAR has over 600,000 members, associations in all 50 US states and a number of affiliates.

Offer: A bid to buy a property at a specified price.

Open Listing: A listing of properties for sale given to any number of brokers without liability to compensate any except the broker who first secures a buyer.

Plat: A plan or map of a specific land area.

Point: An amount equal to 1 per cent of the principal amount being borrowed. A lender may charge a borrower several points as a fee for providing a loan. See also **Discount Points**.

Prepayment Penalty: A penalty sometimes imposed on a borrower when a loan is paid off before the end of the mortgage term (maturity).

Principal: The amount of money borrowed to buy a property and the amount still owed. Also one who owns or will use a property.

Principal and Interest Payment (P&I): A periodic (usually monthly) mortgage payment that includes interest charges plus an amount applied to the amortization of the principal balance.

Principal, Interest, Taxes and Insurance (PITI): Monthly mortgage payment (P&I) plus an amount deposited in escrow against future property tax and insurance payments.

Private Mortgage Insurance (PMI): See **Mortgage Insurance Premium (MIP)** above.

Property Taxes: Taxes based on the assessed value of a home paid by the homeowner for community services such as schools, public works and other costs of local government.

Purchase-Money Mortgage: A mortgage given by a buyer to a seller in part payment of the purchase price of a property.

Real Estate: In law, real estate is land and everything built on or attached to it.

Real Estate Broker: A person who has passed a state broker's examination and is licensed by the state to represent buyers and sellers in real estate transactions. A brokerage is the business of being a broker.

Real Estate Salesperson: A person who has passed a state examination and who works under the supervision of a broker.

Real Estate Taxes: Property taxes levied on land and buildings charged to owners by local government (e.g. county) agencies.

Realtist: A member of the **National Association of Real Estate Brokers (NAREB)**.

Realtor: A real estate broker who's a member of the **National Association of Realtors (NAR)**, a professional association. Not all brokers are realtors.

Refinance: To replace an old loan with a new one, either to reduce the interest rate, secure better terms or increase the amount borrowed.

Seller's Agent/Broker: A real estate agent employed solely by the seller and under obligation to obtain the best price and terms for the seller.

Remodeling: Remodeling is the name used in the US for modernization, renovation and restoration of a property. Also called rehabilitation.

Settlement: See **Closing**.

Single-Family Home: A detached property built on its own lot (plot or parcel of land).

Subdivision: A tract of land divided into lots for homebuilding purposes.

Survey: A process under which a parcel of land is measured and a blueprint produced showing its measurements, boundaries and area. Note to be confused with a British home survey, which is called a home inspection in the US.

Tenancy in Common: A form of ownership in which two or more persons buy a property jointly, but with no right of survivorship. Owners are free to will their share to anyone they choose, which is the main difference between this and joint tenancy. Often used by friends or relatives buying together.

Term: The life-span of a mortgage, e.g. 15 or 30 years.

Title: The right of possession and evidence of ownership.

Title Company: A company that issues title insurance and which may also perform escrow functions.

Title Insurance: Protects lenders and homeowners against loss of their interest in property due to legal defects in the title (e.g. liens or encumbrances) discovered after the change of ownership.

Title Search: A professional investigation of public records to establish the chain of ownership of a property and note any outstanding liens, mortgage, encumbrances or other factors that may affect clear title.

Variable Rate Mortgage (VRM): See **Adjustable Rate Mortgage (ARM)**.

Zoning: The procedure that classifies land and property for a number of different uses such as residential, commercial or industrial, in accordance with a land-use plan. In some counties an area must be specifically zones for short term rentals.

APPENDIX F: SERVICE DIRECTORY

This Service Directory is to help you find businesses and services both in Florida and the UK, serving both residents and visitors. Note that when telephoning Florida from abroad, you must dial your international access number (e.g. 00 from the UK) followed by 1 (the country code for the USA), the area code and the subscriber's number. Please mention *Buying a Home in Florida* when contacting companies.

BUSINESS SERVICES

Florida Property and Business Services, Inc., c/o Jan Marie Doughty, PO Box 41, Chichester, West Sussex PO20 6US, UK (tel./fax UK 01243-536026).

CLUBS & ORGANIZATIONS

Florida Brits Club, c/o Peter and Jean Stanhope, Stanhope House, 18 Grange Close, Skelton, York YO3 6YR, UK (tel./fax UK 01904-471900).

CONDOMINIUMS/VILLAS

Timberwoods Vacation Villas, c/o Diane Hoode, 7964 Timberwood Circle, Sarasota, Florida 34238, USA (tel. 941/923-4966, fax 941/924-3109).

EMPLOYMENT SERVICES

First Point International, c/o John Harper, York House, 17 Great Cumberland Place, London W1H 7LA, UK (tel. UK 0171-724 9009, fax 0171-724 7997).

International Jobsearch, c/o Artena Greene, Nationsbank Tower, 111 North Orange Ave, Suite 950, Orlando, Florida 32801, USA (tel. 407/246-0990, fax 407/246-1512).

FLIGHTS

Florida Homes and Travel, c/o Kathleen Harpham, Freepost, Fleet, Hampshire GU13 0BR, UK (tel. UK 01252-626273, fax 01252-811770).

HOLIDAYS

Florida Select, c/o J. Paul John ARICS, 7852 West Irlo Bronson Highway (192), Kissimmee, FL 34747, USA (tel. USA 407/390-0550, fax USA 407/390-0560, tel. UK 01782-595880, fax UK 01782-394433).

IMMIGRATION/VISAS

Chastang, Ferrell, Sims & Eiserman, PA, c/o Lawrence J. Chastang CPA, 1400 W. Fairbanks Avenue, Suite 102, Winter Park, Florida 32789, USA (tel. 407/629-1944, fax 407/740-0671).

First Point International, c/o John Harper, York House, 17 Great Cumberland Place, London W1H 7LA, UK (tel. UK 0171-724 9009, fax 0171-724 7997).

Frank W. Ricci, P.A., c/o Bettina, 4360 Northlake Blvd, Suite 205, Palm Beach Gardens, Florida 33410, USA (tel. 407/694-2400), fax 407/694-6629).

George C. J. Moore, Barrister (UK) and Attorney (Florida), Suite 812, 105 South Narcissus Avenue, West Palm Beach, FL 33401, USA (tel. 407/833-9000, fax 407/833-9990).

Law Offices Leon J. Snaid, c/o Leon Snaid, 438 Camino Del Rio South, STE. 101, San Diego, CA 92108, USA (tel. 619/297-0771, fax 619/296-5056).
Monty J. Tilles, P.A., Attorney at Law, 5673 Hendee Way, PO Box 1221, Quechee, Vermont 05059, USA (tel. 802/296-8270 and 1-800/818-8472, fax 802/295-3104).
US Visa Consultants, c/o Mr. I.H. Levy, 27 York Street, London W1H 1PY, UK (tel. UK 0171-224 3629, fax 0171-224 3859).
Walter F. Rudeloff, Attorney at Law, 4 Kings Bench Walk, London EC4Y 7DL, UK (tel./fax UK 0171-267-1297). Featuring L-1 and E-2 treaty visas.

INTERNATIONAL REMOVALS

Crown Worldwide Movers Ltd., c/o Miss Norah Franchetti, Security House, Abbey Wharf Industrial Estate, Kingsbridge Road, Barking, Essex IG11 0BD, UK (tel. UK 0181-591 3388, fax 0181-594 4571).

LEGAL SERVICES

Frank W. Ricci, P.A., c/o Bettina, 4360 Northlake Blvd, Suite 205, Palm Beach Gardens, Florida 33410, USA (tel. 407/694-2400, fax 407/694-6629).

PROFESSIONAL SERVICES

Frank W. Ricci, P.A., c/o Bettina, 4360 Northlake Blvd, Suite 205, Palm Beach Gardens, Florida 33410, USA (tel. 407/694-2400, fax 407/694-6629).

PROPERTY EXHIBITIONS

Overseas Property Match, 532 Kingston Road, Raynes Park, London SW20 8DT, UK (tel. UK 0181-542-9088, fax 0181-542-2737/0181-543-4932).

PROPERTY RENTALS

Florida Brits Club, c/o Peter and Jean Stanhope, Stanhope House, 18 Grange Close, Skelton, York YO3 6YR, UK (tel./fax UK 01904-471900).
Riverside Properties, Sales and Rentals, c/o Victoria Josberger (Broker, Realtor), PO Box B, Marco Island, Florida 33969, USA (tel. 813/394-4707, fax 813/642-4707).
Timberwoods Vacation Villas, c/o Diane Hoode, 7964 Timberwood Circle, Sarasota, Florida 34238, USA (tel. 941/923-4966, fax 941/924-3109).

PROPERTY SERVICES

Babet Sales Ltd., c/o Mr. J.G. Esplen, The Mill House, Moorlands Road, Merriott, Somerset TA16 5NF, UK (tel. 01460-76213, fax. 01460-76153).
Florida Brits Club, c/o Peter and Jean Stanhope, Stanhope House, 18 Grange Close, Skelton, York YO3 6YR, UK (tel./fax UK 01904-471900).
Florida Property and Business Services, Inc., c/o Jan Marie Doughty, PO Box 41, Chichester, West Sussex PO20 7RB, UK (tel./fax 01243-536026).

REAL ESTATE AGENTS

The Florida Dream, c/o Tom Cowell, PO Box 15, Bangor, Gwynedd LL57 2JD, UK (tel. 01248-670006, fax 01248-371489).

Florida Select, c/o J. Paul John ARICS, 7852 West Irlo Bronson Highway (192), Kissimmee, FL 34747, USA (tel. USA 407/390-0550, fax USA 407/390-0560, tel. UK 01782-595880, fax UK 01782-394433).

Prudential Florida Realty, c/o Patricia Hale, 3100 E. Commercial Blvd., Fort Lauderdale, Florida 33308, USA (tel. 305/771-2600 or 305/491-8796, fax 305/772-3012).

Riverside Properties, Sales and Rentals, c/o Victoria Josberger (Broker, Realtor), PO Box B, Marco Island, Florida 33969, USA (tel. 813/394-4707, fax 813/642-4707).

Tangerine Realty Corporation, 201 Gulf of Mexico Drive, Longboat Key, Florida 34228, USA (tel. 941/383-8018, fax 941/383-2092).

SELF-CATERING

Florida Select, c/o J. Paul John ARICS, 7852 West Irlo Bronson Highway (192), Kissimmee, FL 34747, USA (tel. USA 407/390-0550, fax USA 407/390-0560, tel. UK 01782-595880, fax UK 01782-394433).

TRAVEL

Florida Homes and Travel, c/o Kathleen Harpham, Freepost, Fleet, Hampshire GU13 0BR, UK (tel. UK 01252-626273, fax 01252-811770).

Timberwoods Vacation Villas, c/o Diane Hoode, 7964 Timberwood Circle, Sarasota, Florida 34238, USA (tel. 941/923-4966, fax 941/924-3109).

ORDER FORM

There are other Survival Handbooks including *Buying a Home Abroad*, *Buying a Home in France* (summer 1996) and *Buying a Home in Spain* (autumn 1996). We also publish a best-selling series of *Living and Working* books for AMERICA, BRITAIN, FRANCE, SPAIN and SWITZERLAND, representing the most comprehensive and up-to-date source of practical information available about everyday life in these countries. Written in a highly readable and humourous style, they are packed with important and useful data, designed to help you **avoid costly mistakes and save time and money.** Regardless of whether you're planning to stay for a few months or indefinitely, these books have been written for you!

Survival Handbooks are available from good bookshops in many countries or direct from Survival Books, 25 Kenilworth Road, Fleet, Hampshire GU13 9AX, United Kingdom. If you're not entirely satisfied simply return them to us within 14 days for a full and unconditional refund. **Order your copies today!**

ORDER FORM

Please send me (by air mail) the following books by David Hampshire:

Qty	Title	Price Europe	Price World	Total
	Buying a Home Abroad	£11.45	£13.45	
	Buying a Home in Florida	£11.45	£13.45	
	Buying a Home in France	£11.45	£13.45	
	Buying a Home in Spain	£11.45	£13.45	
	Living and Working in America	£14.95	£17.95	
	Living and Working in Britain	£13.95	£16.95	
	Living and Working in France	£13.95	£16.95	
	Living and Working in Spain	£13.95	£16.95	
	Living and Working in Switzerland	£14.95	£17.95	
	ORDER TOTAL			

NAME: _____

ADDRESS: _____

_____

Send with payment to: Survival Books, 25 Kenilworth Road, Fleet, Hampshire GU13 9AX, United Kingdom

INDEX

A

Air-Conditioning 174
Airlines 30
Apartments & Townhouses 144
Appendices 199
  A: Useful Addresses 200
  B: Further Reading 203
  C: Weights & Measures 205
  D: Map of Counties 210
  E: Glossary 212
  F: Service Directory 217
Areas 49
Arrival 187
  Arrival/Departure Record 188
  Customs 191
  Finding Help 193
  Immigration 189
  Registration 192

B

Banking 92
  Check Usage 95
  Checking Accounts 94
Brokers
  Business 22
  Real Estate 151
Buying a Home
  Agents & Brokers 151
  Air-Conditioning 174
  Avoiding Problems 124
  Closing 164
  Community Properties 144
  Contracts 157
  Conveyancing 156
  Cost 134
  Fees 137
  Florida Homes 132
  Garages & Parking 155
  Heating 174
  Inspections 154
  Location 125

Mobile Homes 148
Moving House 167
Moving In 168
New Homes 138
Remodeling 165
Rental Income 176
Resale Homes 142
Security 168
Surveys 154
Utilities 170

C

Capital Gains Tax 115
Car
  Insurance 36
  Rental 40
Checklists
  After Arrival 195
  Before Arrival 194
  Moving House 195
Choosing The Location 125
Climate 46
Closing 164
Communications 25
Community Properties 144
Condominiums 144
Conveyancing 156
Cooperatives 144
Cost of Living 120
Counties
  Map 210
Credit Rating 91
Crime 75
  Car 37
  Home Security 168
  Legal System 78
  Prevention & Safety 76
Currency 88
Customs 191
  Pets 70

D

Directory of Services 217
Driving 33
　Car Crime 37
　Car Insurance 36
　Car Rental 40
　Driver's License 35
　General Road Rules 38

E

Education 80
Electricity 171
Estate & Gift Tax 117

F

Fees 137
Finance 87
　Banking 92
　Capital Gains Tax 115
　Checking Accounts 94
　Cost of Living 120
　Credit Rating 91
　Estate & Gift Tax 117
　Importing/Exporting Money 89
　Income Tax 104
　Mortgages 97
　Property Taxes 113
　Sales Tax 117
　US Currency 88
　Wills 119
Finding Help 193
Finding Your Dream Home 123
Flights 30
Florida Homes 132
Furniture & Furnishings 69, 140
Further Considerations 45
Further Reading 203

G

Garages & Parking 155
Garbage Collection & Disposal 175
Gas 172
Geography 48
Getting Around 31
Getting There 30
Glossary 212

H

Health 52
Health Insurance 54
　Residents 54
　Visitors 58
Heating 174
Home Inspections 154
Home Security 168
Homeowner's Insurance 59
　Casualty 60
　Liability 63

I

Immigration 189
Income Tax 104
　Deductions & Exemptions 108
　Federal 105
　Rental Income 112
　Return 109
　Taxable Income & Rates 107
Insurance 53
　Car 36
　Casualty 60
　Health 54
　Holiday/Vacation 64
　Homeowner's 59
　Liability 63
　Travel 64

K

Keeping in Touch 25

L

Legal System 78
Leisure 81
Location 125

M

Map
  Counties 210
  Florida 6
Metric Conversion Tables 205
Mobile Homes 148
Money 88
Mortgages 97
  Types 99
Moving House 167
  Checklist 195
  Moving In 168

N

New Homes 138

P

Part-Ownership Schemes 149
Permits 17
Pets 70
Post Office Services 29
Property Taxes 113
Public Transport 31
Purchase Contracts 157
  Basic Details 159
  Contingency Clauses 162
  Standard Clauses 160

R

Radio 74
Real Estate Agents & Brokers 151
Regions 49

Registration 192
Remodeling 165
Renovation & Restoration 165
Rental Income 176
  Taxation 112
Renting
  Cars 40
  Property 130
Resale Homes 142
Retirement 20

S

Sales Tax 117
Schools 80
Self-Employment 22
Selling a Home 182
Service Directory 217
Settlement 164
Settling In 188
Shared Ownership 149
Shopping 65
  By Telephone 68
  Factory Outlets 67
  Furniture & Furnishings 69, 140
  Household Goods 70
  Mail-Order 68
  Sales 67
  Sales Tax 117
  Warehouse Clubs 67
Sports 81
Surveys 154

T

Tax
  Capital Gains 115
  Estate & Gift 117
  Income 104
  Property 113
  Real Estate 113
  Sales 117
Telephone 25
Television 72
Timeshare 149
Travel Insurance 64
Treaty Investors 24

U

Useful Addresses 200
Utilities 170
  Electricity 171
  Gas 172
  Telephone 25
  Water 173

V

Visas 17
  Treaty Investors 24
  Visitors 18
  Waivers 19

W

Walt Disney World 81
Water 173
Weather 46
Weights & Measures 205
Why Florida? 15
Wills 119
Working 21